NOSTALGIA IN ANGLOPHONE ARAB LITERATURE

NOSTALGIA IN ANGLOPHONE ARAB LITERATURE

Nationalism, Identity and Diaspora

Tasnim Qutait

I.B. TAURIS
LONDON • NEW YORK • OXFORD • NEW DELHI • SYDNEY

I.B. TAURIS
Bloomsbury Publishing Plc
50 Bedford Square, London, WC1B 3DP, UK
1385 Broadway, New York, NY 10018, USA
29 Earlsfort Terrace, Dublin 2, Ireland

BLOOMSBURY, I.B. TAURIS and the I.B. Tauris logo are trademarks of
Bloomsbury Publishing Plc

First published in Great Britain 2021
This paperback edition published 2023

Copyright © Tasnim Qutait, 2021

Tasnim Qutait has asserted her right under the Copyright, Designs and
Patents Act, 1988, to be identified as Author of this work.

Series design by Adriana Brioso
Cover image: The Mahmal, from The David Collection.
(© Fine Art Images/Heritage Images/Getty Images)

All rights reserved. No part of this publication may be reproduced or transmitted in any form or by any means, electronic or mechanical, including photocopying, recording, or any information storage or retrieval system, without prior permission in writing from the publishers.

Bloomsbury Publishing Plc does not have any control over, or responsibility for, any third-party websites referred to or in this book. All internet addresses given in this book were correct at the time of going to press. The author and publisher regret any inconvenience caused if addresses have changed or sites have ceased to exist, but can accept no responsibility for any such changes.

A catalogue record for this book is available from the British Library.

A catalog record for this book is available from the Library of Congress.

ISBN: HB: 978-0-7556-1759-3
PB: 978-0-7556-4193-2
ePDF: 978-0-7556-1760-9
eBook: 978-0-7556-1761-6

Typeset by Deanta Global Publishing Services, Chennai, India

To find out more about our authors and books visit www.bloomsbury.com and sign up for our newsletters.

CONTENTS

Preface	vi
Note on transliteration	ix
INTRODUCTION	1
Chapter 1	
THE CHAOS OF LOST EMPIRES: RABIH ALAMEDDINE, SABIHA KHEMIR AND YASMIN ZAHRAN	33
Chapter 2	
REWRITING COLONIAL ENCOUNTERS: AHDAF SOUEIF, FADIA FAQIR AND JAMAL MAHJOUB	61
Chapter 3	
NATIONAL HISTORIES AND FAMILY NARRATIVES: HISHAM MATAR, LEILA ABOULELA AND RANDA JARRAR	89
Chapter 4	
REIMAGINING BELONGING IN THE DIASPORA: ROBIN YASSIN-KASSAB, SELMA DABBAGH AND RAWI HAGE	123
CONCLUSION	153
Notes	163
Work cited	169
Index	184

PREFACE

In the spring of 2012, I was sent a copy of a family photograph taken in Tripoli, Libya, in 1955, during a fund-raising meeting attended by Ahmed Ben Bella and other representatives of the Algerian independence movement.[1] Libya had become a sovereign country just four years earlier in 1951; for Algeria the battle for independence would last until 1962. In the photograph, the Algerian flag and the Libyan flag hang from the windows behind the gathering. Ahmed Ben Bella sits in the middle of the row; the man in the foreground is my grandfather.

To paraphrase W.J.T. Mitchell, looking at this photograph I ask what it demands of me, and what I want from it (xv). Is the nostalgic mood it evokes for me simply a function of the image? Monochromatic and sepia images have been described as possessing an 'aesthetic of the authentic figured around a basic quality of pastness' (Grainge, 'TIME's past' 384). This quality of authenticity may be part of what draws me to this image, along with the fact that the photograph brings together a family member and an iconic figure of anti-colonial struggle, making the historical personal.

Aside from this personal investment however, I am aware of the nostalgic narrative around Ahmed Ben Bella, as a hero of the Algerian independence struggle and elected president who was deposed by a military coup and lived for decades under house arrest. Ben Bella's fate was shared by Mohammad Naguib in Egypt,

Shukri al-Quwatli in Syria and Abdulkarim Qasim in Iraq: all were overthrown in the early years of independence, and today are often mythologized as rulers who could have created the basis for modern and prosperous countries. This narrative is part of a pervasive nostalgia for an era when independence had just been realized, or was on the verge of being realized, a nostalgia which is heightened by the contrast between then and now. As Svetlana Boym puts it, nostalgia works through the 'superimposition of two images – of home and abroad, past and present, dream and everyday life', a superimposition Boym describes through the 'cinematic image' of a 'double exposure' (xii–xiv). The nostalgia this photograph evokes for me works through such a 'double exposure', where the present situation in both Algeria and Libya (a military regime after years of civil war in Algeria, an ongoing civil war in Libya) is contrasted against the ambitions and dreams of the independence generation.

When I began writing this book, the tricolour flag hanging in the window in the photograph was once again visible everywhere on the streets of Libya, though it had been banned since 1977, when the Gaddafi regime instituted the green flag as a symbol of Gaddafi's Green Book. The reappearance of the flag of independence during the 2011 uprisings, which later came to be called the 'Arab Spring', was one instance of what seemed to be a new beginning for a region often described as having failed to join the modern world. In an article published in February 2011, David Hirst expressed just this, stating: '[i]n rallying at last to this now universal but essentially Western value called democracy, they [Arabs] are in effect rejoining the world, catching up with history that has left them behind' (Hirst). The uprisings were even described as 'amounting to a second round of decolonisation' capturing a cyclicality that paradoxically combines revolution and stagnation (Mishra). The idea of an Arab world left behind by history would, it seemed, be forever altered following the 2011 uprisings. However, in the tumultuous years since, the term 'Arab Spring' has changed, negating the idea of an epistemic shift which it is suggested was always illusory, naïve or facile. The uprisings that erupted after over thirty years of authoritarianism revealed fractured societies, ultimately leading to internecine strife and new heights of repression. Looking back on photographs of the initial months of the uprisings now leads to a telescoped version of looking at photographs of the independence generation: the future imagined in both cases clashes with the reality known in the present. Susan Sontag writes that 'the photograph eclipses other forms of understanding, of remembering' (89). She argues that photographs 'haunt' us but are constrained, in contrast to 'narratives [which] can make us understand' (89). The photograph that was the starting point for this project led me to think about nostalgic narratives and how narratives can make us understand.

There are many people to thank for their support during the time it took to complete this book. I am greatly indebted to colleagues at the English department at Uppsala University. My thanks go in particular to Ashleigh Harris, Robert Appelbaum, Stuart Robertson and Stephen Donovan, whose invaluable advice and feedback shaped the development of this book. I am also very grateful to Gail Ramsay, Roger Allen, Lindsey Moore and Wen-chin Ouyang for sharing their critical insights at key stages of this project. Warm thanks are due to Sindija Franzetti, Maria Zirra, Sanja Nivesjö, July Blalack, Krista Riley, Fatima Ahdash and Khadeja Ramali, who have been a source of inspiration and encouragement. Last but foremost, I thank my family for their patience and support.

Chapters 2 and 3 include revised versions of work which appears in the article '"Like His Father Before Him": Patrilineality and Nationalism in the work of Hisham Matar, Jamal Mahjoub and Robin Yassin-Kassab' in *Postcolonial Interventions*. Chapter 4 includes sections which appear in an earlier version as 'Qabbani versus Qur'an: Arabism and the Umma in Robin Yassin-Kassab's The Road from Damascus' in *Open Cultural Studies*.

Transliteration

The names of authors, characters and place names are rendered in Anglicized forms dictated by common usage, omitting diacritical marks. The names of authors whose works have been translated are rendered according to the form in which they appear in the English-language translation. Where quotations include transliterations, these are not altered.

INTRODUCTION

After Edward Said's death in 2003, the Palestinian poet Mahmoud Darwish wrote an elegy for his friend, giving the poem the title 'Ṭibāq' in reference to Said's concept of the contrapuntal.[1] Structured as a series of questions and answers between Darwish and Said, 'Ṭibāq' presents an interplay of perspectives around topics which both writers have been concerned with throughout their work: nationalism, exile and the formation of identity between 'self-invention' and the 'inheritance of the past'. Darwish dwells in particular on the complications of language for Said, existing between English with its 'yielding phrases' and Arabic which 'does not yield to [Said's] imagination' ('A Contrapuntal Reading' 177). The imagined dialogue between the two personas at times becomes contentious, in particular in a passage instigated by a question about *daʾ al-ḥanīn*, or 'the malady of nostalgia'. Said, as imagined in Darwish's poem, sees the potential of *ḥanīn* as a method to retain hope, a '[n]ostalgia for a higher, more distant tomorrow' (179). As for 'nostalgia for yesterday', Said dismisses this form of *ḥanīn* as 'a sentiment not fit for an intellectual', a dangerous attachment to the past which implies a retreat from the present (179). However, the speaker representing Darwish questions this resolute response, asking what, in that case, motivated Said to return 'to that house, your house in Talbiya, in Jerusalem?' (180). This moment of tension speaks to the poem's concern with the ethics and poetics of exile. What motivates the gesture of remembrance of or return to the illusive, and elusive, past and place of nostalgic feeling? To what extent is it possible to resist or to dismiss nostalgia in favour of a view of identity as self-creation? And what functions do nostalgic feelings serve in the context of geographical and linguistic displacement? The questions which Darwish poses in his elegy to Said, questions about identity, belonging and the impulse to return to the past, are questions which are more urgent than ever today, at a time when the effects of globalization are spurring on narratives that view the past not only as better than the uncertain present but, given that uncertainty, better than any imaginable future.

This book examines nostalgia as a literary trope in Anglophone Arab novels, placing this growing body of literature in the context of Arab diaspora and in relation to theoretical work about the role of memory and history, mourning and melancholia, loss and trauma. The purpose of the book is twofold. First, I undertake a sustained examination of nostalgia as an aesthetic strategy in Anglophone Arab fiction, making the case that nostalgia and nostalgic feeling ought not be dismissed, but rather should be analysed within a critical framework which accounts for the functions and effects of nostalgic discourse in literature, as well as exploring its ethical and political importance in Arab diaspora. Second, I draw connections between Anglophone Arab literature and Arabic literary traditions, making the argument that nostalgic tropes cross linguistic boundaries, and that a bilingual approach is important to bring light to nostalgic narratives across these connected but distinct literary traditions. I agree with Hilary Kilpatrick that Arab literature in English 'requires familiarity with both (or all) the literary traditions on which the individual work draws', addressing connections between the Arab novel in English and Arabic literary traditions ('Arab Fiction' 46). I therefore locate the novels examined in relation to nostalgic discourses in Arabic-language literature, grounding the discussion of Anglophone Arab literature in a comparative framework. I am interested in tracing connections between the emerging field of Anglophone Arab literature and Arabic literary traditions, identifying recurring homological patterns, similarities and differences, as writers in diaspora reiterate or alter pervasive nostalgic discourses, responding to similar political conditions and contexts of political and social upheaval. The comparative approach I take allows what I see as a much-needed integration of cultural production across Arab diasporas and Arabic-speaking countries, reflecting connections across borders while being aware of how language colours experience.

Nostalgic discourses saturate contemporary reflections on Arab politics and culture. In 'On Lost Causes,' Said writes, 'how does the cause of a people, a culture, or an individual become hopeless? We had once believed as a people that there was room for us at the rendezvous of destiny' (355). The acclaimed novelist Hanan al-Shaykh asks, 'why is it that we didn't complete our cultural journey and how is it that we have ended up today in the very worst of times?' (19). In *Black Wave* (2020), which traces the modern history of the Middle East, journalist Kim Ghattas argues that the question 'what happened' has haunted the region over the past forty years. In *Becoming Arab in London*, Ramy Aly describes the 'burden' of failure carried through generations and into the diaspora: '[f]or generations now, Arabs have carried the burden of failing themselves somehow, of betraying their glorious civilisational past, of becoming a vassal, occupied, impoverished and enfeebled nation' (4). In *Considération sur le Malheur Arabe* (2005), translated into English as *Being Arab* ([2006] 2013), Samir Kassir states that '[a]fter its golden age, Arab history is viewed as no more than a string of failures, a single continuum of misfortunes' (38), and describes the nostalgic turning to the past to find out what went wrong as a 'crime novel version of history', casting a present deemed lacking against some romanticized image of the past (80). The various lamentations of the present described here and in the preceding paragraphs suggest a search for the turning point, the point at which the present divorces itself from the past, appealing to various idealized eras from narratives of the 'golden age' Arabo-Islamic civilization, to the cultural renaissance (*Nahḍa*) beginning in the late nineteenth century, to various ideological movements which sought to redefine nationhood during the twentieth century. To pose the question 'what went wrong' in the region in order to dislocate history from these pasts (often represented as potential imagined futures) speaks to the capacity of nostalgia to render loss into narrative and to make sense of historical events that continue to rankle as grievances in the present.

Contemporary Arabic literature is deeply invested in grappling with the question of what went wrong. As Saree Makdisi puts it, Arabic literature today is a 'literature of "crisis"' that 'helps to produce not merely the expression or articulation of crisis but rather the reality of crisis itself' (98). The decades of internal division and conflict alongside entrenched authoritarian rule across Arabic-speaking countries are represented in literatures from the region as a contradictory reality, simultaneously stagnant and chaotic. Anglophone Arab writing is not detached from this context, being very much informed by the multiple crises of the Arab world, yet it offers something new in negotiating the hyphenated identities that are the result of diaspora experiences. While many canonical Arab writers have produced their work in exile, writing in English for a mainly Western audience overlays physical geographical displacement with a linguistic rift that further complicates 'the unhealable rift forced between a human being and a native place, between the self and its true home' (Said, *Reflections* 173). Nostalgia is a hallmark of contemporary Anglophone Arab literature, providing a way to negotiate concerns with the diasporic condition, with linguistic displacement and with the contemporary Arab condition as seen from the perspective of exile. I am not arguing here that shared nostalgic rhetoric proves that there is a unified tradition of the Anglophone Arab novel. Rather, I suggest that nostalgic narratives in this literature are a measure of the historical conditions that place the notion of 'Arabness' under stress, a way to work through essentialist exploitations of identity within the region, as well as stereotypical representations of the so-called Arab world outside the region.

This book follows a temporal progression, examining the nostalgic narratives that relate the past to the contemporary moment. I begin with the juxtaposition of the present against the ruins of great empires, examining the narrative of living in the shadow of great civilizations, which extends across the region in various guises and forms the essential backdrop to the nostalgia for more recent times. I then turn to a second strand of nostalgic sentiment, the idealization of precolonial notions of authenticity, which I explore in conjunction with the nostalgia for the era of anti-colonial nationalism. This discussion of the ideological narrative casting tradition against modernity paves the way for a consideration of nostalgic narratives surrounding the project of pan-Arab nationalism and the failure of this project under the weight of state repression. Finally, the study focuses on diaspora sites, investigating nostalgia for the homeland in relation to the formulations of migrant identity. Through these four strands, I discuss texts by Rabih Alameddine, Sabiha Khemir, Yasmin Zahran, Ahdaf Soueif, Fadia Faqir, Jamal Mahjoub, Hisham Matar, Leila Aboulela, Randa Jarrar, Robin Yassin-Kassab, Selma Dabbagh and Rawi Hage. Many of these writers do not easily fit into established subcategories of immigrant writers from particular countries, not having settled in one location for long enough to claim a particular hyphenated identity. In many cases, the variety of backgrounds and contexts to which the writers belong highlights the difficulty of locating or consolidating a tradition of Anglophone Arab writing. The word

'Arab' itself of course raises the question of what this appellation signifies, and to speak of 'the Arab world' is a fraught endeavour, positing a distinct geographical or cultural 'world' as a totality, and homogenizing a vast and vastly heterogeneous region. I use the term Anglophone Arab literature as a shorthand; as with all attempts to definitively propose a category based on ethnic and national identities, the term obscures the amorphousness of these notions. While I do not take the position that the identity of the writer inevitably defines the text, the classification of texts emerging out of immigrant and minority contexts is inevitably linked with the already established frameworks of identity which locate them as separate or marginal literary sub-cultures. As the politics of marketing literary texts ties them to particular cultural and geographic contexts, national and ethnic categories continue to guide production, distribution and reception, despite the proliferation of 'migrant', 'transnational' or 'transcultural' literatures, to mention only some of the labels increasingly used to describe texts which cannot be categorized under a single national tradition.

I focus on novels published from the 1990s to the present, the era that has seen the development and consolidation of Anglophone Arab writing as an emergent category. I focus in particular on the realist novel not in order to argue that nostalgic discourses are more or less ambiguous or interesting in fiction as opposed to other genres, but in order to set parameters to my analysis and define the scope of the project, exploring how particular modes of realist engagement respond to the present moment. Though writers of Arab background who have produced work written in English include growing numbers of poets and playwrights, the genre of the novel has been dominant, in particular in the contemporary period. Notably, within criticism on Anglophone Arab writing, nostalgic tropes are often associated with poetry as a genre which is deemed to slip more easily into the lachrymose. For example, Lisa Suhair Majaj argues that Arab American writing has turned away from poetry to prose as an anti-nostalgic reaction, stating that 'it is as if the turn away from nostalgic celebration toward more rigorous and self-critical explorations mandates a move away from the lyric compression of poetry toward the more expansive and explanatory medium of prose' ('New Directions' 71). While I agree that nostalgic celebration may be well-suited to lyric poetry, I depart slightly from this point in seeking to expand the concept of nostalgia beyond the celebratory. Rather than identifying nostalgia as more or less prevalent in particular genres, I consider genres as modes which allow us to organize our response to the present in various ways, in line with Laura Berlant's discussion of crisis as 'an emergency in the reproduction of life, a transition that has not found its genres for moving on' (2). The notion of finding a genre for moving on is helpful to me in thinking about nostalgic discourse, projecting as it does the urgency of seeking modes which expand the cultural imaginary by constructing new narratives in response. Novels, in their expansiveness, range across spaces and times and reflect on a complex range of emotions associated with nostalgic feeling, including lingering on the disabling emotions that are associated with this emotion and the critical consequences of the inability to move on.

To begin to draw out some of the implications of nostalgia in Anglophone Arab fiction, I turn to two examples relating to the Egyptian singer Umm Kulthum as a touchstone of nostalgic emotion. In the last few pages of Ahdaf Soueif's *In the Eye of the Sun* ([1992] 2012), the protagonist Asya returns to Egypt after years living abroad, and drives through Cairo listening to a song by Umm Kulthum, reflecting on the nostalgia the song evokes: '[w]hat is it that the song makes her nostalgic for? How can she be yearning for Cairo and the feel of the Cairo night and the voice of Ummu Kulthoum [*sic*] while she is actually here in the middle of it all?' (780). This passage does more than represent a yearning for an idealized version of the past; it also represents the protagonist's questions about the object, function and meaning of such yearning. Asya is at once experiencing nostalgic feelings and simultaneously standing at a critical distance from these feelings, an expression of nostalgia intertwined with doubt. The reflective quality of the protagonist asking herself '[w]hat is it that the song makes her nostalgic for?' expresses and questions nostalgia in the same breath, suggesting that the source of the yearning evoked by Umm Kulthum's song is more elusive than it would appear. Similarly, in a passage of Robin Yassin-Kassab's novel *The Road from Damascus* (2008), the protagonist reflects on why he should be affected by the singer, '[t]he voice of Arab nationalism', who is 'singing about the days that are gone. The weak spot: the pathos of past time' (170). In this line, the 'weak spot' indicates a recognition of nostalgia's pejorative connotations as futile sentimentality, while 'pathos' suggests a recognition of nostalgia's evocative power and emotional appeal. This ambivalence towards nostalgia, questioning its triggers and its functionality, is characteristic of contemporary Anglophone Arab fiction, exploring what it means to yearn for earlier times, while also critiquing idealized versions of the past, thereby opening up a space for discussing nostalgia's phenomenological and aesthetic implications.

Literature is a medium of memory. Birgit Neumann uses the term 'fictions of memory' to describe literary works which reflect on cultural memory, and the 'stories that individuals or cultures tell about their past to answer the question "who am I" or collectively, "who are we?"' (334). These questions, central to the work of diaspora writers, are in the case of Anglophone Arab fiction also inextricable from 'crime novel version[s] of history' which seek to render comprehensible 'what went wrong' (Kassir 80). Anglophobe Arab writers' reflections on these interrelated questions involve grappling with the idealized past and its present repercussions, but also formulating cultural narratives for the future. What are the implications of vivifying the past while vilifying the present? Jill Bradbury notes that 'narratives of the past may serve not to restore an earlier time or the place of "home", but to dislocate our positioning in the present, to open not only windows on the world, but new ways of viewing ourselves' (348). As I will discuss in what follows, Arab diaspora writing is saturated with nostalgia, the bittersweet emotional state of yearning for what is lost, in part because writers have been so invested in questioning the triggers, functions and implications of what Darwish identifies as *daʾ al-ḥanīn*, the pervasive malady of nostalgia.

The malady of nostalgia

In common parlance, nostalgia is a shorthand for fixity and absolutism, associated with sentimental forces which attempt to preserve parochial identities. Among nostalgia's defining characteristics, in Linda Hutcheon's description, is that it 'sanitises as it selects, making the past feel complete, stable, coherent, safe from the unexpected and the untoward, from accident or betrayal – in other words, making it so very unlike the present' (195). To be nostalgic is to distort the object of yearning, screening out anything that might disturb the idealized picture. It is only relatively recently that the variety of nostalgic sentiment has been examined more closely as nostalgia has become the subject of systematic study, often in ways aimed at recuperating it from its negative connotations, as I will explore in further detail later. In the field of psychology, researchers such as Tim Wildschut, Constantine Sedikides and others have worked on defining nostalgia's key features, studying the content, triggers and functions of nostalgic feelings (Wildschut et al. 2006), and identifying the palliative effects of nostalgia as a source of physiological comfort (Sedikides and Wildschut 2016). In these studies, nostalgia is seen as a significant social emotion which fulfils particular psychological functions, rather than a one-dimension sentimental feeling. Within the field of memory studies, meanwhile, critics such as Svetlana Boym, Paul Grainge, Marianne Hirsch, Astrid Erll and others have sought to reposition nostalgia as a strategy to lend coherence to life. For Boym, nostalgia is 'not merely an artistic device but a strategy of survival, a way of making sense of the impossibility of homecoming' (xvii). In these reworkings of the concept, nostalgia is not necessarily uncritically accepting of the value of the past but can potentially facilitate critical engagement with the past and with cultural memory.

In much of the writing focusing on the resurgence of nostalgia and memory, the draw of the past is linked to the impact of neoliberal globalization and the information technology revolution, resulting in the emergence of what Robert Hassan has called the 'chronoscopic society' (Hassan 2003). Famously, in his identification of nostalgia as a symptom of postmodernity and consumer capitalism, Fredric Jameson uses the seemingly oxymoronic formulation 'nostalgia for the present', to discuss how films blur markers of contemporaneity, reading this as 'an alarming and pathological symptom of a society that has become incapable of dealing with time' ('Postmodernism' 117). Andreas Huyssen, addressing the connection between the appeal of cultural memory and the compressed, accelerated times and spaces of globalization, suggests that 'the turn toward ancestral residues and local traditions' represents the 'attempt to break out of the swirling empty space of the everyday present and to claim a sense of time and memory' (Huyssen, *Twilight* 28). According to Arif Dirlik, meanwhile, the pull of the past is an intrinsic aspect of contemporary culture, suggesting that 'a willingness to listen to invocations of cultural legacies' emerges not as 'reactionary responses to modernity, inimical to its achievement, but as the very conditions of a global modernity' (Modernity 25). In these discussions, the turn to the past is identified as resulting from and intrinsic to a cultural acceleration under the impact of technology. While many identify this trend as harmful or even pathological, there is nevertheless a recognition of the need to account for how cultural time is changing. In Paul Virilio's work on deterritorialization in contemporary political ontology, an argument is made for the need to examine 'the time systems administered by various technologies' in an environment where '[t]here is a movement from geo- to chrono-politics: the distribution of territory becomes the distribution of time' (126). Yet as various critics have recognized, the study of our political systems today remains 'overtly pre-occupied with spatial rather than temporal relations', highlighting the need to pay greater attention to the temporal order and to our cultural temporalities, including the impulse towards nostalgia and the impact of nostalgic narratives which seek to recover the past (Hutchings 11).

The question facing memory discourse as it has continued to grow is whether its concepts offer the appropriate forum for such explorations of how we understand temporality. Kerwin Lee Klein describes a growing 'memory industry' (127), where 'memory is replacing old favourites – nature, culture, language – as the word most commonly paired with history' (128). Klein argues that this industry has led to a dangerous 'privatization of history as global experiences splinter into isolate chunks of ethnoracial substance', finding the ethno-national tendencies of cultural memory to be a withdrawal from the realities of circulation and exchange (144). Along similar lines, a number of critics have questioned the concept of memory as an over-personalization of the political, evaluating in particular the usefulness of framing trauma, associated with the individual psyche, as a collective experience. For example, Fatima Naqvi critiques 'the millennial appeal to victimhood' where discourses of trauma and melancholia are reconceptualized as mechanisms for dealing with loss (3). Questioning the implications of memory discourse and its consolidation into the transdisciplinary subject area of memory studies in recent years highlights the extent to which, nearly a century after Maurice Halbwachs's definition of memory as a social phenomenon, terms such as collective, cultural and social memories remain both pervasive and contentious, seen as a transference of psychological terminology to the social field.

The critical discourse around Anglophone Arab writing tends to align with predominant understandings of nostalgia as a self-indulgent and sentimental emotion unsuited to the rigours of truly creative literary writing. While there has been some work on nostalgia in Arabic literature, including Wen-chin Ouyang's important study *The Politics of Nostalgia in the Arabic Novel* (2013), there are no comparable in-depth studies that examine the subject of nostalgia in relation to the diaspora and the Anglophone Arab novel. Understood as the uncritical romanticizing of the past, the aesthetic implications of nostalgia in Arab diaspora contexts are almost invariably framed as something immigrant communities must push beyond in order to open the doors for critical and creative approaches. For example, Tanyss Ludescher celebrates a transition away from nostalgic writing in her article 'From Nostalgia to Critique: An Overview of Arab-American

Literature'. Identifying nostalgia with culturalist logic, Ludescher traces a shift away from the romanticization of the homeland towards a more critical tone, suggesting a move beyond the nostalgic attachment to the past that belongs in the 'old country' as the primary referent for identity. Posited in opposition to critique, nostalgia is seen as the evocation of simplistic images of family and homeland, associated with pandering to a largely non-Arab audience and with a tendency to self-exoticization to appeal to the market. For example, Mara Naaman argues for an Arab American literature 'bold enough to [. . .] write against the market – against nostalgia for a static homeland (that familiar refrain of the immigrant) and against the fetishising of the romance of ethnic difference' (380). Naaman's use of the word 'static' suggests that the wistfulness or longing for an irretrievable place or temporality detaches the nostalgic subject from the evolving present. Nostalgia for the homeland is suspect because it seems to respond to the ethnographic 'romance of ethnic difference', giving expression to an ethnic identity, while metropolitan literature gives expression to universal values. Moreover, nostalgia suggests a focus on theme, which as Pheng Cheah has noted, it often separated from the more valued attention to formal qualities: '"[t]heme" is implicitly associated with the crudeness and simplicity of postcolonial politics and "form" with universal aesthetic value' (15). For these and other reasons, there is a hostility to, or dismissal of, nostalgia which has resulted in relatively little critical work on how nostalgia is deployed in Anglophone Arab writing, despite the prevalence of nostalgic discourse in this literature, and the frequency with which such nostalgic discourses govern conversations about the history of the Arab world.

This book argues for the value of attending to nostalgic discourses in literature, examining nostalgia's role in constructing cultural memory, which is not inherently there to be recovered or possessed but rather is constructed, and manipulated, in the present. As Said puts it, '[m]emory is not necessarily authentic, but [. . .] rather useful' ('Memory' 179). The usefulness of memory, the basic notion that the past is never a given but is produced, has an important bearing on nostalgic discourse in literature as a medium of memory. For Ann Rigney, literary works function as 'portable monuments', that is, as repositories of cultural memory, which tell us something about past experiences, a monument being not an autonomous phenomenon but socially and historically situated. Neumann argues that works which represent the past involve 'an imaginative (re)construction of the past in response to current needs' (334) and stresses that the 'mimesis of memory' produces rather than reflects the past: '[n]ovels do not imitate existing versions of memory, but produce, in the act of discourse, that very past which they purport to describe' (334). This slippage between construction and representation is inherent in the nostalgic gaze which selects what stories of the past will be sanitized and idealized. As Boym puts it, nostalgia works through the 'superimposition of two images – of home and abroad, past and present, dream and everyday life', a superimposition Boym describes through the 'cinematic image' of a 'double exposure' (xii–xiv). To be nostalgic is thus to perform a gesture of return to a time or place which is contrasted to the present, but which always involves confrontation and comparison, situating us in multiple places at once. Nostalgic meaning can only be generated through revising narratives about the past while experiencing a disconnection from the present, and thus nostalgic tropes in literature necessarily involve thematic, stylistic and formal choices which negotiate between memory and narrative, and which have a bifurcated temporality, unfolding forward in time while looking towards the irrevocably lost past.

Much of the criticism directed at the representation of the nostalgic immigrant calls for a focus on the here and now, suggesting that an investment in the idealized past is necessarily in opposition to living fully in the present. The problematic status of the nostalgic subject speaks to a tendency to identify the multicultural society as 'happy object', where, according to Sara Ahmed, the unhappy subject is not only 'an obstacle to his or her own happiness, but also to the happiness of the generation to come, and to national happiness' (48). Through such a lens, the nostalgic's refusal to let go of the past is a tendentious retreat from difference, plurality and the realities of contemporary life. Yet nostalgia is always involved in negotiating the dislocation of attachments and allegiances in contexts of political and social upheaval, as well as negotiating the issues raised by displacement both linguistic and geographic. Ghassan Hage suggests that it is possible to see nostalgia as an 'active insertion of memory in the construction of the present and the future' rather than only a helpless homesickness which takes 'refuge in the memories of the past from the potentially traumatising encounter with the present' (417). According to Hage, nostalgic strategies can improve life in diaspora:

> intimations of lost homelands as well as more obviously intimations of 'new homelands' should be seen as affective building blocks used by migrants to make themselves feel at home where they actually are. They are part of the migrant's settlement strategies rather than an attempt to escape the realities of the host country. (418)

This view sees nostalgia as a strategy of diaspora existence, interlinked with the need to generate new myths of belonging in what Said has called the 'age of the refugee, the displaced person, mass immigration' (*Reflections* 174). To focus on the nostalgic impulse within immigrant communities would seem to further what Hage describes as 'a "miserabilist" tendency in the study of migration that wants to make migrants passive pained people at all costs' and which turns the 'yearning for home into a single "painful" sentiment' (417). However, rather than turning away from the nostalgic subject, perhaps the singular lens on nostalgic discourse as painful should be diversified, to understand how nostalgic emotions can involve more than melancholic sentiment. Nostalgia, as a multifarious, bittersweet phenomenon, can involve narratives that are escapist, comforting, questioning or cynical, encompassing a range of physical, emotional and cognitive attempts at reconnection while experiencing various forms of disconnection.

In what follows, I explore the potential and limitations of nostalgia as a psychosocial strategy for shoring up fragments of identity. I turn to Said's 'Freud and the non-European', which reads Freud's last text, 'Moses and Monotheism', in order to explore an understanding of identity that necessarily contains otherness.

Said argues that 'in excavating the archaeology of Jewish identity, Freud insisted that it did not begin with itself but, rather, with other identities' (44). Said's reading of Freud's meditation highlights how collective identities, whether based on religion, ethnicity or nation, always contain irrepressible differences which complicate attempts to narrate the past. As he writes, 'identity cannot be thought or worked through itself alone; it cannot constitute or even imagine itself without that radical originary break or flaw which will not be repressed' (53–4). Acknowledging this reality allows us to recognize complexity, 'refusing to resolve identity into some of the nationalist or religious herds in which so many people want so desperately to run' (53). Jacqueline Rose, in her afterword and response to Said's text, describes how his reading of Freud's work articulates 'a vision of identity as able to move beyond the dangers of identity in our times' (78). Such a vision reformulates the narrowness of identity to an articulation of an ethics of difference, and as Said sees it, a notion of identity as interwoven with and emerging from otherness which is transferable to other contexts: 'the strength of this thought is that it can be articulated in and speak to other besieged identities as well [. . .] as a troubling, disabling, destabilizing secular wound' (54). However, Said's work has been critiqued by Richard H. Armstrong as offering a simplistic 'gospel of hybridity that will cure the Israelis (and by extension, all of us still plagued by national myths) from the nasty habits of essentialising the past' (245). A similar critique is evident, though less overtly stated, in Rose's response, where she raises the point that 'the fixity of identity – for Freud, for any of us – is something from which it is very hard to escape – harder than Said, for wholly admirable motives, wants it to be' (74). Having highlighted the inexorable draw of identity, Rose points out that the opposite of such fixity is not necessarily empowering. Beginning with the question '[a]re we at risk of idealising the flaws and fissures of identity?' (76), Rose goes on to enumerate some of the ways such flaws and fissures can lead not to inclusivity but 'towards dogma, the dangers of coercive and coercing forms of faith' (76). This is so 'not only because [. . .] history re-presses the flaw, but because the most historically attested response to trauma is to repeat it' (77). Rose takes up the idea that history is 'always that which comes after, and all too often, either overrides or re-presses the flaw' and notes that this petrification of the past is not only a consequence of the writing of history, but an understandable response to traumatic injury (54).

The subtle critique in Rose's response suggests that Said's valorization of unresolved identity does not go far enough. What is needed is further examination of how coherent narratives work as a response to traumas which 'far from generating freedom, openness to others as well as to the divided and unresolved fragments of the self' cause 'identities to batten down' (76). Rose's discussion highlights the contradictory impulses of coherence and fragmentation in Said's work, between the valorization of an unresolved identity and the battle 'over the right to a remembered presence and, with that presence, the right to possess and reclaim a collective historical reality' ('Invention, Memory and Place' 184). According to Said, Freud's writing on Moses raises questions about how a historical narrative that does not 'repress the flaw' might be written. Said asks:

'can so utterly indecisive and so deeply undetermined a history ever be written? In what language and with what sort of vocabulary?' (55). Such an undetermined history would mean acknowledging the unsettling presence of other histories we would rather not acknowledge, pointing to the political and ethical significance of studying narratives about identity and memory, including the contemporary pervasive mode of nostalgia.

The proliferation of studies on nostalgia today raises questions not only around the implications of cultural memory's resurgence but also the cultural parameters according to which nostalgia is being redefined. Nostalgia, as Kathleen Stewart points out, is mutable, 'a cultural practice, not a given context; its forms, meanings, and effects shift with the context – it depends on where the speaker stands in the landscape of the present' (252). While I find memory studies useful in discussing narratives which remember the region's fraught history, I also draw on other critical frameworks to reframe nostalgia in relation to Arab literary history, as I discuss in the following section.

Nostalgia and Eurocentrism

The term 'nostalgia' was coined in 1688 by Swiss physician Johannes Hofer from the Greek *nostos* (home) and *algos* (suffering), initially to describe homesickness as a psychopathological disorder in the context of war. The particular context that surrounds this etymology has lingered in the negative connotations that attach themselves to nostalgia, even as the concept has shifted from the original understanding to encompass several overlapping affective states. Tracing this shift, Linda Hutcheon describes a transition from geographic homesickness to the mourning of past time:

> nostalgia was no longer simply a yearning to return home. As early as 1798, Immanuel Kant had noted that people who did return home were usually disappointed because, in fact, they did not want to return to a place, but to a time, a time of youth. Time, unlike space, cannot be returned to – ever; time is irreversible. And nostalgia becomes the reaction to that sad fact. As one critic has succinctly put this change: 'Odysseus longs for home; Proust is in search of lost time.' (45)

The shift in the concept of nostalgia, from the spatial dimension of homesickness to the temporal longing for the past, raises the question of how to approach other traditions of longing. In *The Future of Nostalgia* ([2002] 2008), Boym broaches this question when she refers to pervasive tropes of longing, mentioning both 'Chinese and Arabic poetry where longing is a poetic commonplace', to show that 'there had been plenty of longing before the seventeenth century' and 'not only in the European tradition' (7). However, Boym goes on to articulate a binary conceptualization of nostalgia which is inextricable from the etymological roots of the term in that tradition:

Restorative nostalgia stresses *nostos* and attempts a transhistorical reconstruction of the lost home. Reflective nostalgia thrives in *algia*, the longing itself, and delays the homecoming – wistfully, ironically, desperately. Restorative nostalgia does not think of itself as nostalgia, but rather as truth and tradition. Reflective nostalgia dwells on the ambivalences of human longing and belonging and does not shy away from the contradictions of modernity. Restorative nostalgia protects the absolute truth, while reflective nostalgia calls it into doubt. (xviii)

Boym separates between the predominant perception of nostalgia, which emphasizes returning to the past as origin, and a more affirmative idea of nostalgia which grapples with physical or emotional alienation and estrangement, creating a model of yearning for the lost past on the one hand and confronting the inability to reconnect with that past on the other. Similarly, Paul Grainge distinguishes between 'nostalgia as mood' and 'nostalgia as mode', where the former relates to nostalgia as a mood of yearning, seeking to reconnect with the irrecoverable past and the latter is a strategic mode that acknowledges the impossibility of such reconnection, through it seeks to recover elements of the past for the present. According to Grainge, the 'proliferation of nostalgic modes' offers 'a new kind of engagement with the past, a relationship based fundamentally on its cultural mediation and textual reconfiguration in the present' ('Nostalgia and Style' 33). In Fred Davis' work on the sociology of nostalgia, meanwhile, there is a tripartite gradation of increasing complexity. The simplest form of nostalgia holds that 'things were better (more beautiful) (healthier) (happier) (more civilised) (more exciting)' (18). A more reflexive form 'summons [. . .] certain empirically oriented questions concerning the truth, accuracy, completeness or representativeness of the nostalgia claim' (21). In this case, there is an introspective quality to the simple nostalgic claim that 'things were better' which questions the extent to which this is in fact true. Finally, interpreted nostalgia involves asking analytical questions: '[w]hy am I feeling nostalgia? What may this mean for my past, for my now? [. . .] What uses does nostalgia serve for me? For others? For the times in which we live?' (24–5). In each of these theorizations of nostalgia as multiple, nostalgic emotion is identified as a binary or as existing on a spectrum, yet in moving from a simple and conservative nostalgia to a more introspective and reflective nostalgic these various theorizations remain inextricable from the negative connotations that linger in nostalgia's initial definition as a psychiatric disorder. The focus on rehabilitating nostalgia from its origins as a disease already locates the discussion in the European cultural context.

The culturally specific meanings of nostalgia highlight the issue of the often monocultural frameworks through which cultural memory more broadly is explored. Michael Rothberg points out that the structures of canonized national memory that have been developed within memory studies seem to fit uneasily with the reconceptualization of identity in contexts 'of colonialism and globalisation, that dislocate the organically defined groups that interested Halbwachs and that continue to interest many students of memory' (362). Rothberg notes that 'memory studies has largely avoided the issues of colonialism and its legacies' but also argues that postcolonial critics have often 'left the category of memory out of their theory and the practice of their field' (359). Richard Werbner similarly argues that despite the 'greatly reawakened interest' being directed at the work of cultural memory in public life, 'the importance of this theoretical interest for the study of postcolonial political subjectivities in the making is only beginning to be recognised' (15). This is not to say that representations of the past have not always been central to postcolonial studies; given that '[m]emory and its representations touch very significantly upon questions of identity, of nationalism, of power and authority' (Said, 'Memory' 176), the awareness of this vitality of memory leads writers to 're-excavating and recharting the past from a postcolonial point of view' (182). However, memory as a category is framed differently in these respective fields, the insights developed within memory studies differing from theorizations of memory as a category in postcolonial theory.

These arguments for 'decolonizing' cultural memory are often brought up in contending with the imperative to focus on the present and the future as we confront a range of political and ecological crises. Memory studies scholars often return to the social and political imperatives of studying narratives about the past in order to make a claim for not only the validity but the urgency of memory work. For example, taking issue with Gavriel D. Rosenfeld's claim that in a post-9/11 world 'the study of memory [. . .] may increasingly appear to be a luxury' (147), Astrid Erll makes the case for examining

> paradigms that were formed in long historical processes – via cultural memory, [. . .] to understand the different ways in which people handle time, and this refers not only to their 'working through the past', but also includes their understanding of the present and visions for the future. (*Memory in Culture* 172)

Erll goes on to discuss how 'current wars in Afghanistan, Iraq, and on the African continent, the rise of China and India, global warming' are evidence for the inextricable connection between what Erll calls the 'hard facts' of economy, politics and environment, and the 'soft factors' constituted by 'cultural processes grounded in cultural memory' (173). Rather than cultural memory being a luxury which an age of crises cannot afford, Erll suggests that the study of culturally framed narratives about the past is vital in order precisely to understand these crises. However, the passage quoted above is the only reference to Iraq and Afghanistan in the book, while Africa, India and China appear only in a few more scattered references, speaking to the gulf between the statements of global political relevance articulated within these fields of study and the areas of the world which tend to be the focus of this research.

Efforts to expand the use of memory studies within postcolonial contexts are in parallel with similar efforts to expand the related field of trauma studies through considering the traumatic legacies of colonialism. As Stef Craps argues in *Postcolonial Witnessing* (2013), there is a need for 'a commitment not only to broadening the usual focus of trauma theory but also to acknowledge the traumas of non-Western or minority populations' (19). Craps, along with Gert

Buelens, edited a special issue of 'Studies in the Novel' with the title 'Postcolonial Trauma Novels' that frames the reorientation of trauma studies through Frantz Fanon's 'classic example of insidious trauma due to systematic oppression and discrimination' ('Introduction' 3). However, as Saadi Nikro points out, this special issue 'eschew[s] any consideration of the colonial, decolonising, and postcolonial circumstances and related discursive articulations in which Fanon's work is empirically, phenomenally, and hermeneutically embedded' (15). Expanding this point, Nikro notes that there is a 'lack of attention within postcolonial trauma studies to Arab and Islamic majority demographics and geographies' (15). This lack highlights the consequences of a larger problem, the relative lack of attention to Arab contexts in postcolonial studies. As Waïl Hassan notes, though colonial discourse analysis began with several theorists who wrote about colonialism in the region, including Fanon, Albert Memmi and Edward Said, it has developed into 'a sophisticated theoretical apparatus that rarely takes Arab literary and cultural production into account' ('Postcolonial Theory' 45). There are then several challenges which must be negotiated in relation to the issue of theoretical frameworks and their applicability: first, the relative lack of cross-fertilization between postcolonial studies on the one hand and memory and trauma studies on the other, despite their overlapping concerns, and second, the relative disregard, in all three fields, to the regional and cultural contexts of North Africa and the Middle East, and the diasporas related to these regions.

Meanwhile, the lack of critical attention to nostalgia in Arabic literary studies, and the relative paucity of theoretical material relating to issues including melancholy, mourning, trauma and loss, cannot be separated from unease about the deployment of Western theoretical concepts. For example, Moneera Al-Ghadeer in her analysis of Bedouin women's poetry critiques 'the failure of Arabic studies to think critically about mourning' which she sees as 'symptomatic of a recurring ambivalence – a resistance to the theoretical in relation to its perceived foreign origin' (40). Nouri Gana, in *Signifying Loss* (2011) puts the gap in critical work on mourning in the region more starkly:

> What is even more startling, however, is that there has not been any sustained work at the juncture between contemporary Arabic literature, which hovers at the margins of the unbendingly Anglophone postcolonial studies, and the recent theoretical work on mourning and melancholia, despite the many palpable convulsions and decolonial wars that have marked and continue to mark Arab contemporaneity. (11)

Gana speaks of the long-established relationship between mourning and poetry in both 'Western tradition of elegiac poetry and the poetic genre of *marthiya* (i.e. elegy) in the Arabic literary tradition', suggesting the potential for a more engaged exploration of mourning and melancholy in relation to Arabic literature (*Signifying Loss* 10). A comparative frame would allow for an exploration of the issues that arise in relating the *marthiya* and the elegy, for example, or connecting the black bile disorders of *sawdāwiyya* and melancholy. There is clearly much work to be done when it comes to "translating" theoretical terms in relation to Arabic literary tradition given the lack of attention to the cluster of theoretical concepts relating to loss in Arabic.

The challenges of transferring concepts across different contexts recalls Edward Said's reminder, in 'Travelling Theory' (1982), about 'processes of representation and institutionalisation different from those at the point of origin' (226). Theories that come to operate in contexts other than those from which they derive are filtered through conditions that can temper or modify political implications and how they apply to genres developed in other situations. Genre, as Berlant describes it, is always based on a process, as a 'loose affectively-invested zone of expectations about the narrative shape a situation will take'. Berlant goes on to suggest that '[a] situation becomes-genre, finds its genres of event. Any historical present is an impasse that appears in multiple temporalities of movements that have anchored themselves to a cluster of conventional genres' (2). The emphasis on process suggests the need to consider how aesthetic forms respond to and take on different expectations in an ongoing, situational recalibration of terms.

In the case of nostalgia, the particularity of the term's development as a disorder leads Bo Holmberg to argue that, despite the centrality of 'nostalgic sentiments' which 'are important in Arabic tradition even apart from the classical ode', there is no single word in Arabic that corresponds precisely to the term nostalgia as it is used in English (184). Holmberg asserts that '[e]ven in Modern Written Arabic it seems one has to resort to circumlocutions in order to express the idea of nostalgia' (183). The argument that a word taken up in critical discourse simply does not exist in Arabic is a recurring claim in Arabic literary criticism. For example, writing about medieval satire, G. J. H. van Gelder notes that '[t]here is no exact equivalent in Arabic for "satire"' and so to use that word is 'to impose a Western concept on a tradition that has its own system of modes and genres'. Yet van Gelder also notes that 'there is a considerable body of classical Arabic texts that may be called satirical' (693). In these cases, stating that there is no equivalent Arabic concept seems to perform the work of a space clearing gesture, to avoid translating or equating between terms. I use the term nostalgia without making a claim for its untranslatability, instead focusing on the multiplicity of translations possible, which may help to extricate nostalgia from a framework that seeks to rehabilitate this concept from being a disorder or a sentimental force. Within Arabic, the words that might be translated as nostalgia include *ḥanīn, lahfa, ṭawq, shawq* and *ishtiyāq*, among others, and the connotations of each of these words vary from a joyous longing to a lyrical yearning. Feelings of *ḥanīn*, a word which stems from the same root as the word tender (*ḥanān*), might be used more in the context of a nostalgia for childhood or for the homeland, while *lahfa* involves a sense of anticipation, a nostalgia that is future directed. The spectrum of Arabic words for longing or yearning, which involve various nuances of nostalgic emotion, offer a potential avenue to explore nostalgia as a multifaceted emotion that includes celebratory and creative dimensions, encompassing a variety of discourses about emotional attachment, adjusting to new conditions and seeking cultural continuity provided by narratives about the past.

Longing and yearning for the past, and for home, are recurrent tropes in Arabic poetics, rooted in the pre-Islamic literary tradition and in particular, in the classical ode or *qaṣīda*. Traditionally, the ode opens with the *nasīb*, the section in which the speaker stops by the traces of the beloved's abandoned campsite and laments the passing of time, establishing 'a space and mood of unparalleled melancholy in its invocation that all is lost' (Seigneurie 17). This elegiac topos of *al-wuqūf ʿalā al-aṭlāl* or 'standing by the ruins' continues to be invoked in modern literature. Perhaps the most famous lines of Arabic poetry are the opening of Imruʾ al-Qays's *muʿallaqa*, or hanged ode, from the sixth century. The ode begins: '[h]alt, let us weep, you two and I, as we remember beloved and campsite/at the winding dune's crest between al-Dakhūl and Ḥawmal' (qtd. in Stetkevych 110). This tradition continues to reverberate in contemporary Arabic literature. Palestinian writer Jabra Ibrahim Jabra is one of many writers who have cited this line in his writing. In Jabra's novel *The Ship* (1985, *al-Safīnah*, 1973), one of the narrators, Wadi, a Palestinian businessman living in Kuwait, points to the plethora of place names in premodern Arabic poetry, reciting the opening lines of al-Qays' *muʿallaqa* to prove that '[r]eal alienation is alienation from a place, from roots. This is the crux. Land, land, that is everything' (74). As suggested here, the connection to the *aṭlāl* topos is often part of a commentary on exile. For example, Walid Mounir in his essay 'Riḥlat al-manfā fī al-shiʿr al-ʿArabī al-ḥadīth' (The Journey of Exile in Modern Arabic Poetry) compares the necessity of movement for 'the ancient poets' and the 'inward' estrangement of 'modern poets':

> [t]he ancient poets were outwardly estranged, travelling from place to place in a quest for the bounties of nature [. . .] or for the beloved who did not leave any trace but the ruins of her encampment. The modern poets are [. . .] inwardly estranged, forced often despite themselves to leave the homeland [. . .] carrying with them their nostalgia. (193, my translation)

The elegiac mode of the *nasīb* expands from being the formulaic opening of a classical form to become an emotionally resonant touchstone for contemporary narratives about exile and alienation. The invocation of this trope of standing by the ruins resonates, as it turns the abandoned campsite into the metaphorically or literally ruined homeland, the homeland from which one is estranged. This deeply entrenched mode of estrangement presents Arab writers with a tradition to contest and negotiate the past, specifically the relationship between what Said has called the 'dialectic of memory over territory' between place and identity ('Memory' 176).

Though Arabic-speaking countries have until recently barely featured in memory studies, the memory industry has been a significant factor in the growth and the proliferation of projects seeking to construct national pasts across this region. Anthony Downey, editor of the volume *Dissonant Archives: Contemporary Visual Culture and Competing Narratives in the Middle East* (2015), argues that there is 'an imminent critical need to ask why a commitment to working with archives has become an apparently dominant aesthetic strategy for contemporary artists' (14). Lebanon has been a locus of memory work in the region, including for example The

Arab Image Foundation, established in Beirut in 1997, which collects and preserves photographs from across the region and the diaspora. In order to overcome the paucity of historical materials and difficulty of accessing archives, fictional collections such as The Atlas Group project seek to 'locate, preserve, study and produce audio, visual, literary and other artefacts that shed light on the contemporary history of Lebanon' (Ra'ad). Discussing the need for such creativity in relation to archives in the region, Iraqi art historian Nada Shabout highlights the problem of producing alternative historical narratives given the difficulty with accessing archives:

> [a]rchives as an active site of remembering would give us the tool [sic] to challenge the grand narrative produced by the state, and imagine alternative, globally-connected local narratives [...] archives are seemingly not available or accessible in the Middle East, which misleadingly presents the contemporary as rootless and ephemeral, and consequently heightens the question of identity in the region. (Shabout)

Shabout examines the role of the archive in relation to developing art history, however the questions she raises are relevant to historical imagination and cultural memory in the broader sphere of cultural production. The upsurge in archival projects by artists in recent years speaks to a recognition that, as Jacques Derrida notes, the archive is 'more than a thing of the past, before such a thing [...] it is a question [...] of the future itself, the question of a response, of a promise and of a responsibility for tomorrow' (36). This concern with constructing an archive for the preservation of cultural heritage has been a theme in a variety of projects concerned with Arab cultural memory. For example, a joint UNESCO and Arab League project entitled 'The Memory of the Arab World' is concerned with developing an internet portal as a 'bilingual gateway [...] to connect the younger generations of Arabs with their cultural identity' and as a way to 'maintain the collective memory of the people of the Arab World' ('Memory of the Arab World'). Perhaps the most visible manifestation of memorialization in the region is the museum boom in the Gulf states, where the last few decades have seen the construction of museums such as the Sharjah Museum of Islamic Civilisation and the Museum of Islamic Art, museums that are concerned with the preservation of Arab and/or Islamic heritage, which provide an illustration of the strategic use of the past for the present. These projects speak to increased awareness about the uses of cultural memory, including the very aspects of nostalgic discourse which render it suspect, creating cultural frameworks which serve to repress the flaws, in Said's phrasing. However, as I will suggest in what follows, rather than suspending or shying away from nostalgia due to its deployment in the service of essentializing narratives, it is important to explore how nostalgia functions in society, and literature, as a medium of memory.

Anglophone Arab literary criticism

At the time of its publication in 1992, Ahdaf Soueif's first novel *In the Eye of the Sun* was a rare example of literature written in English from the Middle East and North

Africa. In his discussion of Soeuif's text, Said remarked that the 'tiny number of writers in English' from this region is especially anomalous when compared to the 'explosion of literature in the Arabic language' and (I would add) to more established Francophone writing by Arab writers (*Reflections* 407). Geoffrey Nash similarly describes Anglophone Arab literature as minimal in 1998, noting that 'although a trickle of novels by Arabs writing in English is beginning to appear, it can hardly be placed on a par with the established English writings of Africa or India' (*The Arab Writer in English* 1). Though the first Anglophone literary works by Arab writers date back to the early twentieth century, it is only in recent decades that there has been a marked increase in the works of poetry and prose produced in English by writers with an Arab background, encompassing the work of immigrants and writers of mixed heritage in a variety of diasporic contexts, a resurgence which, as Nouri Gana argues, 'deserves a measure of critical attention and commentary' ('Introduction' 3). Academic scholarship on Anglophone Arab criticism has been rapidly increasing in recent years, but as Layla Maleh points out, until recently, 'anthologies and critical scholarship approaching Anglophone Arab writing remained scanty' (ix). The critical discourse has grown in correspondence to the emergence of what has come to be termed Anglophone Arab literature, providing nuanced engagements with the texts. Examples include *The Edinburgh Companion to the Arab novel in English* (2013), edited by Nouri Gana, Waïl Hassan's *Immigrant Narratives* (2011), *Arab Voices in Diaspora* (2009), edited by Layla Maleh, and *The Arab Diaspora*, edited by Zahia Salhi and Ian Netton (2006).

One aspect of this growing field of study involves returning to the earliest texts to construct literary histories of English-language literature by Arab writers. Evelyn Shakir and Layla Maleh have each separately described Anglophone Arab literature as falling into three chronological stages, a division which has been widely accepted. The first period, according to both critics, includes the early twentieth-century immigrants known as the Mahjar writers in the United States, Khalil Gibran and Ameen Rihani, as well as their contemporaries, such as George Antonius and Edward Selim Atiyah, who spent time in the service of the British administration in the Arab world. The second group, in Shakir and Maleh's accounts, are writers including Edward Attiyeh, Waguih Ghali and Jabra Ibrahim Jabra, whose work 'mostly reflected their British educational and intellectual formation' during the 1950s and 1960s (Maleh 7). According to Maleh, there was an instrumental quality to their English rather than 'an appropriation or subversion of it, or [. . .] a desire to challenge its dominance' (7). In comparison with the Mahjar writers, who formed the Pen League literary society (*al-Rābiṭa al-Qalamiyya*), works published during the mid-century were more scattered; Nash describes them as 'either an overture [. . .] or a fortuitous handful of disparate texts' (*Anglophone Arab Encounter* 47). Ghali, for example, only wrote one novel, and most of Jabra's fictional works are in Arabic.

The two previous groups correspond to distinct periods, with the selection of the texts focusing on establishing distinctions on the basis of the writers' country of settlement. The last category includes a much more amorphous and heterogeneous group of writers since the 1970s, splintering, as Nouri Gana puts it, into 'such fictional varieties as Arab American, Arab Canadian, Arab Australian and Anglo or British Arab' (9). The focus here is on a national (yet cosmopolitan) framework, the articulation of various subcategories on the basis of ethnic or national communities established in the diaspora. Defining such an amorphous group as part of one tradition highlights '[t]he difficulty of pinning down an author to a cultural "home" or a single geographical location' which marks all migrant literature (Maleh 52). Saadi Nikro illustrates this difficulty when he differentiates between what he calls 'diasporic' and 'multicultural' writing. Defining these terms in relation to Arab Australian fiction, Nikro suggests that diaspora writing 'structures an existentially concentrated movement across space' while multicultural writing 'is more preoccupied with inhabiting a certain place' ('Arab Australian Novel' 305). Diana Abu Jaber's *Arabian Jazz* (1993), for example, exploring the lives of Palestinian/Jordanian immigrants to the United States, might be described as multicultural, concerned with 'inhabiting a certain place'. Hisham Matar's *Anatomy of a Disappearance* (2011), by contrast, is more concerned with 'movement across space', with the narrative moving from Cairo to Geneva to London, and thus might be described as a novel of diaspora. This distinction however is necessarily one of degree. Moreover, the first category, where writers are able to explore the nuances of creating new hybrid identities in a multicultural society, is in part dependent on a sense of community which is not always equally apparent in all experiences of immigration.

The often tentative nature of group identity in diaspora is suggested by Jordanian-British author Fadia Faqir, in a conversation with Lindsey Moore. In the interview, Moore refers to 'two phases of migrant and/or minority fiction' identified by Mark Stein in *Black British Literature* (2004), the first phase being the bildungsroman and the second 'novels of transformation that deconstruct Englishness and transform the national topography', and asks Faqir how her novel attempts to 'remap British space' ('You Arrive At A Truth' 8). Faqir responds that for such remapping to happen 'you need a critical mass' (9) and points out that in Britain 'the ethnic category Arab is not even on the census, although it will be included in the next one'. Her comment about being included in the census, described as 'slowly [. . .] being quantified and recognised', highlights an emerging sense of an Arab-British community, which is related to the categorization of a literature from and about this community (9). The particular history of immigration and assimilation of Arabs in Britain has a relatively short time span, given that the majority arrived after the Gulf War. This has meant that British Arab identity has only recently been articulated through the establishment of bodies such as the National Association of British Arabs and the British Arab Association. The nebulous nature of 'Arab-British identity' has an impact on the sort of writing produced, and a framework which focuses exclusively on the extent to which these works address the British context would be lacking.

Discussing the US context, Lisa Suhair Majaj's article 'The Hyphenated Author' explores the issue of locating texts by describing two ways in which

Arab-American literature has been viewed. Majaj asserts that there is always 'a discernible inclination toward one or the other side of the hyphen':

> [t]he first view is that Arab-American identity is in essence a transplanted Arab identity, turning upon a preservation of Arab culture, maintenance of the Arab language, involvement in Middle Eastern politics, and a primary relationship to the Arab world [. . .] The second view, however, is that Arab-American identity [. . .] should be understood in relation to the American context and American frameworks of assimilation and multiculturalism. ('Hyphenated Author')

Much of the critical discourse around the Anglophone Arab novel can be mapped onto these two approaches, locating the texts either in relation to the writers' countries of origin or their countries of settlement. The former approach includes several studies focused on the Lebanese diaspora in the wake of the civil war in that country, which lasted from 1975 to 1990. Examples include Syrine Hout's *Postwar Anglophone Lebanese Fiction* (2012) and Jumana Bayeh's *The Literature of the Lebanese Diaspora* (2014), accounts that focus on the renegotiations of belonging and nationality outside the homeland. Critics who take the latter approach, on the other hand, attempt to define the characteristics of a body of texts produced by Arab immigrants in relation to the diaspora context. Geoffrey Nash for example has focused on Arab-British writers in *The Anglo Arab Encounter* (2007), and there have been some studies of Arab authors in Canadian contexts, by Elizabeth Dahab, and Australian contexts, by Saadi Nikro.

Most of the critical work on Anglophobe Arab novels has been on Arab American literature. Studies of this literature as a particular phenomenon include Carol Fadda-Conrey's *Contemporary Arab-American Literature* (2014) and Steven Salaita's *Modern Arab-American Fiction: A Reader's Guide* (2011). As Majaj makes clear, the focus on the creation of new hyphenated identities, on the particularities of an Arab American experience in this case, places the emphasis on inhabiting the new space, the country of settlement, rather than looking back at the homeland or seeing immigrant narratives as representing 'a transplanted Arab identity'. This focus is possible at least in part because a developing Arab American identity allows for an investigation into 'the process of ethnogenesis, the creation of something new and different out of the conjunction of Arab and American cultures' ('Hyphenated Author'). To some extent, this approach is also dependent on a cosmopolitan framework that distances itself from a particular connection with the Arab world. For example, Maleh argues that 'Anglophone Arab writers are perhaps the furthest away from paradigmatic Arabs, themselves being the progeny of cultural espousal, hybridity, and diasporic experience' (1). Similarly, though less definitively, Steven Salaita points to the 'different cultural values' among Anglophone Arabs 'as a result of their different social circumstances' in comparison to people living in Arabic-speaking countries (35). This emphasis on the distinction and the distance between the English-language writing of Arabs and the Arabic literary tradition also helps to explain why nostalgia, oriented as it is towards the past and the homeland, tends to be dismissed within the growing field of Anglophone Arab literary criticism.

Audience is another factor relevant to the critical framing of this body of literary work, especially given that the current increase in Anglophone Arab writing has occurred during a period where political events have brought Arabic-speaking countries to the forefront of the news cycle. While part of the audience for English-language literature by Arab writers may be readers in the region or the diaspora, the choice of English positions this body of work as literature for a 'global audience' which is identified with the Anglosphere. Nash points out that addressing such a readership involves 'all the problems inherent in trying to present an alien culture to the globally dominant one' (*Anglophone Arab Encounter* 12). This work of cultural mediation is particularly charged in a political context where interest in this literature is related to what Nash calls 'Arab and Islamic oriented events in recent history' which 'feeds into a dissemination and consumption of texts that might be deemed to inter-face with (and even partially "explain") those events' (16). As Waïl Hassan points out, immigrant Arab writers face the imperative to explain and speak about the 'other side' simply because they are in a position which 'represents a merger of the two classic stances of the native informant and the foreign expert' (*Immigrant Narratives* 29). In Susan Muaddi Darraj's description, Anglophone Arab literature usefully 'bypasses the need for translation [. . .] poised between East and West' and 'speaks directly to English-speaking audiences about the world on the other side of the divide' (123). Mohammed Albakry and Jonathan Siler similarly describe 'Arab writers who use English as a medium of creative expression' as 'mediators who, by bypassing the need for translation and speaking directly to Western audiences, popularize and humanize their culture to non-Arab readers' (Albakry and Siler 120). This focus on the bridging role of literature centres the mainstream Western reader. Critiques of nostalgic tropes in this literature seem inextricable from a wariness about reinforcing stereotypes, which is predicated on certain assumptions about the reader, on the need to humanize the characters, and on the celebration of hybridity and fluidity. Moving away from this fear of playing into expectations about homesick morose migrants would allow for an exploration of the nuances of nostalgic narrative, rather than reducing nostalgia to a one-note painful emotion or experience.

While Anglophone Arab writers can be seen as playing a role as cultural mediators, their attempts to represent a more nuanced view also responds to their own need to see their experiences reflected in mediated forms, countering representations of Arabs in English-language media. For example, Soueif discusses her confrontation with 'distortions of [her] reality' in the introduction to her collection of essays *Mezzaterra* ([2004] 2012) where she describes moving to London in 1984:

> it troubled me that in almost every book, article, film, TV or radio programme that claimed to be about the part of the world that I came from I could never recognise myself or anyone I knew. I was constantly coming face to face with

> distortions of my reality [. . .] and world geo-politics meant that interest in where I came from was growing. (2)

Soueif cites a number of historical events during this period that had an impact on her writing, including the Afghan-Soviet war from 1979 to 1989, the civil war in Lebanon, the Israeli invasion of Lebanon from 1982 to 1985, and the Gulf War and sanctions against Iraq from 1990.[2] Political conflicts have continued to play an important part in propelling an increase in cultural production from the region in English. The increase in English-language literature seems to be driven in part by a perceived need to counter the prevailing view of the region and to portray it in a more nuanced way, as well as to create new narratives for life in the diaspora. In the introduction to an anthology of Arab American fiction, the editors raise this point in discussing the cultural politics of migrants in the United States, living '[w]ith their place of origin still beckoning and their place of relocation continuously wincing at their presence [. . .] on unsettled ground, biding their time, waiting to be invited to tell their stories' (Kaldas and Mattawa xix). The editors go on to note that the impact of global politics, in particular following the 9/11 attacks, prompted more 'politically conscious' literary interventions:

> [p]ost-September 11, the invasion of Afghanistan, the extralegal treatment of Arab Americans, and the war on Iraq must be considered turning points not only for the community but also for the larger American public's awareness of this community's existence. [. . .] More ethnically and politically conscious, the current generation of Arab American writers sheds a more critical light on issues of heritage, gender, nationalism, and assimilation within the Arab American community. (xix, xx)

In comparison with earlier writing where writers exhibited an 'uncertainty about the usefulness of the label [Arab], about what kind of light such identification would shed on one's work', in more recent years, the editors argue, writers have been 'emboldened with a sense of urgency and confidence' (xvii). The urge that many of the writers acknowledge they feel, particularly at times of political crisis, to influence the representation of the region is a reminder that the burden of representation is not simply an external imposition. However, many writers are wary of the expectations imposed on them in this regard, as their books are packaged in terms that reinforce the orientalist framework that their writing seeks to challenge. Faqir discusses this problem in an interview, describing how her third novel

> was published with the title, *The Cry of the Dove*, in the United States, and [. . .] has a totally covered woman on the cover in the courtyard of a mosque. Totally Orientalist. If you look at the cover of Leila Aboulela's *Minaret* (2005); a serious text, regardless of my reservations about the Islamic world vision it propagates, you will see that the novel was reduced, exoticised, clichéd. ('Interview' 7)

In other words, the content of the work has little impact on the marketing: the cover for Faqir's novel has the same ubiquitous veiled woman imagery as the cover for the novel by Aboulela, despite the marked difference in their politics and writing styles. The commercial considerations for marketing these texts draws on well-established iconographies which evoke familiar narratives and promise a satisfying read. In another example of how orientalist tropes geographically locate the texts, marking them as from this particular region, Rabih Alameddine has discussed how his novel *The Hakawati* (2008) was received as a 'new Arabian Nights': '[a]s much as I loved the great reviews *The Hakawati* got, a lot of it was about, "Oh look at how exotic these little people are, isn't that fun? You know, like Scheherazade"' (Srinivas). If writers are aiming to challenge the marketing of their work in these predetermined frames, it can be argued that evoking the term nostalgia runs the risk of further overloading clichés about the region. However, this fear does not negate the importance of attending to the pervasive nostalgic tropes across Arabic and Anglophone literature, to engage with the narratives of Arab cultural time, and the perennial issues related to modern Arab culture's embattled relationship with its own past. The multiplicity of nostalgia as a psychological comfort for the uprooted and the displaced means that it can be a cultural battleground for what it means to exist within, or outside, the borderlines of identity. Studying the literary strategies used to deal with the burden of history specifically can speak to how literature takes its cues from and produces cultural narratives relating to memory and imagination.

The pervasiveness of nostalgia in Arab discourse can ironically call forth a nostalgia for a culture which is not so bound to its past, a nostalgia for a time when there are narratives which valorize moving on. To give an example of this nostalgia, I will now turn to a recurring anecdotal story that contrasts a stagnant present against a premodern age perceived as having an immaterial culture. The story appears in a number of both Arabic and English texts. In Jabra's *Hunters in a Narrow Street*, the story is recounted by a Bedouin character, Towfik al-Khalaf, who castigates the city-dwellers for their romanticizing of desert life: '[d]o you know the story of the Bedouin who once felt the urge to make a statue? [. . .] he had a quantity of dates. So he made it of dates. Next morning, he was hungry, so he ate the statue. And rightly too' (83). Here, al-Khalaf uses the story of the date-idol to critique the static nature of discourses that fashion a satisfying vision of the past at the expense of the present. The Bedouin, he asserts, is reasonable enough to remember his idol is something he created and to abandon it when physical needs becomes a more pressing concern, an assertion of 'now time', in Walter Benjamin's words, over the '"eternal" image of the past' (*Illuminations* 262). Among many iterations, the date-idol story also appears in Emile Habibi's novel *al-Waqāʾiʿ al-gharība fī ikhtifāʾ Saʿīd Abī al-Naḥs al-Mutashāʾil* (1974, *The Secret Life of Saeed, the Pessoptimist,* 1989). Here, the anecdote is a critical comment: '[i]n the so-called Age of Ignorance [. . .] our ancestors used to form their gods from dates and eat them when in need [. . .] You might say it is better for people to eat their gods than for the gods to eat them' (5). Habibi's passage then forms the epigraph to Palestinian-American Randa Jarrar's *A Map of Home* (2008), where the protagonist takes a critical stance against the notion of an 'unflawed' history connecting distant origins to the present. Yet another version of the story appears in Robin Yassin-Kassab's *The Road from Damascus* (2008). In this novel, the protagonist's father tells him: '[w]e'd always had gods [. . .] We always knew they were our creations. We invented them and destroyed them [. . .] We used to make gods from date stones when we were bored' (52). There is, in other words, a common thread in the variety of ways the date-idol narrative appears in Arab literary narratives, in both Arabic and English: the story of the date-idol celebrates the prosaic anti-nostalgic approach to the past, but also expresses a nostalgia for this attitude, a yearning for the ability to let go of what has come before and to see what has passed as a creative field, a cultural resource for the present.

The emphasis on the prosaic is particularly clear in Elias Khoury's *Bāb al-Shams* (1998, *Gate of the Sun* 2012), where the priority of the present is represented in terms of hunger:

> [a]nyone who talks of eternity exits history, for eternity is history's opposite, something that's eternal doesn't exist. We even ate our god. During our age of ignorance, we – we Arabs – would model gods out of dates and then eat them, because hunger is more important than eternity. (131)

The moral of the date-idol story in *Gate of the Sun* is that the demands of the present should be prioritized over the 'idols' of tradition. The critique of eternity is richly symbolic in Khoury's novel, which deals with the Palestinian refugee experience. Set in a hospital, the novel takes the form of a long monologue, where the narrator Khalil addresses his friend Yunes as he lies in a coma. The section quoted above comes as part of a discussion where Yunes critiques nationalist myths as 'foolish' attempts to defy history. Khalil recalls Yunes commenting: '[w]hat is this silly slogan of theirs – "Jerusalem, Eternal Capital of the Jewish State"! Anyone who talks of eternity exits history, for eternity is history's opposite [. . .] an eternal capital? [. . .] It's foolish – which means that they are becoming like us, defeatable' (128). Through Yunes, Khoury explores the danger of accepting the narrative of unchanging historical continuity, 'a trick to make people believe that we've been alive since the beginning and that we're the heirs of the dead' (21). Without explicitly mentioning Arab nationalism, these passages seem to critique the Ba'ath slogan ('a single Arab nation with an eternal mission'). Khoury takes aim at one of the most influential Arab nationalist ideologies, implying that this attachment to continuity is at least partly responsible for the Arab world's 'exit from history', a phrase that evokes the sense of failure which built up in the decades following the 1967 war. Through this association with nationalist mythology, the story of the date-idol has added resonance, suggesting that nomads in 'our age of ignorance' had a grasp of the essentials lost to nationalist mythmakers, who create a nationalist myth and then come to believe in it, to their own detriment.

In tracing the various manifestations of the date-idol story across texts written in Arabic and English, we see the entanglement of the thematics of loss and mourning in reflecting on consuming or being consumed by the idols of the past, in the simultaneous insistence on present needs above the worship of the past, while situating the past as nourishment for those needs. The emphasis is on the need to recognize the past as a cultural resource, yet there is a paradoxically nostalgic staging of the critical distance from nostalgia, a melancholy tone of 'what went wrong' to lead us to our present situation of idol-worship. The challenge, for writers who use English, is how to refer back to this tradition while negotiating their own estrangement, the probable lack of familiarity of their audience with the material they cite, and the multiple ways nostalgia is transmuted when physical dislocation overlaps with the impossibility of returning to a yearned-for time and place. When Said asks how an 'indecisive' and 'undetermined' history might be written, he adds 'in what language and with what sort of vocabulary?' (55). In the next section, I explore the question 'in what language' in both its metaphorical and literal capacity, exploring the politics of language choice which are unavoidable for Arab novelists who write in English.

Language and loss

In his discussion of Soueif's novel, Said poses a question to be asked of any Arab writer who uses English: '[w]hy English and not Arabic is the question an Egyptian, Palestinian, Iraqi, or Jordanian writer has to ask him or herself right off' (*Reflections* 407). This question clearly preoccupied Said himself, as he reflects in his memoir *Out of Place* that languages represent a split in his life:

> [e]veryone lives life in a given language; everyone's experiences therefore are had, absorbed, and recalled in that language. The basic split in my life was the one between Arabic, my native language, and English, the language of my education and subsequent expression as a scholar and teacher, and so trying to produce a narrative of one in the language of the other – to say nothing of the numerous ways in which the languages were mixed up for me and crossed over from one realm to the other – has been a complicating task. (217)

Yasir Suleiman notes that in this passage 'linguistic displacement is no less foundational than the physical displacements [Said] lived through' (78).³ The 'unhealable rift' is a corollary to the 'basic split' between the native language and the language of education that concretizes dislocation. Loss is intrinsic to language, as Jeffrey Sacks explores in his work on loss and aesthetic form, where he argues that 'loss does not come to language as if it were an accident – as if it came later to language – but points to an essential dimension of what language is' (11). In Arabic literature, this intrinsic sense of loss resonates in the centrality and valence of the notion of *ghurba*, denoting a feeling of estrangement, and implying a break from an earlier state of being in harmony with one's surroundings. The root of the word *ghurba* is itself ambiguous and multivalent. As Jonathan P. Decter notes '[a]l-tagharrub and al-ightirāb – emigration and estrangement' like 'the English pair "travel" and "travail" [. . .] share a common root (ghrb) that underscores the intimate relation between moving from one place to another and resigning oneself to the burden of alienation' (1). In the contemporary era, the term has come to relate both to the physical dislocation of immigration and to metaphorical estrangement. This is the understanding of the term that is captured in the titles of two studies by Halim Barakat, *Ghurbat al-Kātib al-'Arabī* (The Estrangement of the Arab Writer, 2011) and *Al-Ightirāb fī al-thaqāfa al-'Arabiyyah* (Alienation in Arab Culture, 2006). In the present context, *ghurba* and its derivations are often used to describe an internal alienation stemming from disillusionment with the present. Lorenzo Casini highlights this metaphorical understanding of exile when he notes that *ghurba* has come to signify 'an exclusion [. . .] from the nation and other forms of collectivity. It is an exile from History that takes the form of the impossibility for the characters to be active actors' (7). The multiplicity of the term therefore provides a useful lens to discuss the work of Arab writers in the diaspora, which Peter Clark characterizes as 'the literature of exile, of *ghurba*, of *ightirab*' (183).

In Anglophone Arab literature, the space of *ghurba* is further complicated through the disconnection of linguistic identity from the contexts around which their narratives revolve. Libyan novelist Hisham Matar, reflecting on his use of English rather than Arabic, writes: '[i]t never ceases to unsettle me that I am operating in a language my grandparents would have not understood.' In the same interview, Matar goes on to state that 'to write outside one's language' is 'the deepest and most peculiar dimension of exile that [he has] experienced' ('An Interview'). Elsewhere, Matar describes the use of a language other than Arabic as a form of betrayal, aligning linguistic and political identity: '[i]t never feels completely okay that I'm not writing in Arabic. On some level it's sort of a betrayal' ('Reluctant Spokesman'). Matar's sense of unsettlement speaks to how the use of English can amplify the very 'unhealable' nature of dislocation. This rupture heightens the urge to re-envision to the past, to imaginatively bridge geographic and linguistic rifts, relating to the homeland left behind and to the histories that continue to have an impact on the present.

The issue of language also leads to a line of self-questioning which is evident everywhere in the words of writers such as British-Sudanese novelist Jamal Mahjoub, who highlights the problems of being outside a literary community or 'tradition':

> [b]ecause you don't have a people behind you and are not speaking from with-in an established voice – whether that is national or literary – you question: What tradition do I belong to? I don't think many people would include me as a British writer. Do you include me as a Sudanese writer? Well, no, not really, because I don't write in Arabic. ('Novelist, Nomad')

Mahjoub describes writing in a void, without a sense of tradition that he can either claim or break away from. At the same time, for writers from the Arabic-speaking world, there is a confrontation with the lack of knowledge about this region. Commenting on writing his first novel, Mahjoub describes being 'aware of the nonexistence of the world I came from' for most of his audience, which meant 'in order to tell my story, I first had to tell the story of Sudan' ('Accidental Arab'). Given the relative marginality of Anglophone Arab writing, Mahjoub's suggestion that he is 'not really' a Sudanese writer and yet needing to 'tell the story of Sudan' raises questions about the implications of addressing an English-speaking and primarily Western audience.

In an article published in July 2016, Hani Al-Barghouti discusses the phenomenon of Arabs writing in English and raises the following questions of legitimacy and audience:

> [t]he reader can understand the objections to the writing of Arab literature in English, considering that it is the language of the coloniser [and] connected to particular structures of publication, and considering that in using this language writers are primarily addressing a non-Arab audience. However, when it comes to asking about the connection between language and cultural identity and the legitimacy of literature written by Arabs in English, the answers may show other aspect of the case. Can writers express their cultural context without the use of language associated with that context, or is this connection [between language and identity] so intertwined that it is impossible to separate the two? (Al-Barghouthi, my translation)

To write in English opens the writer up to critique, as writers face 'their critics "back home", who take them to task [...] relentlessly construing both their choice of foreign tongue and their subject-matter as a reflection of disaffection or lack of national feeling' (Maleh 14). These issues of categorization and methodology have been long-standing topics in the more established tradition of Francophone literature by Arab writers. In contrast, there has been relatively little critical engagement with the relationship between Arabic literature and Anglophone Arab writing, even though, as Ahdaf Soueif observes, at this point, 'the use of English by Arab authors is expanding at a faster rate than the use of French' ('A Correspondence' 60).

The reasons for and responses to this use of English are varied. Soueif simply states that she writes in English because it was '[her] first reading language'. Elsewhere, she comments: '[i]t is very difficult to explain that this was not a choice, that you work with the tools that are best for you' (Brooks). Moroccan-American writer Laila Lalami explains her own answer to 'Why English and not Arabic?' in the following passage:

> A braver writer – a Ngũgĩ say – might have immediately cast aside the colonial tongue and returned to the native one, but my literary Arabic was not good enough to allow me to produce a novel. The Arabic language is often referred to as 'al-lugha al-'arabiyya al-fusha' [sic] or 'the eloquent Arabic language.' I sorely lacked that eloquence. One day I thought, why not try my hand in English? [...]

> After a few tries, I noticed that the linguistic shift enabled me to approach my stories with a fresh perspective. Because English had not been forced upon me as a child, it seemed to give me a kind of salutary distance. ('So to Speak' 20)

Lalami finds something positive about the 'distance' that English gives her, because (unlike French, the language she used to write in previously) it 'had not been forced upon [her]' ('So to Speak' 20). For Lebanese Canadian writer Rawi Hage, his use of English is also a considered choice over French, and he remarks that '[l]anguage is not an ideological thing for me, it's just a tool [. . .] It's just circumstances' (Tousignant). Hage uses the same word as Soueif here, identifying language as a 'tool'. Similarly, Matar explains the 'practical reasons' for his writing in English:

> [s]ince I was a boy I attended English schools. For this reason, my English tends to be better than my Arabic. This is the practical reason behind my writing in English. That is not to say that it is 'natural,' as you call it, to write in English. In fact, what interests me about my situation is how unnatural it continues to be. ('An Interview')

Matar's experience resembles that of Soueif, attributing his use of English to his schooling and familiarity with English, which consequently is better than the language that should be his mother tongue. This is a common theme in Anglophone Arab writing. Like Matar, Rabih Alameddine describes his use of English as the result of his education:

> I read Shakespeare when I was 14 because it's what we were taught. I think that's a problem, a remnant of colonialism, still. In school in Lebanon we were not allowed to speak Arabic during breaks – it had to be French or English. Because if you speak a foreign language, my god, you're educated. (Srinivas)

Though the attitudes to the use of English differ between writers who see it as a choice which gives them a certain freedom, to those who use it for the simple reason that it is the language of their education, for many Arab writers, certainly those who are first-generation immigrants, their use of English is mostly a result of education. Though some, such as Alameddine, ascribe this education system to 'a remnant of colonialism', these conditions stand in contrast to postcolonial writers whose writing in English is a more direct result of colonialism and/or forced displacement.

The novelists examined in this study are at a generational remove from a context which centred the postcolonial as a term: though their texts could be described as postcolonial, they postdate the literary and critical focus on 'writing back' as postcolonial strategy. Mahjoub elucidates this difference in relation to categorization, noting that he feels that he 'came after the old postcolonial generation, the so-called Empire Writes Back gang, [Salman] Rushdie, Anita Desai, Timothy Mo, and so on'. Mahjoub concludes: 'I didn't really belong to them, but whatever was coming next hadn't really arrived' ('Which Africa'). Elsewhere,

Mahjoub describes this disconnection as the development of a 'no man's land of the third world cosmopolitan' ('The Writer and Globalism'). Here, the 'cosmopolitan' indicates a transnational mode of living with multiple, complex identities and affiliations, while the term 'third world' indicates the extent to which Mahjoub feels he remains imbricated in the particular postcolonial history of Sudan. The juxtaposition of these terms speaks to a need to refine the theoretical tools used in reading literatures from postcolonial contexts. To return once more to Said's memoir, there are tensions between the liberating and devastating consequences of exile in the assertion that 'nothing more painful and paradoxically sought after characterises [his] life than the many displacements from countries, cities, abodes, languages, environments that have kept [him] in motion all these years' (*Out of Place* 217). Without acknowledging this ambiguity and the simultaneity of the emotions associated with exile, the critical discourse around migrant or diaspora literatures risks collapsing diverse experiences into the oneness of hybrid experience. Waïl Hassan describes how this prism leads to an 'emergent canon of postcolonial-literature-as-world-literature' which 'inscribes "writing back," diaspora, migrancy, border-crossings, in-betweenness, and hybridity as the defining features of the "postcolonial condition"' ('Horizons' 60). These modes are understood as catalysts for post-national identities, the experiences of displacement and negotiating 'in-betweeness' celebrated as means of a postmodern questioning of essentialist narratives. Along similar lines, David Bevan describes how in discussions of hybrid modalities

> the sense of release, of critical distance, of renewed identity, of fusion or shock of cultures and even of languages, is interpreted as productive; generating a proposition whose originality of vision must almost necessarily derive from the transgressing and transcending of frontiers. (4)

Having laid out these positive associations, Bevan goes on to ask 'whether the experience [of exile] is predominantly one that invigorates or mutilates' (4), a question which recalls Rose's response to Said, discussed earlier, in asking whether we are 'at risk of idealising the flaws and fissures of identity' (76). These frameworks often do not include within their scope the negative ramifications of loss and exile as a mutilating experience, a paradoxically exclusionary aspect beneath the promise of inclusion.

In what follows, I explore nostalgic discourse as a source of comfort and sense-making that mediates dislocation, including creative and inventive hybrid forms, but also the painful losses that evoke nostalgia in the first place. In his posthumously published article entitled 'Living in Arabic', Said reflects on how languages create new realities after the erasures and destruction left behind:

> [h]aving left behind locales that have either been ruined by war or for other reasons no longer exist, and having very little by way of property and objects from my earlier life, I seem to have made out of these two languages at play, as experiences, an environment that I can carry about with me, complete with

timbre, pitch and accent specific to the time, the place and the person. ('Living in Arabic')

Said describes 'living' in languages, as the creation of an environment that is both rooted in remembering and specificity, and that is disconnected, shaped by 'two languages at play' that alter and impact each other. Perhaps here we can read the two languages as not only English and Arabic but also as two modes of exploring identity which in Darwish's elegiac poem appear as 'self-defence' and 'self-invention', the pull to consolidate and the push to invent, which are often simultaneous and equally complex, rather than involving a binary or spectrum of simple negative forms and more ambiguous, critical forms. Nostalgic discourse can be engaged as a creative and inventive cultural resource without precluding or dismissing the comforting, palliative functions nostalgia performs. It is this entanglement and complexity which I seek to examine in the chapters of this book, situating Anglophone Arab literature as neither distinct and separate from national narratives nor as deterritorialized extensions of national literatures.

In the first chapter, I examine the narrative of a transcendent golden age, an imagined time outside of history, which is contrasted against the contemporary realities of the protagonists. In Rabih Alameddine's *The Hakawati* (2008), Sabiha Khemir's *The Blue Manuscript* (2008), and Yasmin Zahran's *A Beggar at Damascus Gate* (1995), the nostalgia for various lost empires responds to and is inextricable from a pervasive sense of present failures, bringing a more illustrious past into conversation with the disappointments of the present. The protagonists experience nostalgia for historically distant eras, attempting to seek out traces of various times which can be loosely identified as a golden age. However, as the narratives unfold, the writers reflect on the fact that ancient ruins, artefacts and literary fragments do not allow for unmediated connection to history, requiring interpretation, translation and adaptation. These processes complicate the nostalgic subject's attachment to the past and detachment from the present.

In the second chapter, I examine the fictional rewriting of colonial history in Ahdaf Soueif's *The Map of Love* ([1999] 2000), Fadia Faqir's *Pillars of Salt* (1997), and Jamal Mahjoub's *In the Hour of Signs* (1996). These novels confront the historical amnesia of the colonial period and how this history is brought to bear on the present. I explore how the writers dramatize the nostalgia for a precolonial authenticity consolidated as tradition, and the extent to which this nostalgia functions as an escapist fantasy from the conditions of (post)modernity. The novels discussed in this chapter complicate the dichotomous representations of pervasive discourses about 'tradition' and 'modernity' that continue to be central today through tracing their interrelationship.

In the third chapter, I examine novels that explore nostalgia for nationalist discourse and represent the disintegration of the promise of independent nationhood. Focusing on the superimposition of the nation onto the family, I examine Hisham Matar's two novels, *In the Country of Men* (2007) and *Anatomy of Disappearance* (2011), Leila Aboulela's *Minaret* ([2005] 2015) and Randa Jarrar's *A Map of Home* (2008). These novels rewrite nostalgic narratives of nationalism to include the intra-national violence excluded from official discourse. The trauma of the authoritarian state's violence at the level of the home results in a disintegration of home as the locus of stability and security, a disintegration that represents the failures of the national project. The time lapse between experiences of political violence in the homeland and the reliving of these traumatic experiences later compounds a sense of alienation and dislocation from the national framework.

Finally, I turn to nostalgia in the context of diaspora, and examine Jamal Mahjoub's *Travelling with Djinns* (2003) alongside Selma Dabbagh's *Out of It* (2011) and Rawi Hage's *Cockroach* (2008). I focus on the ways these writers explore the measures people take to anchor themselves in their country of settlement, from attempted assimilation, to nationalism as resistance to acculturation, to adapting Islam as an alternative framework for a cosmopolitan identity. I argue that the many evocations of belonging in these novels function strategically to reconfigure ways to be 'at home' in the diaspora, ways of living that involve a shift away from territorial frames.

Through these four chapters, I explore how nostalgia as a longing for a time that is irredeemably past grapples with the rifts of estrangement, *ghurba*, reconstructing the past through the perspective of the present. Anglophone Arab literature is shaped by the predicaments of being dislocated from the past, from homeland, from a native language. Nostalgia contends with that dislocation, and with that sense of an impasse, seeking modes which would allow a transition from the production of crises to the discovery of genres appropriate for moving on. Confronting the impossibility of direct engagement with history, the nostalgic tropes deployed in Anglophone Arab literature speak to the need to better understand narratives of the past in order to produce new ways of relating to the world.

Chapter 1

THE CHAOS OF LOST EMPIRES

RABIH ALAMEDDINE, SABIHA KHEMIR AND YASMIN ZAHRAN

In her essay 'Mobile Identity and the Focal Distance of Memory', published in 2001, Tunisian writer and art historian Sabiha Khemir writes about making what she calls 'far-reaching memory [. . .] part of the present identity, not just the ugliness of war and conflict'. Discussing artefacts from various Islamic empires, Khemir frames what she calls 'far-reaching memory' as necessary for the present, arguing that these artefacts can animate the present by reconnecting to a past 'rich in harmony, in contrast to our recent history where that harmony has been broken'. Despite the undeniably nostalgic aspect to this contrast, Khemir asserts that she is not 'advocating nostalgia for a glorious past' but rather arguing for a strategic re-imaging of the past for the present and the future ('Mobile Identity' 46). As an example of such reimagining, Khemir discusses the romanticized image of Andalusia through a future-oriented framework, as 'a promising token of the possibility of positive coexistence and interaction' (48). This framing of what William Granara calls the Andalusian chronotope highlights how nostalgia can be felt 'not for the past the way it was, but for the past the way it could have been. It is this past perfect that one strives to realise in the future' (Boym 351). The focus on the future shifts the frame from the lamenting look back, to anachronistically using the past as a promise of what could be, particularly in the context of the 'ugliness' of contemporary conditions which in Khemir's argument is at the heart of the idea of *ghurba* ('Mobile Identity' 46). Here Khemir quotes a statement attributed to tenth-century philosopher Abū Hayyān al-Tawhīdī, *al-ghurba hiya ghurbat al-awṭān,* which she translates as 'exile is when one feels in exile at home'. According to Khemir, '[t]he problems of Arab identity impose themselves on an individual abroad not only because of [. . .] displacement. The identity of the Arab world is in turmoil at home too' ('Mobile Identity' 45). Khemir here describes the experience of Arab migrants as an extension of a metaphorical exile, rather than opposing an immigrant perspective to the nationalist politics of rootedness and belonging – in a sense, physical exile overlays internal exile or *ghurba* from a sense of coherent cultural time.

Imaginatively returning to the golden age is often framed as a melancholic lament for a lost better past. It is this sense of a debilitating, disabling nostalgia that Samir Kassir critiques as emphasizing the past at the expense of the future, arguing that 'what is most urgent, what is indispensable to recovery' is to 'abandon our fantasy of a matchless past' (92). As novelist Hanan al-Shaykh expresses it: 'we Arab today have no connection with the Arabs of Andalusia [. . .] we didn't complete our cultural journey [. . .] how is it that we have ended up today in the very worst of times?' (19). Edward Said has also discussed this logic of glorifying the past in relation to the defeats of the present in his article 'Andalusia's Journey', where he describes the notion of a golden age as attaining a particular power in conditions of 'defeat and violence':

> [b]ut for me, and indeed for many Arabs, Andalusia still represents the finest flowering of our culture. That is particularly true now, when the Arab Middle East seems mired in defeat and violence, its societies unable to arrest their declining fortunes, its secular culture so full of almost surreal crisis, shock and nihilism. ('Andalusia's Journey')

Andulasia offers respite from 'a modern world of disillusionment, strife, and uncertainty' in an utopian model of *convivencia* as 'a model for the co-existence of peoples, a model quite different from the ideological battles, local chauvinism, and ethnic conflict that finally brought it down – and which ironically enough threaten to engulf our own 21st century world' ('Andalusia's Journey'). Having laid out the logic for this nostalgic narrative, later in the same article Said questions the yearning for what could have been as 'a rather too facile, moral lesson', and asks instead how one might go about 'seeing and understanding the place beyond illusion and romance'. Seeking traces of a 'composite Andalusian identity' involves recognizing the historical palimpsest of this place, in ways that challenge culturalist claims to the past ('Andalusia's Journey'). The effort to move beyond the idealization of Andalusia demonstrates what Said describes elsewhere as 'the need [. . .] for deintoxicated, sober histories that make evident the multiplicity and complexity of history without allowing one to conclude that it moves forward impersonally' (*Humanism* 141). Narratives of ancient glory by their very nature are intoxicated by the idea of an ideal era, involving a one-dimensional vision of history that is necessary to sustain any notion of a golden age.

In this chapter, I examine the strategic use of the fantasy of a golden age and nostalgic tropes related to idealized pasts. The novels I discuss explore various forms of profound nostalgia for the glorified eras of ancient Arabo-Islamic and pre-Islamic civilizations, yet in their focus on material traces of the past they dramatize the impossibility of ever fully comprehending or reconnecting with the past. I begin the chapter by discussing how nostalgic discourses of the golden age appear in Arabic literature, focusing on Moroccan writer Abdelkarim Jouaiti's short story 'Madīnat al-Nuḥas' ('The City of Brass', 1999), which exemplifies many of the recurring tropes in representations of an elusive golden age. I then discuss briefly some of the ways nostalgia for the ancient past is deployed as an aesthetic strategy in Anglophone Arab literature, with the writers at once staging the pathos of nostalgia and undercutting it through ironic juxtapositions. I focus on three novels: Rabih Alameddine's *The Hakawati* (2008), Sabiha Khemir's *The Blue Manuscript* (2008) and Yasmin Zahran's *A Beggar at Damascus Gate* (1995), the last two having received little critical attention thus far.

Narratives of a golden age

Narratives of a golden age are particularly compelling because they set the complex recent past of society against a simplified account of the distant past. Egyptologist Jan Assman speaks about the distance between recent 'communicative memory' and a distant 'cultural memory'. According to Assman, 'the cultural memory of the people who share it extends into the past only as far as the past can be reclaimed as "ours"' (113). Picking up this description in relation to the use of archaeology to further nationalist feeling, Philip Kohl points out that the past that is reclaimed as 'ours' extends as far back as possible. In particular, '[t]imes defined as "golden ages" are in strong demand, and if they cannot be found as such, they can be invented or manipulated creatively' (Kohl 19). Since the golden age functions as an origin story, the examination of narratives about such culturally significant eras opens up an investigation into the political uses of the past in the present.

Across Arabic-speaking countries, the myths of a golden age are shared by the ideological camps of pan-Arabism and pan-Islamism which overlap and compete in their efforts to integrate the region through narratives of religious predestination and nationalist teleology.[1] The historical utopianism in contemporary Arabic culture, from the abundance of historical television series to the reactionary nostalgia of Islamist fundamentalism, speaks to how the notion of a golden age continues to impact the present.[2] Despite being ideologically opposed, pan-Islamist and pan-Arab discourses often converge in invoking the Arab conquests of the seventh century and the various Islamic empires established thereafter as a golden age. Syrian poet Ali Esber (better known by his pseudonym Adunis) draws on this discourse when he describes the sacking of Baghdad in 1258 as the beginning of a decline compounded by subsequent invasions:

> [t]he retreat of Arab society from the ways opened up by modernity began with the fall of Baghdad in 1258. With the Crusades came a complete halt, prolonged by the period of Ottoman domination. From the beginning of the nineteenth century to the middle of the twentieth – the time of Western colonialism and of contact with its culture and its modernity, the period known as the *Nahḍa* (renaissance, a name which merits a detailed study in itself) – the question of modernity was revived and the debate resumed over the issues which it provoked. (77)

The view expressed here, that Arab modernity was truncated in the medieval past, ties into a broader discourse built on contrasting present failures against eras long past, located in the ancient civilizations of Egypt and Mesopotamia, the Umayyad and Abbasid Empires, or the Ottoman Empire. The destruction of shrines and archaeological sites by Islamist groups that locate their utopian golden age in the seventh century perfectly captures this revivalist obsession with restoring a delimited period of history. The iconoclasm of these groups, and their intentional destruction of particular histories, is inseparable from a rejection of the use of pre-Islamic sites for nationalist purposes.[3] Nostalgia for certain periods of the imagined past shapes politics in the region across the ideological spectrum.

In modern Arabic literature, various historical eras have been represented as mirrors for the present, often as a method to escape censorship. Notable examples include Moroccan novelist Bensalem Himmich's historical novels, such as *Majnūn al-Ḥukm* (1989, *The Theocrat*, 2005), a novel about an eleventh-century Fatimid caliph which is a barely veiled indictment of 'power-crazy' (the literal translation of the title) political elites in the present. Youssef Zeidan's controversial *'Azāzīl* (2008, *Azazeel*, 2012) returned to early Eastern Christianity to examine bigotry, misogyny and the rejection of secular learning, with clear relevance to contemporary Islamism. One of the most acclaimed novels to employ historical allegory in recent years has been Egyptian novelist Radwa Ashour's *Thulāthiyyat Gharnāṭa* (Granada Trilogy), published between 1994 and 1995. The trilogy narrates the lives of the Abu Jaafar family in Andalusia from the fall of Granada in 1492 to their final departure a century later. While the themes of the trilogy are those of loss and nostalgia, in an essay on why she wrote the novel, Ashour differentiates her role from that of simply preserving the past, which she describes as mummification: '[m]y ancestors were masters of preservation [. . .] However, I do not opt for the role of mummification but for the role of an eyewitness and scribe who has an urgent story to tell' ('Eyewitness' 92). Describing this urgency, Ashour refers to a present that was 'too difficult to handle':

> [t]o me Granada was the Granada of the Moriscos, defeated men and women whose resistance was doomed to failure. It was a correlative of my experience of the bombing of Baghdad, a bombing which brought with it the 1967 bombing of Sinai, the 1982 bombing of Beirut, and the persistent bombing of Southern Lebanon [. . .] Maybe the present was too difficult to handle, too scorching. ('Eyewitness' 94)

As Ashour puts it, 'Granada attempts to connect past and present by means of a metaphorical image of loss and resistance in the Arab nation' ('Eyewitness' 96). The Granada trilogy joins a tradition of writing that displaces contemporary issues onto a glorified period seen from the melancholic prism of its failure. While this projection contributes to the nostalgia aura surrounding this culturally significant era, it is combined with an accusatory rhetoric that locates responsibility in the internecine conflicts that lead to the loss of Andalusia; as Said has noted, Andalusia is a vivid metaphor for the successive failures, internal divisions and ideological bankruptcy of the region ('Andalusia's Journey'). In contrast to the kind of nostalgia that seeks to escape present realities, the failures of the past are here used analogically to critique and comment on the present.

Ashour herself located the Granada trilogy as a response to the first Gulf War. In her later experimental autobiography, *Aṭyāf* (1999, *Specters*, 2010), the narrator describes the moment when the project of writing Granada began, as she watched 'still shots of the Basra-Kuwait road: the destroyed vehicles, the corpses. She hadn't realised that these scenes would open up the doors of memory, letting out a flood of images unravelling all the way back to her roots' (*Spectres* 231). The phrase 'flood of images' describes an unstoppable force while 'unravelling' suggests returning to some original moment. Contrary to Ashour's account, the Granada novels were widely viewed as an allegory for Palestine, particularly given the Oslo agreement signed in 1993. The narrator of *Spectres* does not however want to accept this analogy between Palestine and Andalusia: 'I haven't conceded the loss of Palestine and emotionally I cannot get to it by way of Granada' (226). There is thus a layering of loss in Ashour's *Granada*, where a novel about the loss of Andalus (according to the writer triggered by watching media coverage of the first Gulf War) is taken to be about the loss of Palestine. The parallels of Andalus/Palestine might be said to be based on understanding them as lost causes, as outlined in Said's essay 'On Lost Causes' which develops an aesthetic analysis of the concept in literature and nationalism: '[l]ost causes can be [. . .] the debris of a battle swept aside by history and by the victor' (*Reflections* 551). Both Palestine and Andalusia, 'swept aside by history', have become literary topoi, their invocation a shorthand for loss.

Rather than offering a static narrative, nostalgic tropes have much to say about the present potency of the past, in particular as forms of grievance. For example, finding solace in the recalling of the more prosperous past is often represented as disinheritance. In the opening pages of Naguib Mahfouz's novel *Awlād Ḥāritnā* (1959, *The Children of The Alley*, 1981), the narrator describes a severance from the past in terms that capture the intertwining of loss, nostalgia and alienation:

> [e]veryone in our alley tells these stories, just as they heard them in coffeehouses or as they were handed down for generations [. . .] Whenever someone is depressed, suffering or humiliated, he points to the mansion at the top of the alley at the end opening out to the desert and says sadly, 'that is our ancestor's house, we are all his children, and we have a right to his property.' (3)

In Mahfouz's novel, as well as in Ashour's trilogy, the wish for a better past is in fact a desire for a better future. As Ouyang suggests, nostalgia in Arabic literature involves not only 'a profound longing for the past' but also 'more importantly for the future that has yet to take proper and desirable shape' (*Politics of Nostalgia* vi). In the case of Mahfouz's novel, the allegory of the nation as a house and the people as disinherited children makes clear this connection between the nostalgia for the past and its vital function as a cancelled future.

The Moroccan writer Abdelkebir Khatibi offers an alternative to how the rupture between past and present could be experienced in his autobiography *La Mémoire tatouée* (1971, *Tattooed Memory*, 2016). The title references Amazigh tattoos as compelling traces: though what they signify may be lost, they redeem the yearning for an original point of reference. Khatibi's use of the present/absent meaning of the tattoos to discuss the material vestiges of history borrows from the Derridean concept of the trace as a point of contact with historical experience that nevertheless force recognition of the loss of meaning. Such loss can either be experienced as inhibiting (a painful severance) or liberating (acknowledging the irreducible difference of the past). Through reflections on the past as the trace, this chapter examines novels which invoke the poetic topos of *al-wuqūf 'alā al-aṭlāl* ('standing by the ruins'), a topos running through Arabic literary tradition from pre-Islamic odes to the present. The *aṭlāl* topos stages a moment of mourning, where the speaker elegiacally describes the traces of habitation that are under erasure, and then moves on from this site of memory, having acknowledged the transitory nature of this moment. Representing the rewriting, excavating, and translating of the traces of the past allows contemporary writers to stage the complex and multiple emotions attached to nostalgia as a form of standing by the ruins.

Standing by the ruins

In her work on the politics of nostalgia in Arabic literature, Ouyang cites '*Al-kitāba 'amal inqilābī*' (Writing is a Revolutionary Act) by Syrian poet Nizar Qabbani, where Qabbani urges Arab writers to erase memory (*ilghā' al-dhākira*) in order to write new poetry. Qabbani argues that writing should be a revolt against the authority of the past. Although recognizing that literary tradition plays a crucial role in the transmission of culture, Qabbani argued that there is too much reverence of memory in Arabic poetry, represented in the forms and topoi of the canonical odes. As previously mentioned, one of the most pervasive examples is the topos of *al-wuqūf 'alā al-aṭlāl*, or 'standing by the ruins', which dates back to the pre-Islamic ode. Typically, the ode opens with the speaker stopping at a deserted campsite, contemplating the traces that are the remains of habitation. The contemplation of the deserted site, coupled with the psychological frame of the loss of the beloved, prompts cathartic recollection, after which the speaker resumes his travels. The topos has been described by Roger Allen as evoking 'nostalgia for times that are forever gone – of longing, absence, and wistful memories' (102). Al-Ghadeer points out that the speaker 'attempts to narrate loss' even as 'this narrative hinges on the speaker's inability to recuperate what has been lost – the abode, the beloved, or the past' (71). Kilpatrick has described how the *aṭlāl* topos is also 'a symbol of the transitoriness of everything in this world', through the reflection by the poet on 'a landscape where nature has reasserted itself, effacing the signs of habitation from the places he carefully names' ('Aṭlal' 29). The *nasīb* begins with nostalgia and longing but ends with acknowledging the inevitability of erasure and moving on, as even the traces of habitation are erased by winds.

In examining the *aṭlāl* topos in modern Arabic literature, Kilpatrick posits that it is 'connected with the role of memory in literature today as a device for structuring experience'. Kilpatrick argues that whereas the topos is 'confined to the introductory section' in the classical ode, in modern narratives contemplative nostalgia 'tends to continue through the work, increasing in intensity' ('Aṭlal' 42). As an example of how the *aṭlāl* topos filters into modern cultural production, Ken Seigneurie discusses its appropriation in post-war Lebanese film and literature to form 'a new elegiac humanism'.[4] I would add that the increased intensity of standing by the ruins in contemporary literature is often joined to a seemingly opposed critical distance which critiques such melancholic lingering. An example of this doubleness, of nostalgic emotion juxtaposed with cultural critique, is Rashid Al-Daif's novel, *'Azīzī al-Sayyid Kawābātā* (1995, *Dear Mr Kawabata* 1999), which takes the form of a letter from the narrator to Japanese novelist Yasunari Kawabata, ending with a postscript hoping that Kawabata will have the time to reply.[5] While penning this epistolary narrative which seeks an impossible response, the narrator indicts narratives of cultural memory for a similar attitude of waiting, for expecting to arrive at a future that mirrors imagined perfect pasts:

> [m]y fellow-Arabs are generally fed on memory, on Memory in fact – the Memory that we Arabs were once masters of the earth [. . .] My fellow-Arabs know the future well, because the image of it is already in their minds. It is the past as they like to see it, and as they would like it to be. (17)

The grip of memory here perpetuates a dangerous communal delusion, as the narrator goes on to suggest: 'it is for this reason that "Revival" is the objective around which political discourse (and also literature) generally revolves' (17). Revival offers a readily understandable narrative of future utopian redemption but it is a narrative predicated on present lack.

The consequences of the fantasy of a glorious past are dramatized in a short story by Moroccan writer Abdelkarim Jouaiti, 'Madīnat al-Nuḥas' ('The City of Brass'), where the narrator describes his quest for an ancient city which has vanished without trace: '[t]he earth, had it swallowed all traces of the magnificent City of Brass? Or was it the story of an imaginary city that [. . .] inhabited stories and supported the people's need for storytelling?' (98). The narrator constantly compares the lost past with what he sees in his modern-day city: '[t]he unsatisfied desires, the motionless faces [. . .] the uniform steps of the crowd that comes and goes without tiring along the one and only boulevard of the city' (85–6). The city is trapped between dreaming of a future modernity and yearning for the past. This impasse is captured in the description of an urban renewal project which hopes to reconnect the contemporary city to the ancient city of brass: '[a]s if things could not escape their fate, the city improvised a makeshift committee that decided with a strange contempt for the urban environment of the city that the houses would be painted [. . .] A screaming brass-coloured yellow that like belated vomit enveloped the city as though it were closed off by a quarantine for the plague' (100). Katarzyna Pieprzak describes this short story as drawing on 'a canon of Arabic literature on cities, ruins and nostalgia and a global modernist literature on cities, paralysis and disease' (201). The modern-day city symbolizes a nightmarish entrapment, 'that which created feelings in your interior of wanting to choke, that which pushed you to reflect upon an impossible escape, all that makes obvious to you the phenomena of a senseless history that practices an eternal repetition' (101). 'The City of Brass' captures the predicament of loss where the object being sought was perhaps never present. Though the narrator finds literary traces of the fabled ancient city in descriptions by medieval travellers, these traces in themselves do not affirm the actuality of the city: 'nothing affirms that this past glory was ever truly realised outside of these pretty tales' (98). The narrator hopes to conjure the 'pretty tales' into actuality, to reanimate myth, but the city that the narrator searches for seems to exist only in narrative and therefore must be reproduced in narrative. The loss that the protagonist feels is in a sense the loss of a tangible loss, the recognition that 'nothing affirms' that anything has been lost in a tangible way. 'The City of Brass' in part presents us with a familiar story about entropy, the melancholic tone having much to do with the irrevocable otherness of the past. This attempt to narrate the loss of even the traces of the past places the narrator in the position of the speaker in the *nasīb* who stands by the vanishing traces of an encampment. Arabic-language literature is irrevocably bound up with this lyrical mode that goes back as far as the recorded literary tradition. Seigneurie argues that '[i]t would, in fact, probably take an effort to depict memory and longing in Arabic without some intersection with the classical topos' (19). For Anglophone Arab writers too, the *aṭlāl* topos provides a crucial site to explore the tension between the comfort derived from nostalgia and the criticism of escapist romanticization. Moving between these modes involves a double movement of mourning and acknowledging erasure, the same movement that structures the topos of standing by the ruins.

The sometimes contradictory reflection on cultural narratives of the golden age is a dominant theme in early Anglophone Arab novels such as Jabra's *Hunters in a Narrow Street* (1960). *Hunters*, the only novel by Jabra written in English, is narrated by Jameel Farran, a Christian Palestinian who flees Jerusalem in 1948 and travels to Baghdad. Throughout the novel, there are criticisms of those who 'wallow in antiquarianism' (80), yet the narrative is constantly interwoven with nostalgic contrasts between Baghdad now and in a distant past: 'Baghdad had decayed [. . .] the structures of the golden age had fallen to dust centuries ago' (36). Later, we have a similar contrast: 'the great city of the Abbasid empire [. . .] reduced to an ugly little place' (58). The nostalgic threads woven through the text become not only a way of expressing dissatisfaction with the present moment, the turbulent last years of the Hashemite monarchy, but also a comment on trying to find a way out of being 'caught in the web of power politics, oil politics, East and West politics' (*Hunters* 59). The contradictory attitude (both nostalgic and critical) which runs through the novel is encapsulated in an exchange between friends of the narrator, one of whom comments, '[w]e're so obsessed with our present we don't know a thing about our past', while the other contradicts him by reversing the claim: '[w]e're so obsessed with our past [. . .] we don't know a thing about our present' (114). A few pages later, the English banker Brian Finch speaks about Nineveh and Nimrud, and the contrast between the ruins and the villagers 'quite unconscious of the forces that lie petrified in those grass-covered mounds'. The protagonist responds to this contrast between past and present by critiquing the dispassionate knowledge that can 'organise [the past] into historical patterns': '[w]ith your critical eye [. . .] you may observe the irony of such juxtapositions as peasants with gummy eyes sitting in the midst of their asses' dung within sight of the great monuments of an empire they cannot understand. But to us the irony is savage' (116). The use of the word 'irony' here is significant. As Linda Hutcheon notes, irony and nostalgia share a dependency on juxtapositions and the element of response: 'to call something ironic or nostalgic is [. . .] less a description of the entity itself than an attribution of a quality of response [. . .] In both cases it is the element of response – of active participation, both intellectual and affective – that makes for the power' (199).[6] For Jameel, it is the difference in responding to the same reality that is notable: the historian immediately notes the discordant juxtaposition but is too distanced to grasp the emotional weight that the juxtaposition carries, which Jameel feels acutely as a savage irony. Like the examples cited earlier, this passage emphasizes the distance between civilizations of the past and the contemporary age, and it is the 'savage irony' of the discontinuity between past and present that is stressed.

The nostalgic aesthetic involves a 'double exposure' in Boym's terms. Boym describes how nostalgia 'produces subjective visions of afflicted imagination that tend to colonise the realm of politics, history, and everyday perception' (9). The nostalgia for a golden age 'colonize[s]' these realms to an extent that the present is experienced as a nightmare, which is only intensified by the contrast that is set up between an existence in diaspora and the past/place from which the nostalgic diasporic subject feels severed. We see an example of this severance in Robin Yassin-Kassab's novel *The Road from Damascus*, when the protagonist Sami meets Muntaha, an Iraqi woman who immigrated to Britain with her family after her father was arrested by Saddam's regime. Sami sees Muntaha for the first time 'in one of the Mesopotamian rooms at the British museum' (15) and initially connects her with the artefacts from the exhibition:

> Sami turned from an ancient diadem and glimpsed her, the kind of woman who would have worn such jewellery [. . .] she was entirely still, an exhibit herself. A Mesopotamian woman in communion with Mesopotamian art about to launch herself from its past into Sami's life. (15)

Sami's objectification of Muntaha as 'an exhibit herself' identifies her as an authentic link to the past. He is pleased that unlike his own pronunciation of English, '[h]er accent confirmed she was Sumerian, Iraqi'. Sami's interlinking of the ancient past and the present, of Sumeria and Iraq, leads him to ask Muntaha if she is proud of the exhibition because 'it comes from your land'. Muntaha however immediately rejects this framing: 'I'm from Iraq, not Sumeria. We have different gods today. Gods with moustaches' (16). In other words, she undercuts Sami by reminding him of the ideological uses of nostalgia in a repressive authoritarian regime, resisting the use of ancient history for nationalist purposes, which she experienced under Saddam's regime:

> I learned all about this at school in Iraq [. . .] the teacher read nationalist poetry and made speeches about the people and the leader [. . .] It didn't make me

> proud to be Iraqi. It made me think how strange it is to be human. Believing in your gods, thinking you understand things, making beautiful statues and then dying and waiting for people to guess who you were. (17)

While Sami's nostalgia is for the fantasy of reconnecting with the ideal past, for Muntaha the nostalgia she experiences in the Mesopotamian rooms is more personal: 'my father used to bring me here. This was his favourite exhibit. I suppose it makes me feel nostalgic' (16). Yassin-Kassab uses this scene in the Mesopotamian rooms to set up a contrast between Muntaha and Sami: Muntaha resists the nationalist use of the past because of her family's experiences in Iraq, while Sami finds in this past a satisfying contrast to his own confused, hyphenated identity as a Syrian raised in Britain. Standing before the artefacts from Mesopotamia and Sumeria, Sami is standing by the ruins and contemplating the loss of a golden age. Muntaha, meanwhile, critiques the golden age as a fantasy that assumes the past can be fully recovered, eliding the interpretive work needed to 'guess' at the meaning of the artefacts.

A similar use of nostalgia for the ancient past as a reflection of a desire to belong is dramatized towards the end of Ahdaf Soueif's first novel *In the Eye of the Sun*. In the last few pages of the novel, the protagonist Asya recalls a visit to an archaeological excavation. Looking at a recently unearthed stone figure, Asya is struck by 'the composure' on the figure's face:

> the very indignity of her posture makes the pride and grace of her expression – of her bearing – all the more remarkable [. . .] The composure, the serenity, of her smile tells of someone who had always known who she was [. . .] she has indeed found a gentle grace; for here she is, delivered back into the sunlight still in complete possession of herself – of her pride, and of her small, subtle smile. (785)

There is an obvious contrast here between the figure of the woman who knew 'who she was' and the protagonist Asya, who is conscious of how much she does not know where she belongs. This passage comes only a few pages after Asya wonders how she can be 'yearning for Cairo' when 'she is actually here in the middle of it all' and asks herself 'what can she do more than just be, just be here'? (780). Like Yassin-Kassab's strategic use of nostalgia to set up the tension between his characters, here at the conclusion of *In the Eye of the Sun* Soueif presents us with a nostalgically framed scene that adds resonance the novel's open ending. Her protagonist compares her own lack of certainty to the figure of the unknown woman who represents a composed self. The connection with the past gestures to a hoped for cultural reconnection in the future: Boym makes the case that 'creative nostalgia reveals the fantasies of the age and it is in those fantasies and potentialities that the future is born' (351). Again however, as when Muntaha reminds Sami of the ultimate unknowability of the past in Yassin-Kassab's novel, when Asya asks who the stone figure represents, she finds no answers. Instead, she is told '[t]hey think she's from the time of Ramses the Second [. . .] They've found things that say a queen, and things that say Rameses' sister, and things that say a dancing girl at court. Who knows?' (784). In both novels, the writers simultaneously establish a nostalgic mood and complicate nostalgic impulse through the recognition of the impossibility of fully comprehending the past. The fragments of the past are represented as offering a partial, always incomplete testimony.

The golden age narrative can also comment on topical issues in the present which are reframed through a contrast with the past. In Moroccan-American writer Laila Lalami's first novel *Hope and Other Dangerous Pursuits* (2005), the journey of a group of illegal migrants is framed in a way that juxtaposes the present against the age of Islamic conquest to comment on migration politics today. In the opening pages, as the immigrants set out from Tangiers to Tarifa, the main protagonist, Murad, is aware that the journey they are on is the same journey undertaken by Tariq Ibn Ziyad's invading army in 711:

> Murad used to regale tourists with anecdotes about how Tariq Ibn Ziyad had led a powerful Moor army across the Straits and, upon landing in Gibraltar, ordered the boats burned. He'd told his soldiers that they could march forth and defeat the enemy or turn back and die a coward's death [. . .] Little did they know that we'd be back, Murad thinks. Only instead of a fleet, here we are in an inflatable boat – not just Moors, but a motley mix of people from the ex-colonies, without guns or armour, without a charismatic leader. It's worth it, though, Murad tells himself. Some time on this flimsy boat and then a job. (3)

In this opening scene, the contemporary crossing becomes the symbolic inverse of the historical voyage of conquest, with the burned boats paralleled in the word used for illegals, *harraga*, 'those who burn' (their identity papers). The passage between Tangiers and Tarifa illuminates the distance between the past and present, as Murad wonders 'how fourteen kilometres could separate not just two countries but two universes?' (1). Here, the physical distance is mapped onto the vast distance between 'a first world postmodernity with a third world postcoloniality' which seem to exist in different temporal zones (Makdisi 285). Lalami draws on the pathos of a melancholic nostalgia, the lament for a golden age, to make a political point about present inequalities. Lalami herself is clearly wary of the sentimentalism associated with immigrant nostalgia, noting in an interview that 'it can be quite important for those of us who live outside their ancestral homelands to retain a little bit of distance because it's so easy to get homesick and nostalgic and put on rose-coloured glasses' ('Interview'). However, her fiction illuminates how a nostalgic lens can represent immigrant experiences in ways that highlight the intersection of individual, psychological and affective stories with national narratives.

These examples, which combine nostalgic tropes with a critical distance from nostalgia, mediate between projecting a glorious past and the recognition that this glorious past is in fact a fantasy. Pride in the past is often inextricable from the frustrations of the present. Thus, María Rosa Menocal describes Said's writing on Andalusia in the following terms:

> [t]he whole of Said's article veers back and forth between pride in the incomparable achievements of moments like tenth-century Ummayyad Cordoba

and anger, directed first and foremost against 'the self-destructive demise of the Andalusian kings and their *tawa'if* – which he explicitly compares to 'present-day Arab disunity and consequent weakness.' (242)

This ambivalence is characteristic of how Anglophone Arab writers depict the distant pasts constructed as a golden age. Hutcheon speaks of nostalgia as '[s]imultaneously distancing and proximating', since it 'exiles us from the present as it brings the imagined past near. The simple, pure, ordered, easy, beautiful, or harmonious past is constructed [...] in conjunction with the present – which, in turn, is constructed as complicated, contaminated, anarchic, difficult, ugly, and confrontational' (195). In the examples I have discussed, a variety of complex feelings associated with nostalgia are brought to bear on different contexts, but in each case the interest in the emotions inspired by the fantasy of a perfect past becomes an essential part of the characterization of protagonists who feel alienated from the present.

Rabih Alameddine's The Hakawati

Alameddine is a Lebanese American writer who has published several well-received novels as well as a collection of short stories. His novel *The Hakawati* in particular has received wide critical acclaim for its experimental retelling of stories drawing from a wide range of sources, including, to mention only a few of the texts referenced in the author's acknowledgements, 'A *Thousand and One Nights* (uncensored), Ovid's *Metamorphoses*, the Old Testament, the Koran, W. A. Clouston's *Flowers from a Persian Garden* [...] numerous Internet folktale sites, and quite a few books of Syrian and Lebanese folktales' (514). The novel's various borrowings are woven around a story of return to the homeland, with the protagonist Osama al-Kharrat returning to Beirut from Los Angeles when he learns that his father is dying. The novel shifts between the family's vigil at the hospital, Osama's memories of his childhood, and the stories that he has heard growing up. The retellings of myths and legends in Alameddine's novel extends from its structure, as a narrative woven from heterogeneous sources, to its various storyteller characters who insist on the impossibility of identical retellings. Book Two of *The Hakawati* begins with several epigraphs, including a quote from *Tomorrow in the Battle Think on Me* by Javier Marías (1994) asserting that once a story becomes 'common currency', alteration is inevitable, since all stories are 'twisted and distorted' and 'no story is told the same way twice or in quite the same words' (135). This passage captures the spirit of much of Alameddine's work in its emphasis of revisionism.

Alameddine's work has been among the most widely discussed examples of Arab American literature and in particular Anglophone Lebanese literature. Often these readings focus on Alameddine's revisionist style as pushing against the attempt to fix ever-mutating cultural forms, centring instead the fanciful and imaginative forces of storytelling as an evolving form. Syrine Hout, for example, describes Alameddine's collection of short stories *The Perv* as having 'no place for nostalgia', that is for the sentimental yearning for the past ('Memory' 223). In his reading of *The Hakawati*, Alberto Fernández Carbajal refers to Alameddine's 'druzification of history' (altering Salman Rushdie's 'chutnification of history'), arguing that as a Druze, 'Alameddine remains, ethnically speaking, a "queer" form of Muslim' (79). Carbajal also highlights that the explicit reference to the uncensored versions of texts 'demonstrates Alameddine's choice to reinstate in his own narrative those elements deemed controversial or deviant by later editors and translators' (81). In a sense, Alameddine's works fit neatly into what Waïl Hassan calls the canon of postcolonial literature as world literature, given the focus on hybridity and deconstructing authenticity, yet there is a curious twist to locating a particular identity as the secret source for such hybridity, the author's Druze background being located as a factor in the writer's interest in recovering but also reinventing the eclectic traditions he references in his texts.

In a similar formulation, in this case focusing on Alameddine's national rather than religious affiliation, Franck Salameh's brief discussion of *The Hakawati* focuses on a single passage where the definition of the word, meaning storyteller, is described as 'derived from the Lebanese word "haki," which means "talk" or "conversation," with the comment that 'in Lebanese the mere act of talking is storytelling' (*Hakawati* 36). This passage, which has been widely cited in reviews of the novel, is striking for the particularity of its identification of 'haki' as a Lebanese rather than an Arabic word. In a book otherwise devoted to language and identity in the Middle East and focused on the case of Lebanon, Salameh's discussion of Alameddine's novel argues that '[o]pting for "Lebanese" tout court was a statement [Alameddine] was making on behalf of a bona fide "Lebanese" language' rather than as a dialect of Arabic (21). In other words, for Salameh, the claiming of *haki* as a Lebanese word is an argument against 'the futility of trying to pigeon-hole [Lebanese identity] into an ideologically soothing label, Arab or otherwise' (21). While for Carbajal the revisionism, heterogeneity and reinstating of uncensored bawdiness in the text are interlinked with queerness, marginality and Druze identity, for Salameh, the novel primarily reflects the unique 'congenital diversity' of Lebanon against the homogenizing force of the label Arab (21). In both cases, the celebrated aspects of mixedness and hybridity in the text are linked with a smaller scale, more localized identity, Lebanese or Druze, where the writer is culturally situated, which is then seen as significant factor informing Alameddine's writing against religious and cultural forces seeking to enforce homogeneity.

Given the parallels that can be drawn with *A Thousand and One Nights* in particular, and the breadth of references the novel incorporates, reviews of *The Hakawati* tend to instead emphasize the novel's Arabness. Describing one review which presented his novel as 'a bridge to the Arab soul', Alameddine is visceral in his rejection of such readings: 'I mean, 250 million or I don't know how many and they have one fucking soul? And my book is the bridge to that?' ('My Existence'). However, Alameddine goes on to just as explicitly reject the framework through which the fabulist and bawdy richness of his retellings are pitted against stereotypes of austere morality and religious violence, the idea that this is a novel that should be celebrated because it is 'not about a jihadist; it's about a storyteller'. Instead, Alameddine sees his novel as an exploration of the nature of narrative-making itself, an exploration of how 'myths are what make us' and how '[w]e are the stories we tell ourselves about ourselves' ('My Existence'). The novel is both about and composed of the questions that fictions of memory address. It is the insistence on the very unfixed nature of stories themselves which serves as an antidote to and an indictment of essentialist narratives, rather than a particular marginal or 'congenitally diverse' localized group identity.

I would argue that there is something to be gained in paying attention to nostalgia as a vehicle for the preservation, alteration and retelling of stories in Alameddine's novels, since nostalgia appears insistently as an imaginative resource in daily life in Alameddine's work. For example, in his novel *An Unnecessary Woman* (2014), the protagonist Aaliya Saleh is keenly aware of the power of nostalgic emotions and the intimate relationship between loss and nostalgia, arguing that '[n]o loss is felt more keenly than the loss of what might have been. No nostalgia hurts as much as nostalgia for things that never existed' (155). These sentences encapsulate the evocative power of nostalgia even (or rather especially) when the source of nostalgic feeling is acknowledged to be a fantasy. Reaching back to imagined and fictional pasts as a strategy to deal with present loss is strategic, and the wilful blindness to more recent history is self-protective. Later in the novel, Aliyah critiques this selective vision of the past, though she acknowledges it to be a human tendency: 'the Lebanese [. . .] like most humans, consider history a lesson on a blackboard that can be sponged off. We'd rather ostrich life's difficulties' (193). The selective way people approach the past, from nostalgic fantasies to an avoidance of historical realities, is in Alameddine's novels inextricable from the psychological impact of the Lebanese civil war. Rather than critique the nostalgic with a celebratory emphasis on diversity, Alameddine's novels dramatize and investigate the appeal of the lost past, or of an irrecoverably changed place, and the power of imagining this point of putative fixity in an always situated, flexible context.

The Hakawati opens with the first-person narrative of Osama al-Kharrat's return to Beirut from America to visit his dying father Farid, over a decade after the end of the civil war. As Osama looks upon this different Beirut, he contrasts the city he sees now with the city he left, commenting that '[t]he reds of my Beirut, the home city I remember, were wilder, primary. The colors were better then, more vivid, more alive' (8). This paradigmatic nostalgic lament of lost childhood comes as Osama describes himself 'standing distracted and bewildered before my old home, dwelling in the past', a sentence which I read as deliberately invoking the trope of *al-wuqūf ʿalā al-aṭlāl* ('standing by the ruins'), in which the speaker experiences the present while being preoccupied with the past (8). Osama's nostalgic return to the homeland, contrasting the romanticized past against the present, conveys his *ghurba*, his estrangement from this home that is no longer the home he remembers:

> Once upon a time, I was a boy with potential. I roamed the streets of this neighborhood. Once upon a time, this was a neighborhood with possibility. Now it lay decrepit, dying [. . .] Hope [. . .] was nowhere to be found. [. . .] This used to be both my sanctuary and my mystery zone [. . .] I wanted to find my way home. (476)

In this passage, Alameddine layers the nostalgic sites of childhood and home together with a reflection on ruins and ruination, with the 'decrepit, dying' neighbourhood which now offers neither sanctuary nor hope. Later in the novel, Osama will recall how his grandfather spoke of his own childhood, remembering how 'the remnant of the ancient Roman wall was the back wall of our house' and how he would 'climb the wall at night and [. . .] yell at the world: I am here. I'm here, like Abraham' (46). The material presence of the ruins of ancient civilizations, linked here with the myth-making of Abrahamic religions, is implicitly contrasted against the ruins of post-war Beirut. Here displacement is not only the condition of physical exile, but the alienation one feels while at home. Nostalgic tropes are part of an effort to locate the self, to be able to declare 'I am here'. As the novel links the protagonist's memories of his childhood with his grandfather's story, the nostalgia for the pre-war period is refracted through the nostalgia for more distant pasts, for the presence and continuity represented by the material traces of previous civilizations.

The juxtaposition of ancient ruins and the ruination of the war is a recurring trope in novels about the Lebanese civil war. For example, in Tony Hanania's *Unreal City* (1999), the opening pages set up a familiar narrative of decline, as '[p]rophets, generals, Caesars, saints, all have long been forgotten, their memories effaced by the march of pimps, playboys, traffickers, warlords, militiamen' (30). The novel includes a scene where tourists are guided through Sidon. In a passage that clearly invites the reader to mock the nostalgic attachment to some far-off golden age, the tour guide points the tourists to the artefacts celebrating the history of this 'city of [. . .] marble colonnades, caravanserais' (84):

> Harun [. . .] gestures grandly towards the trestle table, as if drawing the curtain from some great panorama; the piles of fruit softening in the heat; on racks behind the apples and bridled water-melons: dusty ceramics, straw donkeys, olive-wood camels. (81)

Here we have a simultaneous invocation of melancholic nostalgia for past glories, and elements of parody and irony that would seem to critique such nostalgia. There are similar juxtapositions of irony and nostalgia in Alameddine's work, where nostalgic tropes are constantly interwoven with bathos. In fact, in the opening pages of *The Hakawati* Osama reminds the reader of the origins of the name Kharrat, which means fibster, wryly noting that '[n]o one thought it strange that a car dealership, and the family that ran it, had a name that meant "exaggerator", "teller of tall tales", "liar"' (9). The grandiose myth-making of what one reviewer calls the 'piquant stew' of the Kharrat family history allows the narrator to interweave stories from many backgrounds, yet rather than suggesting the need to preserve a fixed version of cultural memory, the novel overflows with narrations and re-narrations of the same story, rendering them prosaic, an intrinsic part of everyday life (Schlack).

The novel opens with the injunction to listen: 'Listen. Allow me to be your god [. . .] Let me tell you a story' (5). For Osama, the decline he experiences in post-war Beirut is encapsulated in the failure to listen: '[n]o one listens anymore' (9). As we soon learn however, this is an inherited complaint. Osama's grandfather Ismail couches it in generational terms: '[h]ere I am trying to infuse you with culture, my flesh and blood, my own kin' (45). The syntax of the sentence renders the 'flesh and blood' ambiguous, both an address to Osama as Ismail's kin, and potentially a reference to the *infusion* of culture as a way to confer kinship, with the nostalgic contrast of a better time when people listened inspiring the moment of retelling. Later, when Ismail asserts, 'I come from a time when ink was still liquid and lush [. . .] None of this cheap Biro shit', we have a sense of storytelling itself as liquid and lush, suggestive of the ability to tell and retell rather than to copy (85).

The fluidity of stories is emphasized when Ismail describes his first encounter with a *hakawati* who 'enthralled everyone's attention' as he 'held a book in his lap but hardly looked at it', telling rather than reading the story, which Ismail experiences as '[m]agic' (89). The nostalgia for this moment is not for any notion of authenticity, since Ismail stresses the hybrid nature of the *hakawati*, who 'wore a fez and Western clothing' (89). Rather, the emphasis is on the skilful oration of stories, at a time when being a *hakawati* is a respected profession, and where crucially the storyteller does not read from the book (and therefore does not repeat the story in the same words). This scene of magic is contrasted with the performance of a less admired *hakawati*, who speaks with a 'a pretentious inflection', and who is described as 'carr[ying] a plastic sword in his right hand and a tattered book in his left' (105). Ismail's contempt for this figure is highlighted in the fact that the *hakawati* reads from his book, rather than performing the story he tells. To read is to fix the story, whereas telling is unfixed, as is suggested when Osama's uncle Jihad tells him that it is now his turn to tell stories: '[w]hy don't you tell us a story, Osama? It's time you contributed to our lore' (439). Framing the telling of a story as a contribution to a shared lore locates cultural memory as something valuable not because it preserves the past but rather because of the additive capacity of retelling, which speaks to the constructed nature of cultural narratives.

Osama's uncle Jihad is himself a storyteller, but his more cynical vision stands in contrast to the generational critiques expressed by Ismail. For Jihad, to reflect on the failures of the present acknowledges what is lost yet sees something to admire in the attempt to return from that loss. Hope, from this perspective, is transposed from a future-oriented emotion to a touchstone of complex nostalgic feeling. We see this reversal in temporal orientation when Jihad describes his love for Umm Kulthum because '[e]ver since they lost the last war, she's been on a never-ending tour trying to raise Arab morale [. . .] I love people who are passionate about lost causes' (168). While seemingly a throwaway line, the reference to Umm Kulthum speaks to the novel's theme of repetition with variation. As Alameddine describes in an interview, in recordings of Umm Kulthum 'you can hear the audience encouraging Umm Kalthoum [*sic*] as she's singing. They say "ma sar" – it didn't happen. What you just sang didn't happen, you have to do it again. And she would'

(Crossen). This scene is included in the novel itself, when the narrator Osama and his uncle Jihad listen to Umm Kulthum:

> 'It didn't happen.' a man said to the radio. 'You have to do it again.'
> She did. She began the song again. from the beginning [. . .] Each line became a tease. Will she repeat it? Will she take it further? (167)

The reiterative quality, an erasure in order to allow another rendition, is a request to begin again in order to listen again, like the beginning of fairy tales, which begin not with a definitive once upon a time but rather with '*kan ya ma kan*' (there was or there was not). Story-telling begins with an erasure that encourages repetition, as Osama's mother requests: '[t]ell me another story. Entertain me once more' (439). To repeat something involves a simultaneous presence, the trace of the thing retold, and an absence, its erasure in order for the repeated yet different version to take its place.

The connection Jihad draws between Umm Kulthum and the familiar 'what went wrong' narrative of modern Arab history is at once nostalgic and cynical, admitting the absence that is the lost cause while at the same time admiring the passion which insists on repeating, and retelling, the story of loss. For Jihad, Umm Kulthum's voice evokes the complexity of nostalgic emotion, an emotion which David Werman calls a 'wistful pleasure, a joy tinged with sadness' (393). In a similar formulation bringing together sorrow and pleasure, Lebanese writer Etel Adnan describes Umm Kulthum as 'the tide of history, the tide of all the frustrations transfigured in a kind of bliss':

> [w]hen the Arabs were thinking that they had nothing, they were saying that after all they had Oum Kasloum [sic] and that, all by herself, she represented their will to be [. . .] I heard her when I was twelve in the Grand Theatre of Beirut. It was a beneficial trauma. (12)

Adnan's description here captures the bittersweet nature of nostalgia as an emotional response and psychological state that strangely includes both 'bliss' and 'trauma'. The emotions that Umm Kulthum stirs means that, for Jihad, she can be described as 'the quintessential Arab [. . .] the one person whom all Arabs can agree to love' (168). While positing a person to be a 'quintessential Arab' seems opposed to the queerness and revisionism and mixedness with which Alameddine's writing has been associated, Arabness here is linked not to ethnic or linguistic markers, but rather to this attitude which refuses to abandon the lost cause, to turn away from the past.

It is in part his admiration for his uncle Jihad that inspires Osama to learn the oud with Istez Camil, a musician who had once accompanied Umm Kulthum. As he grows older however, Osama shifts away from the Egyptian icon to another musical icon, Elvis, deciding to buy 'the most expensive guitar [he] could think of, the same kind that Elvis played', because he 'no longer wished to be an old-fashioned Arab' (211). Similar moments of cultural rejection occur in a number of Alameddine's novels, going back to his first novel *Koolaids* (1998), where we have the following visceral rejection of nationalist sentiment: 'I fucking hate the Lebanese [. . .] They think they are so great, and for what reason?' Immediately, however, there is also a struggle with the possibility of self-invention: 'I tried so hard to rid myself of anything Lebanese [. . .] But I never could [. . .] The harder I tried, the more it showed up in the unlikeliest of places' (243–4). From a visceral rejection of the nostalgic attachment to a homeland, we are drawn back into the narrative of identity. Similarly, in *I, The Divine* (2002), though the protagonist Sarah struggles to embrace her 'American half', she is unable to repress her ambivalent attachment to the 'all consuming' aspects of Lebanese culture, and her love-hate relationship to (again) Umm Kulthum:

> I hated Umm Kalthoum [*sic*]. I wanted to identify with only my American half. I wanted to be special. I could not envision how to be Lebanese and keep any sense of individuality. Lebanese culture was all consuming. Only recently have I begun to realise that like my city [Beirut], my American patina covers an Arab soul. These days I avoid Umm Kalthoum, but not because I hate her. I avoid her because every time I hear that Egyptian bitch, I cry hysterically. (*I, The Divine* 299)

Sarah's attempt to erase her Lebanese identity is followed by her realization that she is unable to repress her 'Arab soul', a particularly essentialist framework, which, as I have discussed above, is precisely the framing Alameddine rejects in reviews of his novel, when he mocks the notion of a novel as 'bridge to the Arab soul' (Alameddine, 'My Existence'). Like the idea of Umm Kulthum as a 'quintessential Arab', the positing of identity in such essentialist terms is troubled. For Syrine Hout, Anglophone Lebanese literature is centred on 'the debunking of two myths: the return to a golden age of a romanticized Lebanon and the slavish imitation of a supposedly superior Western lifestyle' (*Post-War* 9). We see these twinned tendencies in Alameddine's novels which clearly question the value of instinctive attachment to group identity, and yet, I would argue, this refusal of romanticization coexists with a recognition of what motivates such behaviour, and particularly how nostalgia can be experienced as a complex psychological minefield, latent in the very human emotion of longing, despite a seemingly enlightened distaste for sentimental feeling.

In *The Hakawati*, we have a similar attempt to divest from nostalgia in Osama's abandoning the oud for the guitar. As in the examples discussed above however, this effort is not entirely successful. Osama seeks to return to the oud and to the musical heritage associated with it when a friend asks him to play something from his country, and Osama attempts to adjust a maqam to his instrument: '[t]he guitar's sound proved awkward [. . .] the frets got in the way. I had to improvise. I slowed down, allowing myself more time to adjust' (342). Hybridity here is discordant, even awkward, requiring time and effort. Coming towards the end of the novel, the scene of playing a maqam on a guitar is symbolically weighed, a reminder of the possibilities that extend from the word maqam itself, a word which is explained in the novel as meaning '"place" or "situation"' implying not only the stability of location but the capacity of changing that stability through a change in situation (164).

As Osama realizes when he recovers his great-grandmother's oud, the passion for what is lost does not make it any less lost: '[y]ou don't just pick up an instrument after all these years and start strumming. This isn't a fairy tale' (342). In a novel infused with fairy tales, this corrective voice of realism connects the instrument which cannot be restored to a recognition of entropy, of something 'aged beyond repair' (342). Even here however, Alameddine interweaves this moment of melancholia for what is irrevocably lost with comedy, describing how Osama and his sister cry over the fact that 'the gorgeous oud' now 'sound[ed] like a ukulele' (397). This juxtaposition of loss and laughter is a consistent theme in the novel. For example, in a humorous yet serious and symbolic conversation between Jihad and Osama's mother about how the poet Mutannabi's poetry survived after his death, Jihad constructs a story where one of the brigands who killed the poet had 'an unexplored sensitive nature' which led him to be 'entranced and bewitched' by the poems (420). Osama's mother posits then that some of the poems may have flown away while the brigand was attempting to repack them:

'Imagine. Poetry still hovering over the skies of Baghdad.'
'Or buried under the desert sands,' my mother said. 'Someone drills a well in Iraq, and out gushes poetry instead of oil.'
'But will the discoverers understand Arabic or appreciate poetry, for that matter?'
'Al-Mutanabbi's basic problem to begin with'. (420)

In this exchange, the poetic image of poetry hovering in the Baghdad sky is transformed into the notion of buried wealth, poetry as oil, something to be excavated. However, the suggestion that through such excavation we will be able to grasp what has been lost, to be in touch with the past, is questionable. In the final line of dialogue, the notions of loss and entropy are shifted from the question of what reaches us from the past to a more expansive question, 'Al-Mutanabbi's basic problem', which has to do with the inherent losses and misinterpretations that are already present in any attempts to communicate. This prosaic approach to how we think about the past reappears in the final paragraphs of Osama's story, when Osama defines depression as a 'necrotizing bacteria [...] flesh-eating gloom' against which he marshals pleasant thoughts, invoking moments and sensations that have a distinctively nostalgic flavour, including 'Maqâm Saba [...] Uncle Jihad telling me stories [...] The Arab voice of Umm Kulthum' (234). In other words, in the final scenes of this novel, Osama recognizes nostalgia as a part of something practical, less about fantasy than a palliative, a personal resource, which can be weaponized against the gloom of negative thoughts.

Alameddine's novels are frequently cited as evidence for the development of Anglophone Arab writing beyond the sentimental nostalgia of the homesick immigrant, a shift from nostalgia to critique. However, nostalgia in *The Hakawati* is far more complex than a sentimental yearning for a better time, varying from a narrativization and making sense of collective loss to a reclamation and retelling of inherited stories and to an individual's consciously deployed weapon against depression. Nostalgia, as Alameddine represents it, is a contradictory and fraught emotion which often coexists with the critique of what nostalgic tendencies may inspire, a nuanced perspective which is carefully negotiated in this novel, Alameddine's first to be written since 9/11, in which he reclaims the names Osama and Jihad for his own narrative.

Sabiha Khemir's Blue Manuscript

Sabiha Khemir is a Tunisian writer, illustrator and Islamic art expert who was the founding director of the Museum of Islamic Art in Doha, Qatar. Khemir's fiction works have not been the focus of much critical discussion; however, her novels provide an interesting lens on the exploration of nostalgia, particularly in relation to the material remnants of an idealized past. Her engagement with nostalgic discourses is already signalled in the title of her debut novel, *Waiting in the Future for the Past to Come* (1993), a contradictory phrase that suggests a critique of nostalgia as a futile reversal of temporality. This first novel follows the protagonist Amina's return home to Tunisia after studying abroad, and then goes further back in time as Amina narrates her memories of childhood. Having at least temporarily returned to her homeland, Amina realizes that the point of origin does not ensure a sense of belonging, describing, not quite tautologically, a 'strange feeling of being a stranger' (20). After her return home to a place she no longer feels is home, the protagonist begins to narrate the story of her childhood, but frames it in terms of a longing to return even further than her own memories: 'I will go as far as I can remember but what I really want to tell you is beyond what I can remember' (28). In the essay cited in the opening of this chapter, Khemir writes: 'the present reality of the Arab world is a difficult one [...] I need and have the responsibility to carry the hope and energy of transformation, of recreating – and I do not mean here reproducing – but recreating my past' ('Mobile Identity' 46). Here, Khemir suggests that present-day political conflicts prompt the need for nostalgic discourses. Significantly, she makes a distinction between 'recreating' and 'reproducing' the past, a distinction which exemplifies the ambiguities I am interested in here.

Khemir's second novel, *The Blue Manuscript*, takes up similar themes, though here the exploration of identity and belonging unfolds in the context of an archaeological excavation. The protagonist, Zohra, is a Tunisian–British translator who is torn between her Arab and Western identities. At the beginning of the novel, Zohra has just arrived in Egypt to join a group of archaeologists searching for a lost copy of a Quran manuscript commissioned during the tenth-century Fatimid dynasty in the village of Wadi Hassoun. Set in the 1980s, the novel sets the archaeologists from abroad amid the villagers and workers. The international team, led by the ambitious Mark, includes a British professor named only as O'Brien, Japanese site surveyor Kodama, German conservator Hans and Egyptian archaeology inspector Monia. The villagers include the go-betweens Rayyes Ahmed, a local contractor, and Mustapha, a museum guard's son and an ambitious entrepreneur, as well as the blind storyteller Amm Gaber whose meditations, interweaving dreams and reality, punctuate the narrative. The narrative switches between these perspectives, a technique that results in shallow and flat characterizations. Yet as one reviewer notes, 'the shallowness of the descriptions is actually how the characters know and perceive each other [. . .] there is little bridging of cultural or personal gaps. Finally, each character is left in his or her own [. . .] reality' (Jones). The constant switching of perspectives and the narrow focalization forces the reader to interpret the world through the solipsistic view of each of the characters.

The novel opens with the archaeological team in Cairo, on a tour of the Fatimid city. The present-day city is described by one of the archaeologists as 'a remnant of a civilisation that had been exhausted' (26). In these opening pages, Zohra reflects on how the urban environment is one of '[l]ayers of time [. . .] interwoven in intricate chaos' (20), yet the presence of the old buildings evoke a sense of loss in her, as 'the gap of time created an inexplicable sense of melancholy' (22). Once they arrive at the village, the proximity of ruins to the village drives Zohra to reflect again on 'the gap separat[ing] the village from the glorious past crumbling nearby', and to ask 'how [. . .] the link between the past and present [had] been severed' (67). What disturbs Zohra particularly is the contrast, 'the present mediocrity of her father's mundane reality juxtaposed with the sophistication of his culture's past' (210). Zohra's juxtaposition of the grandiose 'sophistication' of a lost civilization and the micro-level, everyday mundane present highlights the selectivity of nostalgia which Hutcheon describes as '[s]imultaneously distancing and proximating' (195). In Khemir's novel, this distancing effect is transposed onto the present itself, when Zohra reflects on the villagers' reality as itself anachronistic, lagging behind the world they have access to through media: '[t]he privileged few bathed in the blue light of their televisions [. . .] The gap between their reality and the world on the screen was unbridgeable' (53). The gap has now shifted from that between the ancient past and the present to instead indicate the inequality that separates the villagers from the life they see on the television. Similarly, when Zohra leaves Wadi Hassoun, 'that remote and isolated place' (297), for London, she is aware that 'the villagers remained trapped in their reality, the gap between worlds immense' (302). Again, the 'gap between worlds' is transfigured from a gap between the past and the present to a temporal gap between there (Wadi Hassoun) as the past, and here (London) as the future. The shift highlights the way in which the temporal gaps represented in the novel relate not only to the contrast of past and present but to the power dynamics of juxtaposing 'a first world postmodernity with a third world postcoloniality', as Saree Makdisi puts it, contrasting two worlds which seem to exist in different temporal zones (285).

In an article on the architecture of Cairo, Khemir describes neglected historical buildings as 'stand[ing] bewildered, too close yet far removed from a present reality that has taken over their time but has not managed to make it into the modern era' ('Cairo'). This anthropomorphic description of 'bewildered' ruins in the essay also appears in her novel, when Zohra's attention is captured by the ruins of a minaret which 'looked bewildered [. . .] reduced to a lonely ruin at the edge of a village' (67). The marginality of the ruins, which seem out of place in contemporary settings, is even more pronounced where remnants of the past coexist with the constantly evolving present in a crowded metropolis:

> [n]ew constructions, many of them unfinished, rubbed shoulders with ruins. Old buildings, hundreds of years old, were close, too close, to blocks of flats that rose pompously fast towards the sky. Zohra had heard that in some cases, they collapsed just as fast, killing large numbers of people. (22)

Khemir's reflections on the architectural juxtaposition of ancient and modern in Cairo connects the consequences of buildings rising too fast with the desire to 'catch up' to modernity, to translate the city's present into the global image of a modern society. The juxtaposition of consoling histories and dissatisfaction with the present is heightened when the city's chaotic reality is contrasted against a present elsewhere that seems to exist in a different temporality.

Translation and archaeology are intertwined in the novel. The excavation itself is described in terms of language, as a 'scraping the inside of memory [...] siev[ing] the earth as though wanting to make the silent grains speak' (172). Zohra imagines languages as 'containers' which, when she faces challenges in translation, break 'into perilous shards [...] meanings lost in the jagged chaos' (285). Increasingly, she feels 'as though she was betraying something' and expresses this in an image of antagonistic bilingualism: 'she felt that there were two tongues in her mouth, superimposed in synchronised motion like a pair of scissors editing what came out' (153). This vivid description of bilingualism recalls the medieval writer al-Jahiz's representation of bilingualism as rivalry and hostility. As Moroccan writer Abdelfettah Kilito writes, for al-Jahiz, in the context of the ethnic tensions that marked early Abbasid politics, linguistic encounter involves a contest over dominance where '[t]o speak a language necessitates turning to one side' and to be bilingual is to be 'in constant movement, always turning', to be 'two-faced' (*Thou Shalt Not Speak My Language* 23). Instead of expressing her bilingualism in terms of a celebratory hybridity, Zahra is acutely aware of the predicament of in-betweenness, which is represented not as liberating but as an entrapping zone: 'there were moments when she, the translator, felt trapped in that zone, the zone of the untranslatable' (109).

The connections between language and the past is dramatized in a central scene of the novel which brings the 'untranslatable' to the fore when the villagers refuse to dig near a shrine:

> [t]he workers [...] gathered around the scene. They looked like extras in a film. One wore a red sweatshirt with the English word go written on it in thick white letters. It was large enough to be read from the other side of the circle but he himself did not know what his chest declared. For him the letters were mute squiggles. The professor and the rest of the team stood to one side; the workers were on the shrine's side. A wall of silence stood between them. (155–6)

In this passage, the 'wall of silence' seems to represent the zone of the untranslatable, while the 'mute squiggles' illuminate the constraints of inscription, of traces, to deliver truth. Zohra seeks answers that would help her reconstruct the past and sees the excavation as 'holding within its entrails a fragmented past that could be assembled into meaning' (71). Yet, when the archaeologists begin to reconstruct retrieved fragments, she becomes aware of the contingencies of historical narratives as 'piecing together suppositions' (210). The always incomplete knowledge artefacts offer us is discussed in an essay written by Khemir in a catalogue for the 2006 Louvre exhibition, 'From Cordoba to Samarkand', which describes the 'context of a new "here"' created whenever the vestiges of the past are placed in museum collections, and reinterpreted as they are relocated (Skinner, 'The New Here'). In Khemir's novel, the 'new here' of objects becomes evident as they emerge from the ground, 'speaking a language that had to be deciphered' (200).

The novel's resolution follows Zohra's realization that the only meaning traces can be made to symbolize in the present is their perpetual loss of meaning. Increasingly, the plot is focused on the question of whether all the archaeologists' efforts will be for nothing. When artefacts are brought to the surface, they offer little sense of connection: '[i]t was as though these objects had been made just to be dug up and they had always existed as pieces of archaeology' (203). Each of the characters negotiates the contrast between the monetary value of the finds in the present and their value as mnemonic objects. Towards the end of the novel, this contrast is dramatized when Zohra attends the London exhibition of the finds and realizes that they had become 'art objects': '[m]ore than symbols, witnesses of time, actual carriers of civilisation, now they had somehow acquired an entirely different kind of value' (296). The archaeologist Laurent Olivier describes how 'at the same time that digs uncover vestiges of a past that had been thought lost, they unavoidably produce objects that belong to the present' (xvi). Rather than offering a sense of connection to history, the traces of the past are transformed in the 'new here' into new kinds of objects. Even as the digging progresses Zohra realizes that 'whatever was lying there, hidden in the ground, lay peacefully, unconcerned whether they dug it out or not' (204–5). Once the manuscript is unearthed, she feels that 'the object which has become familiar through descriptions, photographs, accounts [. . .] seems somehow fictitious' (260). This last comment self-reflexively highlights Khemir's own mediation of the actual 'blue manuscript' in her novel of the same name, constructing a fictitious object to reflect on the resonance of the past in the present. The fictitious quality of objects recovered from the ground suggests that the medium of fiction can usefully reflect on the intertwining of the real and imaginary in the nostalgic urge to reconstruct history.

In fact, the object that seems to offer an immutable connection to the past means different things for the various characters: '[f]or some it is a copy of the sacred Quran. For others it was treasure, a useful item to realise a career promotion, or a valuable piece of historical evidence' (272). These tensions between a romanticized quest for the past and a more pragmatic perspective where artefacts are a commercial resource reaches its climatic point after gold coins are discovered during the excavation. The villagers begin to imagine 'a halo of gold' around the site, which drives them to dig it up during the night. Khemir represents this scene through the villagers' collective voice, as they determine to 'split the earth wide open' feeling that 'their hard reality [. . .] had been mocked by the shining riches of the past, dug out from under their feet' (242). The villagers' destruction of the excavation site could be said to prioritize the future rather than the past, at least in part as a protest against the 'gap between worlds' – not only that of then and now, but of here and there. The scene lingers on the connection between villagers' determination to dig up the site and their sense of being wronged: '[a]ll their lives, Haj Salem's sons had walked barefoot on the soil of this village. They could not afford sandals' yet 'a treasure lay under those same bare feet. The barrier of time had isolated them from the gifts of the past' (242). Soon, the villagers digging up the site to search for gold leads to 'irreplaceable objects [being] destroyed, history reduced to powder' (244). This reference to treasure and the 'irreplaceable' is however later revealed as both comic and ironic, as the manuscript, the object for which the team is searching is revealed to be forged, a 'meticulously fabricated illusion' (295). Again, the golden age has less to do with truth claims than with the cultural work of memory. Implicitly at least, the comment on the 'fabricated illusion' of the object of nostalgia, as with the previous comment that describes it as 'fictitious', involves a meta-critical observation on the role imagination plays in negotiating nostalgia for the golden age, and in constructing the fantasy of the matchless past.

Throughout *The Blue Manuscript,* Khemir explores the impossible desire to recover the past, to see the ruins 'alive with their own reality' (22). At several points, the novel dramatizes the impossibility of reconnecting with the present through the metaphor of the desert wind erasing the traces of the past. In an early scene that describes the caravan of the Fatimid caliph Al Muizz, the founder of Cairo, heading into Egypt, Al Muizz watches the horses' shoes 'impressing the principles of the new dynasty into the earth' as he has ordered. However, as the caravan moves forward the letters of these principles 'disintegrate and dissolve, erased by the wind before his very eyes' (45). This scene encapsulates the *aṭlāl* topos, compressing the inscription and the erasure into one. As Zohra later realizes, 'the desert has no memory. There was only the presence of the moment' (250). Through recognizing the desert as the site of timelessness, of 'no memory', Zohra comes to terms with her inability to make of the past a coherent and unflawed narrative that would resolve her identity crisis. Here the novel returns to 'standing by the ruins', but on another note, not that of the melancholic pause, but of the poet moving on as the winds erase the signs of habitation. The figure of the author/poet is transfigured into that of an archivist capturing what is irrevocably erased through the use of language, collecting and translating fragments of meaning. Zohra's eventual acceptance of entropy and the loss of meaning is contrasted with the stance of one of the villagers, Zineb, who, when the excavation team leaves at the end, is left contemplating 'the unbearable absence' of the excavation site: 'Zineb looked wistfully at the site, empty, deserted [. . ..] she stood forlornly, waiting for something she knew would not come' (255). In other words, whereas Zohra finally is resigned to 'the presence of the moment', Zineb is, as the title of Khemir's first novel has it, 'waiting in the future for the past to come' (250). The emphasis on the transitory at the end of *The Blue Manuscript* implicitly critiques forms of nostalgia that offer a narrative of an arrested future that can never match the ideal, the future imagined from the perspective of an ideal past. To wait for the impossible is where the fantasy of the past becomes a burdensome history.

Khemir's use of an archaeological plot, reflecting on the fragmentary traces through which the past surfaces in the present, highlights the processes of interpretation, translation and adaptation that deny an uncomplicated retrieval of the past as a golden age. As Derrida puts it, the 'irrepressible desire to return to the origin, a homesickness, a nostalgia for return to the most archaic place of absolute' often involves the 'failure to remember the distance between the original and the trace' (91). The paradoxical ontological status of archaeological traces, as something present, standing for something past, underscores how our understandings of history take on different meanings according to the concerns of the present.

Yasmina Zahran's A Beggar at Damascus Gate

Yasmin Zahran is a Palestinian writer and archaeology scholar who has written a number of works related to archaeology in the Middle East. Her novel *A Beggar at Damascus Gate* (1995), like Khemir's works, has barely received any critical attention, yet there is a compelling focus in her work on how narratives of the golden age are triggered in relation to Palestinian exile. When the Palestinian protagonist reflects on the 'chaos of lost empires' (49), she seeks reconnection to these empires as a way to combat her experience of being 'born in exile [. . .] without memories', as part of a generation that has grown up outside the country of origin, dreaming of 'a Palestine they have never seen' (81–2). Formally, the text uses the conceit of the 'found manuscript', where the narrator, an American professor, finds and then edits the journals and diaries of a Palestinian woman, Rayya and a British archaeologist, Alex (later revealed to be a spy). The narrative then shifts between the three characters, the professor, Rayya and Alex, in ways that are temporally and spatially disjointed. Like the narrator, the reader must attempt to make sense out of the writings left behind by Rayya and Alex by piecing together the fragmentary passages.

The title of Zahran's novel carries a sense of disinheritance from both the past and from place; the beggar cannot enter through the gate to old Jerusalem. This theme of disinheritance from past and place taps into a broader Palestinian discourse of exile itself as disinheritance.[7] Herself an archaeologist, Zahran employs archaeological motifs to dramatize a sense of being excluded from the past and being exiled from Palestine. Another archaeologist, Ghada Ziadeh-Seely, discusses in 'An Archaeology of Palestine: Mourning a Dream' that there are many obstacles faced by Palestinian archaeologists, which include being prevented from accessing various sites. In Zahran's novel, the fact that studying the Ottoman and Islamic pasts has been problematic for the field is relevant to the representation of neglected ruins and the protagonist Rayya's obsession with them in the novel.

Zahran makes no attempt to disguise her political motivations, from the title to the epigraph that highlights the fictional nature of the material, asserting 'only Palestine is real' (iv). At points, in particular when it comes to Rayya's reflections on Palestine and Arab nationalism, the text reads more like a treatise than a novel. However, notably, the narrative's fictionality becomes more marked in scenes where the theme of disinheritance is bound up with experiences of dislocation, as Rayya symbolically connects her geographical exile from place to her obsession with archaeological sites which she experiences as displaced in time. In one scene, for example, Rayya is 'standing by the ruins' of a sixteenth-century city and reflecting on how out of place it seems:

> the old guardian said that nobody ever came to visit, it was out of the way for tourists [. . .] a whole city in ruins, built and abandoned in the sixteenth century due to some calamity or the whim of a capricious sultan. The town, fallen into debris, was ugly [. . .] no green, no growth, just piles of stones. (112)

Ruins are material exiles, out of place in the present. The reason that ruins evoke nostalgia, Andreas Huyssen suggests, is that they allow us to see 'the imagined present of a past that can now only be grasped in its decay' (12). The novel repeatedly stresses the discontinuity between the present and the golden age of various expansionist empires that Rayya speaks of in one breath: 'Mamluk mosque tombs in Cairo, Tartar tombs in Samarkand [. . .] Moghul tombs in new Delhi' (112). Rayya's melancholy is for what could have been, for the past imagined in the present. For her, these remnants of Islamic empires embody the 'imagined present of a past', in Huyssen's phrase, in that they allow her to imagine how the past imagined its future, and how this future, her present, did not live up to the expectations of this imagining. The fragmentariness of the text in a sense replicates Rayya's experiences of travelling to various ancient cities and standing by the ruins to reflect on their incompleteness, their simultaneous presence and absence. In the reader's piecing together of the remnants of Rayya's diaries, the text itself 'stands by the ruins'.

As in *The Blue Manuscript*, Zahran's novel explores the protagonist's nostalgia for times that are not personally experienced, where the only point of contact with the past is through its material traces. As an exiled Palestinian conscious of 'her foreignness, her rootlessness and her exile', Rayya would like to imagine herself as 'a link in a chain of people who lived there before time began' (42). Against this sense of coherent history, Alex offers the critique that she would not belong if she could return, as he argues that Rayya 'attribute[s] all [her] ills to the loss of Palestine but [. . .] [she] would not have belonged even if [she] were physically in Palestine' (42).[8] Rayya stakes her claim on Palestine in terms of continuity: 'we have always inhabited the land.' Challenged about this 'we', she recites the following list of 'continuous dwellers': 'We the Gebusites, the Edomites, the Canaanites, the Philistines, the Hellenised, Romanised, Arabicised natives of this land.' She finds solace in the 'monuments and ancient ruins' (135) which allow her to hold onto a narrative of unity. Meanwhile, Alex picks apart that same narrative by pointing out its exclusionary focus: '[w]hat about the many Christian sects – the Shiite, the Druze, the Kurds and the Berbers? [. . .] modern and westernised as you are, what do you have in common with an Omani Arab, or a Mauritanian Arab?' (39). As Zahran moves between Alex's critical voice and Rayya's resort to nostalgic, we begin to recognize that Rayya is constructing a strategic narrative in order to overcome the realities of her displacement. When Rayya reflects '[h]ow often did we look forward or look back, picking our way through the chaos of lost empires?' she highlights the fact that nostalgic and utopian modes share the rejection of the present. As Hutcheon puts it, '[i]f the present is considered irredeemable, you can look either back or forward' (204). In both Zahran and Khemir's novels, the protagonists look back in order to redeem a cultural narrative for themselves for the future. Both writers examine the processes of constructing such a 'determined' history, the repression of flaws that allows for a resolved sense of self, but also suggest that this constructed story of identity is a pastiche, drawing our attention to the active and strategic attempt to make the past cohere in the present.

In the context of the identity crisis of a Palestinian who cannot return, Rayya's obsession with ruins becomes 'a search for things past that was mirrored in the search for her fragmented self' (49). Rayya seeks to write herself into a modernity that is understood as European, defending herself against the charge of being 'Westernized' by relocating the term: 'I can accept the term "westernized" if you mean by that the common heritage the Arab world shares with Europe – which begins with the Phoenicians, the Greeks and the Romans' (43). Whereas Alex uses Westernized to mean a positive value, to be part of the progressive, enlightened world, Rayya takes it as a troubling, even threatening, label which undercuts her attempt to construct an authentic identity. She attempts to get around this difficulty by pointing out the connections of a composite Mediterranean past. This does not however resolve the contemporary realities that discredit Rayya's Arab nationalist ideology. As a 'westernised Arab', as Alex calls her, displaced from Palestine, she clings to histories of a golden age as part of her commitment to the 'mirage of Arab unity' even as that mirage is exposed in the failures of identity politics (38). Zahran's novel dramatizes the pull of nostalgic feelings as a strategy the exiled protagonist Rayya uses to root herself in the past and in the place she longs to return to, even as the genealogies Rayya constructs are represented as fantasies, an effortful repressing of flawed history.

A Beggar at Damascus Gate questions the attempt to yoke past and present through material traces. From the first pages, we see the narrator 'trying to convince [himself] that Petra [. . .] had once been a living city' (3–4). This desire to believe in the ability to interpret the past, to have it speak in the present, is tied to the narrator's wish to use Rayya's writings to give voice to a political cause, to 'expose the story of a Palestinian girl to the light, lining up behind her thousands of silent women who lived in the shadows and who, culminating in her, had at last the power to speak' (24). Rayya becomes a witness, a spokesperson, someone who can be used to recover the silenced stories of Palestinian women before her. Through this intertwined attempt to give voice to the past and to the subaltern, archaeological remnants become not only a point of contact with the past, traces that 'speak', but also symbols of the politics of representation and translation. As in Khemir's text, the recoverability of meaning from traces is complicated both in the case of the discovered texts and the material fragments of the past. Early on in the novel, the professor describes '[s]hards of Nabatean pottery' as 'thin and delicate [. . .] as if they had been baked yesterday' (10). Again, there is no inherent quality of pastness that would allow the traces to function as forms of contact with the past. Later, when the professor 'wonder[s] whether these guardians of the dead Nabatean world were descendants', the narrative of continuity collapses with the realization that the 'tribe had moved recently to Petra' (21). Zahran here considers the fascination with the material traces of the past which seem to promise some tangible connection to history, while at the same time foregrounding the difficulty, if not the impossibility, of ever fully knowing that past.

The processes by which remains are interpreted and indeed produced in the present are both a challenge to and constitutive of nostalgic narratives. David L. Eng and David Kazanjian note that loss is 'inseparable from what remains, for what is lost is known only by what remains of it, by how these remains are produced, read, and sustained' (2). In the novels I have discussed in this chapter, the exhortation to move beyond the fantasy of the ideal past can itself be nostalgic in the face of a present that seems overly static and monolithic, like the nostalgia for the *convivencia* of Andalusia as a prefiguration of multicultural life. This paradoxically anti-nostalgic nostalgia captures the ambivalence, the veering between criticism and empathy, which is a defining feature of nostalgic discourses in Anglophone Arab literature. As Said makes clear in 'Freud and the Non-European', the nostalgia for origins, for a linear foundational story of inheritance, involves the construction of a determined history that represses all flaws. The novels discussed in this chapter seek to balance between the prosaic realization of distance from the past and the emotional need for coherent narratives. Through dramatizing various nostalgic modes, the texts alternately linger on and interrupt the melancholic gaze that offers the redemptive satisfaction of contemplating cultural losses. Representing the nostalgia for various distant golden ages, the novelists reflect on how nostalgia satisfies political needs, emotions and experiences. However, through restaging the ancient trope of 'standing by the ruins', the reader becomes aware of a critical edge to the nostalgic narrative, critiquing the unreflective eulogizing and romanticizing of the past at the expense of the future. To varying degrees, Alameddine, Khemir and Zahran reveal the original objects in their narratives to be traces, showing the work done to construct the coherent narrative of origin, and thus revealing that narrative to be itself a 'meticulously fabricated illusion' (*Blue Manuscript* 295). As imaginative narratives, these texts offer a non-absolutist version of history, where the distance between the nostalgic object and the present reveals the constructed nature of any historical account. The at times implicit and at other times overt invocation of 'standing by the ruins' allows the writers to dramatize both the stationary mourning which creates a hermetically sealed history, and the erasures and flaws that interrupt and disrupt the writing and rewriting of historical narratives.

Chapter 2

REWRITING COLONIAL ENCOUNTERS

AHDAF SOUEIF, FADIA FAQIR AND JAMAL MAHJOUB

In Jamal Mahjoub's novel *In the Hour of Signs* (1996), set during the Mahdist war in the Sudan (1881–99), the defeat of the Mahdiyya is described in terms of the encroachment of modernity, '[t]he future [. . .] making its way upstream' (235).[1] Towards the end of the novel, Kadaro, a soldier who is uncertain about his loyalties, comes to see the impact of modernity in terms of a conflict between an anachronistic 'yesterday' and the 'tomorrow' which will inevitably sweep that world aside (230).[2] In Kadaro's description, modernity and colonialism are interlinked and cast in temporal terms as a double moment of rupture, caused not by the encounter with the other, but rather the overwhelming nature of that encounter and its erasure of the present order. The novel's representation of nationalism and insurgent militancy however complicates this dichotomy of yesterday and today, chronicling the rise and fall of an ostensibly anti-modern revolt whose founder became known as '*Abū al-istiqlāl*', the father of independence. Exploring the interrelationship of modernity and nationalism, the novel dramatizes the lead up to the Battle of Omdurman and its aftermath as a transformative point in the long colonial history of Sudan. Mahjoub's novel is one of a number of recent works by Anglophone Arab writers that restage the colonial encounter and dramatize national struggles to gain independence, relating this critical transformative era to the present. Reading Mahjoub's novel alongside Ahdaf Soueif's *The Map of Love* and Fadia Faqir's *Pillars of Salt*, this chapter examines how Anglophone Arab writers explore the triad of colonialism, nationalism and modernity, and shows how the literary reimagining of the initial enchantment with modernization and aspirations for nationhood is mapped onto present-day disillusionment with the postcolonial state.

In the previous chapter, I discussed how a pervasive nostalgia for vanished civilizations offers consolation from the conflicts of the present. I argued that the dismissal of nostalgia as sentimental elides the complex ways in which nostalgic tropes are central to political critique, including the blurring between irony and nostalgia in juxtapositions of distant civilisations and a present characterized by conflict. This chapter continues to examine the potential of nostalgia as a productive ground to explore the nexus of tradition, modernity and nationalism. It argues that nostalgic narratives for the precolonial past and the era of anti-colonial nationalism are intimately related to imagining alternative national projects for the future. In the novels discussed here, nostalgia is deployed as a way to open up an exploration of concepts such as 'the homeland' and 'the people' and their cultural and revolutionary impetus, even as representing these terms nostalgically demonstrates the impossibility of using them unironically in the present. I argue that the writers gear their nostalgic narratives towards an exploration of postcolonial anxieties around national history and memory: they seek not only to represent and bear witness to the upheavals of colonial history but also to examine lasting legacies of traumatic encounter.

This chapter focuses on how writers use nostalgia to explore ideas about authenticity and tradition and the relationship between these notions and nationalist projects. The investigation of authenticity recalls what Fanon describes as the nostalgic objective pursued by native intellectuals who seek to 'renew contact once more with the oldest and most pre-colonial springs of life of their people' (209). Here, Fanon suggests that nostalgia might be used strategically. Nostalgia may be a form of strategic essentialism, to use Gayatri Spivak's term, a method of overcoming the psychological trauma stemming from cultural loss in the wake of colonial domination. It is all too easy to argue that such a re-tooling of the longing for the past, for the authentic, is simply an essentialist position, a repression of the flaws of history. Yet Fanon's writings on nostalgia demonstrate an awareness both of the usefulness and the dangers of nostalgic modes. Alistair Bonnett points out that though Fanon offers 'a clear, bold voice of revolutionary action [. . .] when we approach him from the perspective of the transgressive narrative of radical nostalgia, his voice appears vulnerable and uncertain' (94). Stressing that nostalgia must be self-consciously deployed and future-oriented, Fanon advocated 'us[ing] the past with the intention of opening the future', as an instrumental step which must eventually be overcome (232). The 'passionate search for a national culture which existed before the colonial era' is for Fanon an integral but initial effort to overcome the 'serious psycho-affective injuries' of being 'individuals without an anchor, without a horizon, colourless, stateless, rootless' (218). Nostalgia is legitimatized only in so far as it is useful as a tool to combat the traumas of colonization. This equivocation about the usefulness of nostalgia betrays an ambivalence about the reconnection to the 'most pre-colonial springs of life' and how far it is possible, or even desirable, to 'become unrecognizable [. . .] to cut off those wings that before you had allowed to grow' (221). Fanon's prescription implicitly acknowledges the complicating factors that accompany the notion of a return to the source, which is in itself predicated on the notion of the colonial moment shattering an imagined wholeness.

The writers discussed in this chapter negotiate a colonial history conferred on them by their heritage from a position of temporal and geographic distance. Anglophone Arab writers' imaginative projection of the past and their representation of the traumatic legacies of the colonial era explores the extent to which it is possible to move past these legacies, and in particular beyond the strictures of a progress narrative derived from the encounter with modernity. I begin this chapter by contextualizing the notion of nostalgia in relation to the crises of values that followed the encounter with European modernity. I then examine the ambivalence of nostalgic narratives in the context of colonialism, focusing on *Wāḥat al-ghurūb* (2007, *Sunset Oasis*, 2009), a novel by Egyptian novelist Baha Taher which evinces many of the characteristics of nostalgia discussed in the previous chapter, but does so in a colonial setting that sharpens the irony in the juxtapositions of distant past and present. Turning then to the central texts of this chapter, I trace the trajectory through which writers negotiate the legacies of colonialism, taking up an imperative to reanimate the colonial past in order to examine its repercussions on the present.

Modernity and tradition

Napoleon's expedition to Egypt in 1798 is widely framed as a moment of shocking and simultaneous encounter with both modernity and colonialism. Though such an account elides the influence of earlier contact, including encounters through trade, the processes of modernization during Ottoman rule, and the colonial nature of this rule over the region, it offers a compelling narrative of the sudden shock of modernity as an invasion.[3] Locating this moment of double encounter with colonialism and modernity feeds into a discourse where, as Rashid El Enany puts it, from the moment of encounter, 'Europe was at once the malady and the remedy' (3). Seen as a foreign force sweeping aside the traditional order, modernity represents both a defeat and an aspiration. As Jaafar Aksikas describes, these tensions were negotiated by intellectuals, 'reflecting on the dangers that colonisation presented to tradition, while at the same time worrying about lagging "behind" the Western world materially' (18).[4] Despite ideological differences, the disparate movements that developed during the mid-nineteenth century found common ground and common goals centred on 'anti-imperialism and the search for political independence; the search for unity of all Arabs and/or Muslims; modernity and social development; and cultural authenticity' (Aksikas 16). These issues continue to be significant today, though they have been altered by the political and cultural mobility generated by global neocolonial forces.[5]

The project of national modernization that began during the *Nahḍa* was however undermined by the failures of the state in the post-independence era, particularly in the wake of the 1967 defeat. The recriminatory context that characterized this period was marked by a rise in self-criticism and disillusionment, as the war was seen as a symptom of the collapse of the national dream in the post-independence era, resulting in the recognition that 'a century and a half of trying to build the Western model in the east [. . .] had failed' (El Enany 6). In *Al-Muthaqqafūn al-ʿArab wa-al-turāth* (Arab Intellectuals and their Heritage, 1991) Georges Tarabichi claims that the turn to tradition during this period was a regressive reaction to the narcissistic wound of the defeat. Elizabeth Kassab summarises this 'psychological reading of the authenticity/modernisation problematic' (166) in the following terms:

> the obsessive resort to *turāth* [heritage] is a phenomenon proper to the last decades of the twentieth century. Never before had Arabs turned so emphatically to the past cultural legacy as they did after the 1967 defeat by Israel. In this turn, contemporary thought distances itself from the modern Arab thought of the *Nahḍa*. (167)

The centrality of *turāth* in the decades following the defeat is apparent in the titles of texts across the ideological and political spectrum, from the Marxist writer Tayyib Tazini's *Min al-turāth ilā al-thawra* (From Heritage to Revolution, 1978) to the Islamic reformer Hassan Hanafi's *Al-Turāth wa-al-tajdīd* (Heritage and Renewal, 1980). As the titles of these texts suggest, the affirmation of heritage as the future involves a double position, where change is made possible through affirming tradition. Tarik Sabry, in his introduction to *Arab Cultural Studies: Mapping the Field* (2012) describes a spectrum of ideological positions on heritage, ranging from a *turāth*-based position which sees heritage as the only acceptable civilizational model, to a more rationalist position, which argues for negotiating a local narrative of modernity and making *turāth* answerable to the present, as in Mohammed Abed Al Jabri's ideas about disconnecting from heritage in order to reconnect to it under modified terms. At the other extreme, there is the notion of a radical epistemological break, a stance which tends to characterize the historicist Marxist position, as in the work of Abdullah Laroui, whose work often speaks more definitively of the need to free the present from the past and of extricating oneself from history and the nostalgic draw to the golden age. In *The Crisis of the Arab Intellectual* (1976), Laroui analysed the pull between *ightirāb* (Westernization) and *iʿtirāb* (Arabization) and noted that the first 'signifies an alienation, a way of becoming other, an avenue to self-division (though one's estimation of this transformation may be positive or negative, according to one's ideology)', while the latter is 'another form of alienation [. . .] the exaggerated medievalisation obtained through quasi-magical identification with the great period of classical Arab culture' (121). In identifying this duality, Laroui seems to ask us to dismantle what Oyuang describes as 'the deceptive polarity of the present West-other-based "modernity" and the past-tradition-self-oriented "authenticity" in the post-colonial Arab world' (*Poetics of Love* 1). The difficulty however is the extent to which this polarity has become inextricable from the narrative of crisis, resulting in its perpetuation in various forms.

The dual alienations that Laroui outlined three decades ago between *ightirāb* and *iʿtirāb* continue to inform present-day paradigms. As Larbi Sadiki suggests, scholarship in the region remains focused on 'the irreconcilability of tradition and modernity, of certain cultures and democracy' (332). In fact, Amr Shalakany argues that '[m]odernity/tradition discourse is perhaps the most enduringly popular mode in which the Arab post-colonial condition is theorised'. Shalakany goes on to point out that under this rubric 'one finds writers of many creeds, from the fundamentalist-Islamist to the liberal-secularist, all advocating competing approaches to resolving the tension between modernity and tradition' (155). While some reject certain traditions as a 'reflection of underdevelopment, backwardness and stagnation that must be overcome,' others see 'the past as a model to which the contemporary Arab world must aspire' (Abu-Rabi' 55). The pervasive nature of this framework prohibits the capacity to, in Paul Gilroy's words, 'skirt the sterile opposition between tradition and modernity by asserting the irreducible priority of the present' and instead leads to an advocation of approaches which diverge between the amnesiac and nostalgic (202).

As discussed in the last chapter, anachronistically using the past for the future offers the consolation of an idealized time, of returning, in Said's phrase, to 'the finest flowering of our culture' (Andalusian Journey). In the context of colonial domination, nostalgia for a precolonial era is propelled by what Fanon identifies as a romantic 'secret hope' of a lost paradise, of 'discovering beyond the misery of today, beyond self-contempt, resignation and abjuration, some very beautiful and splendid era whose existence rehabilitates us both in regard to ourselves and in regard to others' (210). However, instead of a rehabilitating history that complicates monolithic, exclusive accounts of modernity, the discovery of such a 'splendid era' can heighten the sense of alienation from the present. This sense of contradictory attachment to and alienation from the past is the central theme in the novel *Sunset Oasis* by the Egyptian author Baha Taher, which explores the responses to the archaeological efforts to uncover Egypt's Pharonic past as a colonial enterprise. The novel is based on the story of a police chief who attempted to destroy the Amun-Ra temple complex in 1897.[6] In Taher's novel, the protagonist is Mahmoud Abd El-Zahir, a policeman who is sent to Siwa as District Commissioner as punishment for a nationalist stance in relation to Ahmed 'Urabi's failed revolt. Once he has visited the temple, Mahmoud comes to believe that destroying the structure is necessary for the future: 'not a trace must remain of the temple. We had to be done with all the stories of the ancestors if the descendants were to wake from their delusions of greatness and their false complacency' (301).

Mahmoud's rejection of the temple is not only a rejection of the fables of the past that negate the present, but also carries a sense that this past glory belongs to those 'revealing' it: 'so this was the glory the British were revealing to us so that we could know we had once been giants and were now dwarves!' (300). In part, the scene plays out a view of ancient Eastern civilizations, or in Zainab Bahrani's terms, the 'Oriental past', as a 'problematic historical domain [. . .] belonging at once to the diachronic progress of civilisation and the synchronic time of the Other' (Bahrani 56). The temple symbolizes the contrast of past and present, the 'ancestors' pitted against the 'grandchildren [. . .] fit only for occupation' (*Sunset Oasis* 300). Mahmoud takes up the ideological narrative of progress that justified colonial domination on the basis that the people being colonized were not yet ready to rule themselves. To be at once in the shadow of an ancient civilization and in the 'imaginary waiting room of history', in Dipesh Chakrabarty's phrase, is a paradoxical, and ultimately untenable position (8).

The need to move on from the obsession with the past is a theme in a number of contemporary Arabic novels. For example, in Ahmed Alaidy's novel *An takūn 'Abbās al-'Abd* (2003, *Being Abbas El Abd*, 2006) the titular character Abbas exhorts the narrator to 'burn the history books and forget your precious dead civilisation. Stop trying to squeeze the juice from the past. Destroy your Pharaonic history' (*Being Abbas* 39). As Tarek El-Ariss points out, this passage 'exposes the discrepancy between Egypt's imagined past and its contemporary social and political reality' (536). The call to destroy the traces of past glory not only critiques the transfixion by the past but also recognizes that '[t]hose who read history in the third world find it painful. They freed themselves from foreign occupation to fall into national occupation' (*Being Abbas* 21). The rejection of glorifying rhetoric is framed as a revolutionary act, crucial to understanding the continuity between colonialism and the postcolonial state (*Being Abbas* 39).

In Anglophone works by Arab writers, representations of the legacies of colonialism are inextricable from linguistic and physical displacement. An example is Waguih Ghali's novel *Beer in the Snooker Club* ([1964], 2014), which features a British-educated protagonist, Ram, who returns to Egypt after studying in London, and struggles to reconcile his conflicting affiliations to Britain and his nationalist revolutionary sentiments. As Lucia Admiraal describes it, Ram is 'unable to unite his now fragmented loyalties and identities' and so 'spends his days drinking, smoking and gambling in the Western cafes and colonial clubs of Cairo, in the midst of the rapid changes following decolonisation and Nasser's presidency' (Admiraal). Though Ram despises the materialism of the elite, he shares their lifestyle, triggering a sense of alienation and hypocrisy. Ghali, like his protagonist, was of the generation that witnessed the revolution and overthrow of King Farouk in 1952, and the novel is set during the upheavals following the 1956 Suez Crisis. Ram's sense of alienation is linked to his disillusionment at the repressions of the Nasser era and its security systems. Ghali makes clear the connections between the legacy of colonialism and the political and social failures of postcolonial nationhood, which he witnessed within his lifetime, through exploring how Ram moves between the alienations of life under a repressive postcolonial state and the effects of immigration which leave him unable to locate himself.

The novelists whose work is the focus of this chapter are at a generational remove from this period and the traumatic events represented in the novels are temporally distant, as well as being culturally distant for a presumed Western audience. Ahdaf Soueif highlights this distance when she disavows anxieties about using the 'language of the colonizer': 'I have often been asked whether I have a problem with English as the language of my oppressor. I understand the question, but I do not feel it. The British occupation was out of Egypt before I was born' (*Mezzaterra* 49). Elsewhere, Soueif responds to the question of whether the weight of colonialism was apparent when she was growing up, asserting: 'I am a child of Nasser's revolution [. . .] I never felt that English was the language of imperialism' ('On Colonialism'). Here, Soueif disavows the anxieties of taking on the language of the colonizer, locating herself as someone looking back upon the era of colonialism. In an interview with Steve Paulson about her second novel, *The Map of Love,* Soueif again shifts the focus from the traumas of the colonial past to the repercussions of this era on the present. Referring to the seventy years of colonial occupation in Egypt as 'kind of a blip' in the country's long history, Soueif reframes the traumatizing impact of colonialism as setting back the processes of political independence:

> [s]o it was seventy years, and in the seven thousand years of Egypt's history, that's kind of a blip. And when the British left [. . .] it wasn't a great war like the French in Algeria [. . .] It was a relatively, relatively painless occupation and withdrawal. However, it came at a time when Egypt was finding her feet, was trying to break free of the Ottoman empire [. . .] and was trying to set up civil institutions, a university, to institute reforms of the law, to set up industries, financial institutions and so on, and a constitution. And the occupation coming at that time aborted all this. Everybody had to be primarily occupied with getting rid of the British [. . .] fighting the economic structures that they put in place, which [. . .] were not for the benefit of Egypt but were for the benefit of Britain. ('On Colonialism')

Soueif's establishment of a longer historical context relocates the traumas of colonialism to a focus on the failures of modernity. The use of the word 'aborted' suggests that Soueif sees modernity as having been pre-empted by colonization, rather than seeing modernizing processes as foreign and imposed, in El Enany's words, 'a transplantation, a foreign organ implanted in a body that needed it badly but could not help but try to reject it' (8). These metaphors of abortion/transplantation are symptomatic of the effort to come to terms with modernity not being fully integrated in society, which in turn creates a sense of belatedness in societies deemed to be incapable of generating or realizing modernity. However, whereas the metaphor of a transplantation uses biological language to describe a regressive turn ('could not help but try to reject it'), the notion of a pre-empted modernity invokes a nostalgia for an alternative modernity that never came to be. It represents the years of colonial control as having inhibited the development of postcolonial societies, rather than seeing modernity as a break that, as Kevin Newmark puts it, 'occurred historically to interrupt once and for all the unified structure of what we continue to call "traditional" experience' (238).

A similar sentiment is expressed in a central passage of Mourid Barghouti's memoir *Ra'aytu Rāmallāh* (1997, *I Saw Ramallah,* 2003), a text translated into English by Soueif:

> [h]ow many bookshops could have been set up in Ramallah, how many theatres? The Occupation kept the Palestinian village static and turned our cities back into villages. We do not weep for the mill of the village but for the bookshop and the library. We do not want to regain the past but to regain the future and to push tomorrow into the day after. (147)

Though Barghouti is responding to the ongoing context of the Israeli occupation, his argument that 'Palestine's progress in the natural paths of its future was deliberately impeded' (147) follows the same logic as Soueif's statement that 'the occupation coming at that time aborted all this' ('On Colonialism'). Both evince a nostalgia not for the recovery of precolonial societies but for a future robbed of its potential. Nostalgia is expressed 'not for the past the way it was but for the past the way it could have been' (Boym 351). Such a nostalgia makes clear that the present reality is, as Slavoj Žižek puts it, 'one possible, and often even not the most probable, outcome of an "open" situation [. . .] that other possible outcomes are not simply cancelled out but continue to haunt us as spectres of what might have been' (86). In this sense, the representation of the era of anti-colonial nationalism is nostalgic not only for a redemptive moral clarity, but also for a vantage point where the current reality is one outcome of an 'open' situation. Dramatizing the 'past the way it was' (or the way the writers imagine it could have been) involves a process of tracing the path that history took to lead to the present, both seeking a reconciliation with this history and foregrounding the ongoing legacies that make such a reconciliation difficult.

In what follows, I discuss the representation of colonial history as explored by three writers, Ahdaf Soueif, Jamal Mahjoub and Fadia Faqir, and consider the entangled ramifications of nostalgia for precolonial and anti-colonial eras. Their re-imagination of the colonial period can be described in terms of what Marianne Hirsch terms postmemory, a process of being 'shaped, however indirectly, by traumatic events that still defy narrative reconstruction and exceed comprehension', events which 'happened in the past, but their effects continue into the present' (*Postmemory* 5). Postmemory explores how generations that did not experience traumatic events experience and reflect on those events, as a form of 'remembering' mediated by 'imaginative investment, projection, and creation' (*Postmemory* 5). Though Hirsch coined the term postmemory in the context of the generational trauma following the Holocaust, she notes that this notion may be used to describe other contexts of belated 'cultural or collective traumatic events and experiences', to explore 'the experience of those who grow up dominated by narratives that preceded their birth, whose own belated stories are evacuated by the stories of the previous generation shaped by traumatic events that can neither be understood nor recreated' (*Family Frames* 22). The notion of postmemory is useful in illuminating how the novels discussed here engage with the violence of colonialism as an ongoing haunting presence. However, rather than the present being evacuated by the stories of the past, I read these narratives as charged with a sense of repeating history, as the reader is lead to see the parallels between the colonial period and present. Either through formal elements, such as parallel storylines, or through evocative references in the text, the writers highlight the continuity of these colonial/postcolonial narratives into the future. In returning to the era of national liberation struggle, the writers reflect on the seeds of the failures of nationalism in the postcolonial era. This analogical patterning of colonial past and postcolonial present brings out the politics of nostalgia as the writers trace the failed promise of independence back to the era of anti-colonial nationalism and show the past to be a force operative in the here and now, shaping contemporary political struggles.

Ahdaf Soueif's The Map of Love

Ahdaf Soueif's second novel *The Map of Love* ([1999], 2000) is a family saga that moves between the colonial and the postcolonial eras in Egypt, revealing parallels between the historical and contemporary moments. The historical narrative begins with the story of an English woman visiting Egypt, Anna Winterbourne, and then focuses on her relationship with nationalist Sharif al-Baroudi, and her friendship with his sister Layla. The contemporary narrative mirrors this triangulated relationship, following the story of Isabel Parkman, an American, and her relationship with Egyptian/Palestinian composer and activist, Omar Ghamrawi, though here the focus is on the main narrator, Omar's sister Amal. As Geoffrey Nash puts it, the novel 'takes its place alongside a whole corpus of postcolonial literature in which terms of empire have been renegotiated' (*Anglophone Arab Encounter* 81). Soueif reimagines a transformative period of Egypt's history, bracketed between the 'Urabi revolt and the 1919 uprising, and incorporates historical figures and fictional characters based on real families, such as the Egyptian Baroudis or the Palestinian Khalidis, all of which leads Amin Malak to describe the novel as a 'revisionist meta-history of Egypt in the twentieth century' (128). With a narrative extending over a 120-year period, the contemporary storyline is superimposed on the narrative set during the colonial period.

In contrast to the autobiographical elements in her earlier novel *In the Eye of the Sun*, in *The Map of Love* Soueif uses a multi-generational family story to explore the reclamation of traumatic pasts. The novel weaves together letters, journal entries and both third-person and first-person narrations. The main protagonist, Amal, sorts through and patches together Anna's story from her journals and keepsakes, 'to see for [her]self the country Anna came to [. . .] to re-imagine it, re-create it' (59). As she does so, the reader puts the novel together through fragmented testimonies. Amal finds solace in this work of reimagining the past, seeing the story unfold with hindsight: '[t]hat is the beauty of the past; there it lies on the table [. . .] You can leaf forward and know the end.' Amal then goes on to make an explicitly self-reflective comment addressing the historical half of the novel: 'you tell the story that they, the people who lived it, could only tell in part' (234). The nostalgic perspective, the 'beauty' of being able to retell the past, suggests the reconciliation with a traumatic colonial history through aesthetic engagement, as Soueif structures her diachronic novel to restage and reflect on Egypt's colonial past and its influence on the present. Yet the novel concludes without resolving the violent event at the centre of the text, the assassination of the nationalist figure Sharif al-Baroudi. Instead, at the very end there are hints that Amal's brother Omar has met with the same fate.

Soueif's reframing of traumatic history ultimately offers no aesthetic redemption. The novel makes clear that despite Amal's efforts to construct a coherent narration, her efforts do not raise the violent events depicted into the sphere of 'beauty'. Instead, the traumatic event at the centre of the historical narrative is repeated in the present. This continuity is reinforced formally, as the colonial period which continues to haunt the present is embedded in the bi-partite time structure, revealing the connections between colonial structures and the postcolonial regime. The parallels are often explicit, such as when Amal links the police crackdown following the 1997 Luxor massacre with the experiences of her great-uncle Sharif and his wife Anna during the British occupation. Since Amal has been reading Anna's letters and is immersed in the nineteenth-century world of occupied Egypt, when she hears an Egyptian soldier referring to the villagers as 'natives' she feels compelled to point out to him that 'these people are your people', hearing the disturbing echo of colonial language (438).

This exchange highlights parallels between colonial and postcolonial authorities in their treatment of the disempowered Egyptian majority. In particular, it foregrounds what Achille Mbembé has described as a transfer of colonial attitudes as the independent nation becomes its colonial antagonist, making 'postcolonial relations not only relations of conviviality and covering over, but also of powerlessness par excellence – from the viewpoint both of the masters of power and of those they crush' (129). The violence of state control as a form of continuing powerlessness is represented in various ways in Soueif's novel, such as when the Egyptian security forces search for Islamist militants in the village of Tawasi, an incident which revives Amal's radicalism, driving her to ask '[w]hose country is it anyway?' (*Map* 298). Amal's comment, 'I see myself going to look for "the government." I wouldn't know where to begin' (126), underlines the split of the 'nation state' into the state, 'exercising a monopoly of coercion and extraction within a given territory' and the nation signifying 'an historic culture and homeland' (Smith 14–15). Soueif highlights the extent of this division, showing governing elites to be alienated from their own people and tracing the inheritance of technologies of repression from colonial powers. For example, in her attempts to help the villagers, Amal realizes they are dealing with land law problems inherited from the days of British colonialism, exacerbated by World Bank subsidies and trade relations. The continuity between the power dynamics of the colonial past and the present are underscored for the reader when Amal reads 'accounts of these long-gone Englishmen and [thinks] of the American embassy and agencies today' who see Egypt only through 'their locked limousines with the smoked-glass windows' (*Map* 70).

In the 1990s narrative strand of Soueif's novel, the equation of modernity and Westernization is part of what Sabina D'Alessandro describes as a 'reflection on the building of identity on the part of the Egyptian (middle-class and intellectual) protagonists, who find themselves hovering between two cultures, in an "in-between" area' (274). In a long scene which dramatizes this sense of limbo, Amal and her friends discuss the reason for the failures following the end of colonialism and the collapse of national projects under the weight of postcolonial corruption. One friend, Deena, asserts that the problem is that 'the interests of the governing class are different – are practically opposed to the interests of the majority of the people' (230). Meanwhile, others in the group wonder what it would take to create a 'national project' capable of galvanizing people for political action. The problem is that of identifying a realistic basis for such a project, contrasting the present with the Nasser era: '[i]n Nasser's time – for all its drawbacks, all the mistakes – there was an idea. A national project. Now what do we have? The Idea of the Consumer? Trying to hang on to America's hem?' (228). The discussion turns on a nostalgia for an era of revolutionary struggle, the socialist third worldism which Mark Berger describes as 'mesh[ing] often highly romanticised interpretations of precolonial traditions and cultures with the utopianism embodied by Marxism and socialism specifically, and "Western" versions of modernisation and development more generally' (3). In this case, Nasser's third worldism, identified with 'a national project', is contrasted with globalizing forces deemed a threat to the autonomy of the nation. Looking back on the Nasserist project is reformulated as an imagining of an alternative future, interlinking nostalgic and utopian modes. Yet, as becomes clear through Amal's struggle to help the villagers, it is the same nationalist project narrative which gives cover to the autocratic measures that keep the repressive government in power.

Seeking to bring the past to life despite their temporal remove from it, Anglophone Arab writers who reimagine the colonial past engage with the disruptive legacies of that history in the present, confronting the violence and erasures that are constitutive of historical narrative. In *The Map of Love*, the event at the centre of the narrative is the assassination of the nationalist Sharif al-Baroudi, and the suggestion is that Omar meets with the same fate in the contemporary narrative. Sharif and Omar are parallel figures; both are represented as committed progressive nationalists whose political activities result in having enemies on opposing sides. The suggestion is that Omar meets a similar end to Sharif, and that his assassination, like Sharif's, could be the responsibility of either side of the conflict. This parallel drives home the point made throughout the novel: the political deadlock that leaves no space for a principled progressive 'middle ground' in the era of anti-colonial nationalism remains the problem confronting the present-day characters.

The recognition of the performative aspects to modernity and tradition is represented in a scene in which Amal recalls the days of the student demonstrations during the 1970s, when the students gathered around Mahmoud Mukhtar's statue Nahdet Masr (which translates to 'Egypt's Renaissance'):

> [t]he statue of Nahdet Masr rises before her: the statue at whose feet they had gathered in the days of the demonstrations [. . .] They had taken Nahdet Masr as their symbol: a fellaha [peasant woman], one hand on the head of a sphinx, rousing him from sleep, the other putting aside her veil; a statue at once ancient and modern. (*Map* 297)

The symbolism of Nahdet Masr, 'at once ancient and modern', appropriates a working class woman as the vessel for securing cultural purity, and simultaneously, by depicting her as putting aside her veil, as an emblem of traditionalism that must be abandoned. The statue thus encapsulates the contradictory nationalist narrative that emphasizes development while asserting the relevance of cultural roots. The statue could be said to embody the three themes of anti-colonial discourse that Alastair Bonnett has identified: 'the use of images of a pre-colonial golden age; the identification of socialism as an indigenous tradition; and the need for anti-colonial intellectuals and political leaders to go "back to the people"' (89). The symbolism of the statue, like the Pharaonic strand of Egyptian nationalism, in fact reorients modernization. The statue represents the embodiment of the discourse articulated when, in response to the message that 'it would take "generations" before they learned to govern themselves', Egyptian elites 'took occasion to remind Mr. Roosevelt that Egypt had attained her maturity a few thousand years before America came into being' (*Map* 457). Here Soueif reflects on the adaptive nature of modernity and its reinvention as a way of narrating the evolving identity of the nation. The idea is that 'Europe could be viewed as an *affine* of ancient Egypt rather than as an alien and external entity, and the adaptation of its culture as a reclaiming of an ancient heritage rather than as a nationalist betrayal' (El Shakry 65). The statue, Nahdet Masr, symbolizes this possibility of re-identifying modernity as having indigenous origins, introducing Egypt as a participant in modernity.

The historical narrative in *The Map of Love* dramatizes the production of modernity through adaptation during the period of the *Nahḍa*. The opening epigraph, taken from Nasser's memoir *The Covenant*, makes this clear: '[i]t is strange that this period [1900–14] when the colonialists and their collaborators thought everything was quiet – was one of the most fertile in Egypt's history' (1). This movement was propelled by Westernized elites who 'converged on the language of nationalism and national modernisation and renaissance' (Aksikas 16). The modern political, economic, and cultural structures introduced under colonial rule contributed to the development of this liberal consciousness which involved both working within the framework of the colonial regime and against it. In her novel, Soueif represents the nationalist Sharif al-Baroudi expressing frustration that the colonial government will fund education 'to produce clerks and workers' but 'does not permit an extra piastre for any project to do with culture or education'. This policy is described in terms of the degradation of national development, 'the generations that should have been educated, the industries that should have been introduced, the laws that should have been reformed' (*Map* 262). The nationalist characters in the novel see an alternative Egypt without British colonization as one that would have undergone a more rapid and far-reaching modernization. This argument about local modernization being impeded by the colonial project re-emerges in the contemporary strand of the novel, where developmental lack is explained as a truncation: 'the British came in at a crucial point in our history, they froze our development: our move towards democracy' (*Map* 223). Again, this captures the 'pre-emption' of modernity, whether as abortion or failed transplantation, expressed by Soueif and Barghouti. Nostalgia for the period of anti-colonial nationalism is directed not 'to regain[ing] the past' but, as Mourid Barghouti puts it, 'to regain the future and to push tomorrow into the day after' (147).

2. Rewriting Colonial Encounters 73

The expressed view that the colonial period is responsible for the contemporary stagnation of Egypt captures what Partha Chatterjee describes as the notion that the 'historical process that has taught us the value of modernity has also made us the victims of modernity' (*Our Modernity* 20). Yet Soueif is careful to include a critique of this victimization narrative, in the form of a counter-argument by one of Amal's friends, Ramzi, who exclaims: 'we have now had 56 years – 56 years of our own – of national government and what have we done?' (223). The issue of agency here remains in tension with a certain fatalistic view of history. As Ramzi narrates the conditions that shaped Egypt's present condition, he traces a progression that seems inevitable: '[o]ur Khedive Ismail loved modernism and Europe. Europe is strong and moving outwards [. . .] Their old enemy the Ottoman Empire is dying. So they [. . .] expand into our part of the world [. . .] The rest is history' (223). The handing over of power from the domination of a failing Ottoman Empire to the European colonial project is represented in deterministic terms, heightening the sense of disempowerment, despite Ramzi's professed rejection of the victim position.

In its historical narrative, *The Map of Love* focuses on the project of reconceiving modernity by anti-colonial nationalists who sought to harness modern ideas to gain independence, even as their modernization projects encounter resistance and ideological backlash. This tension is illustrated in a scene in the novel where Islamists interpret the funding of an art institute as 'collusion with the British to import evil European arts into the country' (264). Equated with an imperialist doctrine, 'collusion' with the ideological schools of the metropolitan world is represented as a betrayal of independence: '[w]ith the British here, people will not say of us "These men are patriots who think differently than us." They will say, "These men are in the pay of the British"' (265). In one of Anna's letters, she elaborates on this resistance to modernization, noting that the conflict between those supporting a slow transition from British rule to independence and those supporting immediate withdrawal is connected to other divisions:

> People who would have tolerated the establishment of secular education, or the gradual disappearance of the veil, now fight these developments because they feel a need to hold on to their traditional values in the face of the Occupation [. . .] the people who continue to support these changes have constantly to fight the suspicion that they are somehow in league with the British. (384)

Change is seen as the loss of tradition and stable identity. In Bhabha's terms, 'what may seem primordial or timeless is [. . .] a moment of a kind of "projective past" [. . .] a mode of negativity' which 'makes the enunciatory present of modernity disjunctive' (*Location of Culture* 169). Similarly, Michel Gilsenan suggests that

> tradition [. . .] is put together in all manner of different ways in contemporary conditions of crisis [. . .] it becomes a language, a weapon against internal and external enemies, a refuge, an evasion, or part of the entitlement to domination and authority over others. (133)

Through tracing the process of tradition becoming an ideological bulwark against the other, Soueif reflects on the crisis of values and disenchantment linked to modernization processes. The nativism that sets up an embargo on anything deemed modern stems not so much from nostalgia for the past as resistance to the dislocation of tradition which is perceived to be a loss of a stable self.

Towards the end of Soueif's novel, Sharif confronts the reality that the dream of a modern nation state is as dead as the generation of intellectuals who drove that project: 'Muhammad 'Abdu is dead and Qasim Amin is dead. 'Urabi is dead. Even young Mustafa Kamel is dead [. . .] And what is it all for? A millimeter by millimeter struggle while the world sweeps by like a hurricane' (498). The references to belatedness and slow change is one which again posits a 'what if' future tinged with a perceptibly nostalgic tone:

> [i]f they had been free to build their country as they had dreamed [. . .] instead their lives had been taken up in this inch-by-inch struggle against the British [. . .] And what had he done about it all? [. . .] He might as well have been like his father, content to slide into senility in the shelter of a mad sheikh's shrine. There was still time, he had thought, there was still time. But time for what? (275–6)

The reference to the father who spends his days 'in the shelter of a mad sheikh's shrine' is significant – though there are very few interspersed references to this figure in the text, at the end of the novel, Amal and Isabel visit the shrine and it is there that they mysteriously find the missing piece of a symbolic tapestry woven by Anna, the woman who connects them (276). On the one hand, this shrine offers a redemptive shelter from the present, on the other, it is a retreat from history and from rational engagement with a difficult political reality, capturing precisely the dilemma of engagement raised by Sharif: 'could we have lived our lives ignoring politics? [. . .] And what space would have been left for our lives to occupy?' (473).

The metaphorical 'space' to live a depoliticized life recurs at various points in the novel, linked in the present narrative to the search for an alternative narrative. For example, Ramzi comments '[a]t least when there were two superpowers in the world, we could negotiate a path between them. Now there is no space' (228). Another of Amal's friends, Mahgoub, substantiates this claim with a litany of contemporary conflicts and crises: '[l]ook at Algeria. Look what happened to Lebanon. Look at the Palestinians. The Sudan. Libya. Look at Iraq', a compounding of recent Arab history as a catalogue of misfortune that occurs elsewhere in the novel (228). For example, in a similar passage, Amal reflects:

> each week brings fresh news of land expropriations, of great national industries and service companies sold off to foreign investors, of Iraqi children dying and Palestinian homes demolished [. . .] of the names of more urban intellectuals added to the Jama'at's hit lists [. . .] of raids and torture and executions. And next door but one, Algeria daily throws up her terrible examples. (101)

Later, Amal will explicitly connect the turn to the ideology of tradition to a disenchantment with the present: 'the sale of the national industries [...] the deals and the corruption and the hopelessness and brutality that drive young men to grow their beards and try to shoot and bomb their way into a long-gone past' (298). For Amal herself, the confrontation with the failure of the national project creates despair at the impoverished conditions around her and leads her to move back to her ancestral village of Tawasi: '[i]f she has any responsibility now, it is to her land and to the people on it' (297).[7] Soueif does not linger on the context prompting Amal's feudal responsibility to 'her land'. Instead, the scene is framed through Amal's pragmatic reasoning about 'what she can do' which is to 'learn the land and tell its stories' (298). As Simon Gikandi suggests, it is the 'failure of the ideology of the modern that produced the desire for a pre-colonial tradition [...] tradition is just the other side of modernity – what Walter Benjamin would call the site of its ruin' ('African Literature' 8). The desire for a precolonial tradition that is disappearing has to do with 'narratives about the failure of the premodern, the defeat of the traditional, and the collapse of old epistemologies' where 'what appears to be a celebration of the premodern is ultimately a witness to its loss' ('African Literature' 8). The move that Amal decides to undertake mimics that of the native intellectuals that Fanon describes, who 'since they could not stand wonderstruck before the history of today's barbarity, decided to go back further and to delve deeper down' (210). Soueif represents Amal's return to her ancestral village as a deliberate seeking of some sense of 'national culture', as Amal describes a hope for a renaissance to come, associating her hope for cultural restoration with her political struggle to re-open the village school that the government has shut down: '[s]he'll record the children's songs and learn to make bread. She'll find some old man who still has an Aragoz and a Sanduq el-Dunya – and a storyteller. There must still be storytellers around' (297–8).

Amal's decision to go to Tawasi is seen as naïve by others, including her old friend Tareq: '[y]ou believe that will help Egypt? [...] looking after a bit of land and keeping a few fellaheen happy? [...] Now you'll say you'll teach them to do their own weaving' (339). The charge of naïvety highlights Amal's position of privilege, which gives her the ability to escape seemingly more unavoidable and insurmountable politics in the city. Yet the idea that retreating to her ancestral village would allow an escape from 'the circumstances we are in today' is undercut by Amal's conversations with the fellaheen themselves, which revolve around World Bank subsidies and police brutality (218). Moreover, like the nineteenth-century nationalists who are accused of being in collusion with imperial projects, Amal and her friends are conscious of their distance from 'the people'. As Amal's friend Mustafa puts it, '[w]e're a bunch of intellectuals who sit [...] and talk to each other [...] We have absolutely no connection with the people. The people don't know we exist' (224). This very positing of the concept 'the people' speaks to that sense of distance, and yet also of the desire to bridge and to connect, which further fuels Amal's personal determination to retreat to the village.

Soueif's *The Map of Love* draws to an end with the rediscovery of a tapestry depicting the ancient Egyptian gods Horus, Isis and Osiris, which Anna weaves as her 'contribution to the Egyptian renaissance' (403). While two of the panels are inherited through the two sides of the family, the third panel mysteriously appears after a visit to the sheikh's shrine. The novel ends with the tapestry being reassembled by Anna's descendants Amal and Isabel, taking on the significance of hybridity in uniting the Pharonic iconography of Osiris, Isis and Horus, the Egyptian myth of creation, with a Quranic verse, '[i]t is He who brings forth the living from the dead' (491). The symbolism of the tapestry is clearly intended to act as an expression of the regenerative effects of recovering the past, as expressed in Amal's hope that her son will visit their ancestral village, and that '[i]f he stays long enough [...] [together] they will feel the presence of [...] their ancestors and perhaps sense – however dimly – the pattern of the weave that places them at this moment of history on this spot of land' (298–9). Amal hopes that in returning to this place, her son will be affectively reconnected with the past; yet the modifiers 'perhaps' and 'however dimly' suggest that this hope is for the recovery of what is now absent rather than something lost that can be recovered, an expression of nostalgia that recognizes its own limitations.

The final scenes of the novel, interweaving diverse traditions in a symbolic tapestry, offer a paradigmatic case of the appeal of hybridity as potentially bridge-building. The novel as a whole has been positioned along these lines, with critics describing the primary narrator, Amal, as someone who lives in-between; as Emily Davis has it, a 'modern-day Scheherazade figure' who 'stakes her politics on the artist's ability to translate experience between cultures and across times' ('Romance'). Significantly, however, rather than celebrating the artist's ability to translate experience, the novel ends with the narrator asserting that it is 'almost impossible' to 'translate from one language to another, from one culture into another' (515). This assertion of the impossibility of translation, at the end of a novel that has translation as one of its central themes, highlights the pitfalls of placing the focus on cross-cultural exchange as the exemplary trope of hybridity. While the symbolism of the tapestry in *The Map of Love* represents an attempt at reconciling disparate cultural influences into a single national culture, throughout her novel, Soueif insists on complex interrelationships rather than clearly defined sides that must be bridged, constructing a counter-narrative that complicates the dichotomy of modernity and tradition.

Fadia Faqir's Pillars of Salt

Pillars of Salt by British-Jordanian author Fadia Faqir reimagines colonial-era Jordan and, as Faqir describes, attempts 'to explore imperialism and sexual politics [...] us[ing] the oral tradition and the tradition of travel writing' ('Interview' 7). Though formally very different from Soueif's novel, there are shared elements between the two texts, including their reworking of Orientalist travel writing. Faqir's novel is centred on two women, Maha and Hanniyeh (known as Um Saad), who are roommates in an asylum during and just after the period of the Mandate. The primary narrator, Maha, is a Bedouin woman whose husband Harb is part of the resistance and is killed early on in the novel. The second woman, Um Saad, recounts her story to Maha, from her childhood to her marriage and family life until she is replaced with a younger wife. Maha's first-person narrative and her revoicing of Um Saad's story are interwoven with the narrative of the storyteller, Sami al-Adjnabi, who spins tales that contradict the women's narrative. The storyteller comments on Maha's story, his perspective alternating between mimicking a colonialist discourse and the judgemental viewpoint of conservative religious forces. The storyteller's last name translates as the foreigner, but it is not clear if he is a traveller, a local spy or a supernatural figure. As Faqir explains it, the storyteller represents an Orientalist discourse: '[h]e is a foreigner familiar with Arab ways. The women's stories [are] supposed to challenge his bombastic voice [. . .] The narrative of the storyteller dramatizes how Orientalists fabricated our history in their romantic yet vacuous narratives' ('You Arrive At A Truth' 7). Faqir's assertion that Orientalists 'fabricated our history' frames her novel as an attempt to imaginatively reclaim this history, couching the reclamation in a language that seems intended to reproduce the syntax of traditional Arabic storytelling in English, a synthesis of English language and Arabic narrative structure, particularly drawing on allegorical forms derived from oral tradition. The novel attempts to interweave the fantastical elements of storytelling with postmodern forms along with more conventional realism. This combination of fabulism and realism has been critiqued as not always convincing, with Diya M. Abdo for example describing the result as a familiar mixture of 'Arabian nights fabulism and social concern regarding the repression of Arab women' (Abdo 266). Yet the fragmentary nature of Maha and Um Saad's stories as they chronicle multiple oppressions highlights the inability to ever narrate a complete history and bear witness to the whole story. The non-linear form Faqir employs is clearly an attempt to convey the effects of traumatic histories. Like Souief's *The Map of Love*, where Amal seeks to 'tell the story' only told 'in part', through disparate testimonies, Faqir foregrounds the discontinuous stories of two 'mad' women who take turns to tell their story in fragmentary forms (234).

Faqir has reflected on how the history of her homeland Jordan informs her writing. Born in 1956, the same year King Hussein of Jordan announced independence by taking control of the army from the British, she remembers walking past 'a large English club [. . .] with a wire fence, dogs, guards and gardens' as a child. She notes that '[t]his image of an affluent, exclusive colonial space has remained with [her] and keeps reappearing in [her] writing'. In the same interview, Faqir speaks of her experiences living with 'the Bedouins who were semi-nomadic then' and describes her novel *Pillars of Salt* as an attempt to 'document that magical landscape', a way to 'preserve the Bedouins' noble way of life which was fast disappearing' ('Interview' 6). Elsewhere, she describes the novel as motivated by a loyalty to a past 'held still' in memory, even if it is being erased by present postcolonial modernity: 'a form of loyalty to the house [. . .] to the garden with its tall palm tree, to the mother's headscarf, to the past, the village; all are images held still in a medium which beautifies' ('Stories from the House of Songs' 53). As with Amal's reflection on the 'beauty' of the past, the description here nostalgically frames the lost past that continues to haunt the present. The nostalgic mode behind

Faqir's impulse to 'preserve' and 'document' Bedouin life is however complicated by the novel's focus on how patriarchal structures work alongside colonial forces when it comes to restricting women's freedom. Faqir's focus on lived experiences and patriarchal oppression works against both the nostalgic aspects of the novel and the romanticizations of the storyteller's Orientalist discourse. Faqir's intersectional approach to the colonial era thus involves negotiating between a nostalgic nationalist framework and an anti-nostalgic, feminist focus on the women left out of official narratives of colonial history.

Pillars of Salt explores the impact of social and religious pressures on women, playing out the familiar postcolonial 'analogy between the relationships of men and women and those of the imperial power and the colony' (Ashcroft, Griffiths and Tiffin 30). Faqir places the two women's stories in the context of the end of the British mandate, reflecting on how oppression by patriarchal forces mirrors the domination of the colonial regime. This analogy begins from the title itself, which references the story of Lot's wife. The woman who is punished for turning to look at what is behind her becomes a deeply resonant symbol for the protagonists who are unable to forget the events that have brought them to the asylum, recounting their lives to each other. The pillar of salt is a widely employed metaphor for the sin of nostalgia: as Svetlana Boym describes it, 'the predicament of Lot's wife, a fear of looking back' speaks to the rejection of a nostalgic attitude which 'might paralyse you forever, turning you into a pillar of salt, a pitiful monument to your own grief and the futility of departure' (Boym xv). Salman Rushdie uses the term 'pillars of salt' in a similar context in his essay 'Imaginary Homelands', where he reflects on wanting 'to restore the past to myself, not in the faded greys of old family-album snapshots, but whole, in CinemaScope and glorious Technicolor' (10). As Rushdie goes on to note, 'writers in my position, exiles or emigrants or expatriates, are haunted by some sense of loss, some urge to reclaim, to look back, even at the risk of being mutated into pillars of salt' (10). Faqir's own use of the term 'pillars of salt' as the title for her novel thus signals an awareness of the dangers of nostalgia and complicates her expressed desire to 'preserve' the past. As we will see, the nostalgic mode of a simple 'better time' is undercut in the novel itself, through the connotations of the title, the representation of traditional, patriarchal and oppressive structures, and the absence of a redeeming resolution. Yet despite the limitations of this urge to 'look back', Faqir does not shy away from linking her novel about rural life on the eve of Jordanian independence with her own need to 'remember' the village, and, crucially, to explore the haunting presence of the colonial past in Jordan.

The narrative of an encounter with colonial modernity is reframed through Maha's story of the death of her husband. As the storyteller retells this story, he describes the Bedouin horsemen attacking a modern army as a 'battle between the English [. . .] and the Arabs backed by their vanity' (121). In the retelling, emphasis is placed on the defamiliarization of modern warfare from the perspective of the tribesmen of Qasim: the tribesmen shoot at 'crawling giant insects' and at the end are killed when 'a huge bird of prey made of metal' flies over their heads and 'drop[s] a metal egg' on them (122). This representation of an apocalyptic landscape conveys a level of decimation which leaves 'no corpse, just a few burnt shreds' (172). Maha's anxieties about the proper rituals of burial recalls Michel de Certeau's comment that the quest for historical meaning 'aims at calming the dead who still haunt the present and at offering them scriptural tombs' (2). Faqir's setting of her novel in a psychiatric institution, with two women telling stories about their pasts, plays out the tensions within postcolonial narrative, and the contradiction that Sam Durrant identifies between its dual commitments to the past:

> Psychoanalysis [. . .] encourages us to exorcise our ghosts, to come to terms with loss and move on. Deconstruction [. . .] urges us to learn to live with ghosts. Postcolonial narrative [. . .] is caught between these two commitments: its transformation of the past into a narrative is simultaneously an attempt to summon the dead and to lay them to rest. (9)

In Faqir's novel, these commitments are twinned in the symbolic power of burial and excavation, which resonate in various forms throughout the novel. Initially, the obsession with the buried past is connected to the colonial archaeological endeavour to claim history. When Maha asks her husband what the colonial forces are doing on the land, Harb responds that they are 'digging out the bones of Salahudin' (56). The language of disinterment related to archaeological excavation and the language of decimated, unburied bodies following the battle are connected, representing the struggle of laying the past to rest. At another point in the novel, Um Saad describes the archaeological projects conducted by the British as digging up 'the restless bones rattling at night, eager to be buried under the ground. No Jordanian – they called the country the Hashemite kingdom of Jordan – no Jordanian would pay ten piasters to see rotting bones and mossy stones' (190). In this passage, the metaphor of the unburied past is juxtaposed with an aside, referring to colonial forces creating and defining the state which then takes on that identity. Um Saad may speak derisively of Jordanians paying to access heritage unearthed by the colonizer, but she at the same time signals an adaptability to the colonizer's frameworks in taking up the term 'Jordanian', speaking to the flexibility with which people adjust to new rulers in the context of a long history of waves of Ottoman and European expansion merging, 'one foreign rule [. . .] replaced by another' (*Pillars* 89).

The need to come to terms with this extended colonial history has a particular resonance in the case of the Levant: unlike Egypt, which has a long-established sense of nationhood if not the borders of today, Jordan was created through the colonial 'game called lands': 'Lord Balfour gave the piece of land extending West of the river Jordan to a tribe without dwellings of their own' (*Pillars* 33). Parcelling out the land and making it the property of various tribes resulted in borders so famously illogical that the sharp zigzag in Jordan's eastern border with Saudi Arabia is known as 'Winston's Hiccup'. As Waïl Hassan notes, 'British and French colonialism drew the current political map of the Middle East; even the naming of the region, which dates back only to 1903, indexes the Eurocentrism of geopolitical discourse' (*Immigrant Narratives* 4). The novel dramatizes this reformulation of nationhood as Jordan becomes a new political kingdom that is asserted as eternal, with the colonial period reinterpreted as brief and inconsequential rather than formative: '[w]e must sing, we must dance [. . .] The English tried to change our lives and our land, but failed. Occupation was like a thin cloud, which was blown away by the wind' (209). Witnessing the celebrations that mark independence, Um Saad remembers: '[t]hey left our country and I saw the celebrations and procession [. . .] The Jordanian flag fluttered on our roof' (190). However, she interjects a note of irony when she describes the colours chosen for the flag, including 'green for our fertile meadows', commenting that most of the country was 'just arid desert' (190). The theatrics relating to the struggle for national freedom are here contrasted with a sobering vision of the future: '[t]he country was happy and free [. . .] The realisation of dreams makes me cry [. . .] I see the future and cry over the days to come' (190). Even within this one scene celebrating the founding of the nation, there is a foreshadowing of the shift from a period of triumphalism to one of disaffection, the 'dictatorship, fundamentalism and the mutilation of the mind' which characterize present-day Arab regimes, as Faqir describes elsewhere ('Stories from the House of Songs' 54).

Faqir's novel interrogates the interrelationship of modernizing and Westernization through Maha's struggle with her brother Daffash, a collaborator with the British who wants to 'move towards the white man', who steals Maha's land, takes her son away from her and commits her to an asylum, a modern psychiatric institution run by an English doctor. Daffash is described by the Orientalist storyteller as a 'bright man full of ideas and keen to modernise his backward village' who 'used to go to the city, talk to the learned English and design together with their engineers plans to develop the valley' (32). This emphasis on development is however soon revealed to be superficial, as Daffash 'talks about modernising the farm' but finally abandons it, while Maha, initially the representative of tradition and the land, saves her orange trees with insecticides (78).

Throughout the novel, the negotiations of change under the Mandate is often reflected through such seemingly mundane details, in particular through Um Saad's perspective, contrasting life in Amman during her childhood and during the turbulence of the end of the colonial period. The focus of the novel is not on the major political battles and leaders of this period, but rather on the domestic lives of the two women. For example, at one point, Um Saad describes her appreciation of consumer goods from Britain, as seen in 'advertisements for lifebuoy soap, Marie biscuits, and Kiwi shoe polish' (49). The focus on the material goods is a reminder of the project of colonial modernity where 'the sign of civilisation was a busy road; the sign of modernity was hygiene' (Rabinow 149). Um Saad, with her ambivalence about the cultural products of modernity, is the anomalous character in a clearly drawn conflict between the collaboration of the obsequious figures of Daffash and al-Adjnabi and the devotion to the land exhibited by Maha and her husband Harb. In contrasting these characters, Faqir borrows from familiar tropes of national resistance, the oppositions of West/East, modernity/tradition, and culture/nature.[8] This dichotomy is however complicated by Um Saad's rejection of the past, of tradition and of familial and national identity, in a refrain that repeats throughout the novel, the desire to 'be invisible like ether [...] to slip into another identity' (86), the imperative to '[r]oll into [...] another identity' (160), or '[g]et rid of your skin [...] of your past' (237). As an urban house-bound woman, a daughter and then wife of abusive men, Um Saad experiences none of the autonomy that Maha initially has as a strong-willed village woman, and none of the positive aspects of traditional culture that the Orientalist storyteller romanticizes. The specificity of each woman's experience thus complicates any simplistic idealization of tradition.

Um Saad is conflicted in her relationship to her own past and to the national narrative. While initially she mocks the archaeological projects of the British and asks '[w]ho wants to remember the past?' (130), later she asserts '[w]e hated looking backwards, seeing the past, learning' (190). At one level, this contempt for an ahistorical life may be related to an internalized idea of primitive peoples possessing no sense of history. Yet Um Saad moves confusingly from condemning this general ahistorical ignorance, castigating the communal ignorance of the past, to turning away from her own personal history, rejecting the idea that she suffers from acute memory loss: '[m]emory loss? Empty talk. I remember everything, even the things I don't want to remember. Forgetfulness is a blessing' (138). Connecting Um Saad's relationship to her own past and her views on the correct attitude to take to a traumatic history, the novel shifts between individual memory and a collective account of the past. As the same person who poses the question 'who wants to remember the past?' and makes the assertion 'I remember everything', Um Saad is represented as having lived through a history that can neither be coherently remembered nor fully forgotten by moving forward with life. Through this complicated character, Faqir links the personal and the national, the trauma of being unable to forget and the trauma of being unable to remember.

In her autobiographical essay 'Stories from the House of Songs', Faqir speaks of her need to 'describe her new world in order to understand it' and to 'write her colours back into the predominantly white tapestry' (60). As with *The Map of Love*, weaving is analogous with storytelling in this novel, as the protagonist Maha finds consolation in the task of completing the weaving of her mother's carpet, her spinning described as 'threads spread over the valley to protect it' (104). The literal weaving of the mother's carpet approximates the metaphorical weaving together of Maha and Um Saad's stories.[9] The metaphor of weaving, referencing a traditional handicraft and a creative process, becomes a symbolic way to speak about the need to connect the past in tangible ways, to connect the stories of the past with the present.

Jamal Mahjoub's In the Hour of Signs

Mahjoub's work involves a similar questioning of 'returning' to the precolonial era as the novels by Faqir and Soueif. In Mahjoub's case, this need to rewrite colonial history is closely linked to the imperative to find a coherent narrative which makes sense of Sudan's present borders. For example, in Mahjoub's novel

Travelling with Djinns (2003) the protagonist Yasin reflects on the absence of any comprehensible narrative of a shared past to homogenize diverse cultures and communities: '[w]hat went before? [. . .] What strange concatenation of forces had given rise to this mixture of peoples which we called a nation?' (*Travelling* 62). In the following passage, the absence is mapped onto the presence of a history that is about 'other people, other places':

> [h]istory, the hard stuff, the earth-shattering events, all involved other people, other places [. . .] In class we learned that history consisted of foreign words like Verdun and the Treaty of Versailles, Auschwitz, Pearl Harbor, Hiroshima, Dien Bien Phu. Those distant lawns and pavilions, those men in wide hats and breeches. We memorised words like Realpolitik and Von Bismarck, the scramble for Africa, without really understanding how they had affected us. (*Travelling* 62)

In this passage, Yasin reflects on missing what Marianne Hirsch calls 'an affective link to the past', the sense of a 'living connection' (*Postmemory* 111). Yasin looks at a photograph of colonial figures 'sitting on the deck of a Nile streamer at dusk, deciding our future', and thinks how 'curiously absurd' it is that 'all of these strangers wearing rows of medals and huge moustaches had something to do with our present situation' (62). The study of history, in Said's words, involves 'a nationalist effort premised on the need to construct a desirable loyalty to an insider's understanding of one's country, tradition, and faith' ('Memory' 176). As a child grappling with how the past is constructed and remembered, Yasin cannot imaginatively bridge the disconnection between the colonial past and the present situation, between the European history he learns about and the absent precolonial past.[10] It is obvious to Yasin that those who fought for a 'nation of equals [. . .] were now just a gang of toothless old grumps who mumbled nostalgically about things nobody remembered' (138). He is left with attempting to connect to the disappearing generation who had witnessed 'those halcyon days, with independence in sight' while realizing that '[i]t had all gone terribly wrong. The great age of national independence had proved to be nothing more than a neocolonial mirage' (140).

This disconnect is the subject of Mahjoub's first three novels, which restage Sudan's past, and, as Caroline Mohsen points out, 'can be read as a trilogy which records the historic progression of political events in Sudan since the inception of British colonisation of Sudan down to the late 1980s' (541). In Mahjoub's first novel, *Navigation of a Rainmaker* (1989) the British-Sudanese protagonist Tanner is unable to accept his father's advice to 'forget about that part of you. You don't need it', deciding to travel from Britain to Sudan in an endeavour to rediscover his roots (18). The second novel, *Wings of Dust* (1994), shifts from a second-generation protagonist grappling with his heritage to the 'Arab student in Europe' theme. It follows the protagonist Sharif and his friends, members of an elite who are educated in Britain so they can return to Sudan to implement their modernizing projects, and charts their trajectory from the high hopes of nationalism to disillusionment and resignation to a life in exile.

The main characters in *Wings of Dust* are 'overinflated intellectuals' (71), representatives of an elite that 'views itself as the only possible solution after the end of colonialism' (Mohsen 547). The novel begins with the narrator's recounting of his memories as a way to 'create a space' or 're-invent a space' which he 'can call home' (*Wings* 5). However, even as he seeks to implement modernizing strategies, the narrator worries that the nationalist elites 'will inherit the land, but [. . .] will also be unable to cross the boundary left by the British [. . .] [they] will become [their] own imperialists' (6). Sure enough, after decolonization, these intellectuals realize that they are reproducing the same power relations. Mahjoub traces the transition from a seemingly self-evident fight against colonial subjugation to the realization that this fight involves, as Fanon pointed out, 'building up yet another system of exploitation', a discovery that is 'unpleasant, bitter, and sickening' (145). The novel traces the social shift in Sudanese society from nationalist modernizing enterprises to a traditionalist backlash. With each return to Sudan, the narrator finds that 'what had been liberal was now conservative, what had been modern was now traditional, what had been free speech was now silence' (*Wings* 107). The failure of the modernizing project is represented through the transition of a once-hopeful intellectual known as Shibshib, who initially calls for 'cultural rebellion' urging the others to 'take their language and turn its inflection into ours [. . .] speak their words through our tongues'.[11] In the context of the post-independence era in Sudan, writers were attempting to forge a syncretic language through which a national literature can be developed. However, with 'the failure of earnest discourses of cultural rebellion to survive and be translated in action' in Mahjoub's text, Shibshib gradually loses his grip on reality, a 'descent into madness' that 'mirrors the estrangement of intellectual projects from the bare reality of things [and] demonstrates that idealism cannot bring social change' (Mohsen 547).

The last novel of the trilogy, *In the Hour of Signs* (1996), continues this reimagining of Sudanese history, returning to an even earlier past, the age of imperial conquest and the country's history of double colonization. *In the Hour of Signs* centres on the Battle of Omdurman and features a large cast of characters. The story of the lead up to and aftermath of the battle is told from multiple points of view, including that of military leaders, nationalists and those on neither side of the conflict. The main protagonist is Hawi, a religious scholar who returns to the country after hearing about the Mahdi. Other characters include Medani the cook, Ellesworth, an English officer, Kadaro the soldier and Noon, a girl believed to be possessed. Alongside the Mahdi and the Khalifa, other historical protagonists include the general of the Mahdist forces Abdulrahman al-Nejumi and Ottoman cavalry officer turned governor-general of the Sudan Ala'addin Pasha Siddiq. The chronological episodic narrative of the novel is structured around the historical events of the Mahdist revolution from the moment when the Mahdi declares himself the 'Rightly-Guided' in 1881 to the string of initial victories leading up to the siege of Khartoum. The revolution culminates in the death of General Gordon in 1885, and the Mahdi's own sudden death and the break-up of his movement under the successor caliphs, until the re-conquest at the hands of the British military leader Herbert Kitchener at Omdurman in 1898. In the following year, there was an Anglo-Egyptian agreement to restore Egyptian rule through the British, who would govern the territory on the Khedive's behalf.

The role of the Khedivate of Egypt has often been side-lined by the dominant version of the British Sudan campaign. As Geoffrey Nash points out, Mahjoub 'revisits the Mahdi episode, inserted into popular British imperial history almost entirely on account of the death of Gordon at Khartoum and the revenge of Kitchener at Omdurman and rewrites it from a postcolonial perspective' (*Writing Muslim Identity* 82). Nash notes that Mahjoub may be the first novelist to represent the Mahdist episode in English from a Sudanese perspective. In this sense, Mahjoub's restaging of the Battle of Omdurman, in Homi Bhabha's terms, 'impels the past, projects it, gives its dead symbols the circulatory life of the sign of the present' (*Location of Culture* 254). Mahjoub's reimagining of this crucial moment in Sudanese history reclaims this past from the erasures of the colonial record and reflects on the devolution of the nationalist dream into repressive autocracy; in the case of Sudan, the autocracy of an Islamist government.

Although *In the Hour of Signs* is entirely set during the colonial period, Mahjoub points out in a personal correspondence with Geoffrey Nash that it is not a 'purely historical novel but a novel which seeks to use history to interrogate the nature of national identity' (qtd. in Nash, *Anglophone Arab Encounter* 95). Through the character of Hawi, Mahjoub interrogates the religious fervour behind the Mahdist movement, and obliquely comments on the Islamist seizure of power in Sudan in 1989. The character of Hawi, who believes he can discern 'a second, hidden meaning' in the scriptures, seems to pay homage to the Sudanese reformer Mahmoud Mohamed Taha, author of a controversial work entitled *Al-Risāla al-thāniya min al-Islām* (The Second Message of Islam) published in 1967 (*Hour* 17). Taha advocated an evolutionary approach to Islamic law, and as a result of this work, was hanged for apostasy in 1985. Through Hawi, a parallel character, the novel examines the way in which the religious conflicts of the 1880s reappear in 1980s Sudan. The present is not evacuated by working through the traumatic past, but rather suffused with a sense of history repeating itself. Hawi, a reforming figure who ultimately fails to implement his utopian project of renaissance, is the lynchpin in a historical parallel between the Mahdi movement and the Islamist takeover of Sudan. Through the parallel between Hawi and the reformist Taha, Mahjoub embeds the contemporary framework within the historical narrative about the Mahdi movement, which has often been described as a precursor of contemporary Islamism. For example, Adam Gopnik writes:

> [w]hat 'history' shows is that the same forces that led to the Mahdi's rebellion in Sudan more than a century ago – rage at the presence of a colonial master; a mad turn towards an imaginary past as a means to equal the score – keep coming back and remain just as resistant to management. ('Does it Help to Know History')

The parallel between now and then necessarily involves reflecting on the narrative that modernity is 'an inorganic process forced upon the Arab world as the aftermath of a colonial encounter which the latter lost' (Shalakany 156). This narrative is played out in the framing of colonialism as a metaphorical, as well as literal, 'war between yesterday and tomorrow' in the words of Kadaro (230). The pivotal Battle of Omdurman is located as the commencement of modernity-as-future: 'they are coming [. . .] This time nothing could stop them. The future is making its way upstream and the riverbed is shaking' (*Hour* 235). The inevitability of this 'future' then determines the choice Kadaro is presented with when he attempts to flee:

> [o]ne day this land is going to be crossed by thousands of miles of track, upon which the finest locomotives will fly up and down from Cairo to the Cape of Good Hope [. . .] You can stay in the stone age [. . .] or you can be in at the start. (*Hour* 232)

Here, the capitalist idiom of investment highlights the opposition between the pair tradition/modernity as an ideological narrative that is part of establishing a civilizing enterprise. As with *Pillars of Salt*, there is an emphasis on modernity as associated with material objects – it is only after seeing 'the mountains of bale wire and fish-plates and spare broilers and machine tools and trolleys and a thousand other things whose purpose he could not even guess' that Kadaro decides to collaborate with the colonizers, understanding that his reality has become an anachronistic 'yesterday' since '[t]he armies of the khalifa could never withstand this force [. . .] the battle was not between men of different colours or faiths, but between two different ages' (230). As in *Pillars of Salt*, Mahjoub stages the moment of encounter with the colonial power by emphasizing the scale of mechanized warfare which decimates the forces opposing the colonial endeavour:

> the battle had taken only four hours or so. Four hours – and eleven thousand enemy dead at the cost of forty-eight Englishmen. A strange mixture of awe and revulsion went through [him] like a shudder [. . .] The age of war was a quaint memory; this was the age of meticulous slaughter. (24)

The technological superiority of the colonial power and the scenes of colonial carnage leave 'thousands of bodies' fragmentary and unburied so that 'for years afterwards some widows went wandering in their black shawls like crows, picking up the bones of men and collecting them as some kind of memorial to the ones they had never found' (237). This image represents the battle of Omdurman as a scene which collapses temporality, not only as the site of an overwhelming defeat rendering the present age into someone else's yesterday, but also in the war remaining relevant and visible in the material remains. As Michael O'Riley reflects, there is an 'imperative of returning to occluded colonial history through a reckoning with the specters of the nation's colonial heritage' (2). In Mahjoub's novel, this imperative to reconstruct the haunting traces of history is underlined by a need to understand the present repercussions of this struggle, a confrontation with what remains as a haunting presence in the present era.

The novel does not end with the decisive scene of the battle of Omdurman. Instead, Mahjoub reflects on what happens in the aftermath of the defeat, when the conflict between the colonizing forces and the Mahdiyya spawns a more complex, multi-sided struggle between the Mahdi's messianic movement, Hawi's transcultural efforts and Kadaro's colonial collaboration. After the battle is over, Hawi begins to preach about social cohesion through a comprehensible narrative of an inclusive past: 'he told them to look amongst themselves to see how different they all were' (244). Hawi attempts to confront the challenge of reconciliation in the message of continual change: '[p]eople say that only that which is imperfect evolves and changes [...] perfection is a fluid state of renewal and progression, not stagnation' (245). Here Hawi displaces the tensions of the vastly oversimplified discourse of modernity/tradition to promote a society 'resistant enough to be itself, but porous enough to invite its transformation' (288). Such a view highlights the traps of nostalgia, and suggests that the solution is not to see the rupture of colonialism as being deprived of a 'true' lost identity, but rather to develop a view of a continually changing society, where the appearance of newness does not threaten the understanding of community. However, the novel ends with Hawi's message of reform leading to his sentencing to death for apostasy at the orders of Kadaro, the representative of tomorrow, symbolically representing the autocratic direction the future will take.

The failures of nationalism are a theme in Mahjoub's other novels, including in his recent crime fiction, written under the pseudonym Parker Bilal. In *Golden Scales* (2012), the first of Mahjoub's detective novels, the protagonist Makana describes the illusion of attempting to reconnect to the precolonial past as a model for modernity. Looking at the Cairo Tower, Makana comments that it was '[m]odelled on a lotus flower, symbol of life in Ancient Egypt', seeking to make the past constitutive of a new modernity. Makana goes on to reflect on the distance between the ambitions of the Nasserist era and the present, noting that the tower was

> built in the late fifties to transmit the Sawt al-Arab radio signal. The legendary broadcasts united the Arabs around the bold leadership of Gamal Abdel Nasser and his defiance of the West [. . .] Nowadays, people looked back upon that era with fond nostalgia. It had never struck Makana as a particularly attractive object. There was a restaurant up there, which revolved while you eat. Spinning around in the air trying to eat struck him as a strange idea. Was that what had become of Egyptian independence? (233)

Like Soueif's *The Map of Love*, where the intellectuals discuss the lack of a national project, Mahjoub's writing often dramatizes the failure of the narratives of Arab nationalism. In this passage, the revolving restaurant captures the sense of being stationary while moving, without arriving at an answer to the question of independence. The psychological struggles that emerge in the wake of colonialism 'forces the people it dominates to ask themselves the question constantly: "[i]n reality, who am I?"' (Fanon 250). In Mahjoub's works, this question haunts the protagonists, who turn to the past out of a need to locate themselves in the present. For example, in *Wings of Dust*, the narrator asks:

> [b]ut who were we really? What united us as a single coherent people? In the ancient graves you can find the seeds of confusion and doubt. People were

buried according to custom with the signs of Isis and Osiris and Apadamac [...] but under their heads was a discreetly placed cross – just in case. Each incursion overlays the previous one until finally nobody really knows who they are and where they came from. (71–2)

Mahjoub transposes the search for a national culture into an intercultural continuum that does not allow for a single answer to the question Fanon articulates. As Jopi Nyman has described, Mahjoub's novels are 'involved in an ethico-political project of historicising cultural encounters' ('Europe' 240). The same might be said for Soueif and Faqir, whose novels reconstruct the colonial past as a way of reworking the discourses of modernity and tradition, and the alignment of the former with the West and the latter with the East. Soueif, Mahjoub and Faqir each relate colonial history to the dimension of the present as a vital point of reference to understand the development of Jordan, Egypt and Sudan from colonialism to independence to authoritarian postcolonial states, leading the reader to reflect on the impasse of considering modernity and tradition as opposed forces. Sharif in *The Map of Love* and Hawi in *In the Hour of Signs* each work to reform their own societies while resisting being co-opted by the colonial civilizing mission. In *Pillar of Salt*, Maha (though not a self-identified reformer like the preacher Hawi and the politician Sharif) strongly rejects the limited lives of the village women. At the same time, she does not suffer from Daffash's inferiority complex and rejects the colonizer's 'civilizing mission' narrative. In each case however, these figures fail to implement their vision: in *The Map of Love*, Sharif feels he has failed as the extremists and the collaborators on either side have erased the middle ground, while Maha and Hawi are victimized by the collaborators, Daffash and Kadaro, who perpetuate the colonizers' oppression, thus foreshadowing the postcolonial state. The writers highlight how intellectual elites took advantage of new governing structures and perpetuated structures of domination as a way of exploring the extension of oppression from the colonial era to the present situation. This critique involves not only examining the enduring legacy of colonialism but also the persistence of the same structures of domination in the postcolonial state.

The novels I have discussed in this chapter were written in the 1990s, in the wake of the first Gulf War, and the writers' perspective on the colonial past of their countries is clearly impacted by the contemporary repercussions of that past. Writing in 2007, in the wake of the War on Terror, and at the height of the violence in Iraq, Michael O'Riley notes:

> there is nothing new about looking at the heritage of colonialism and its influence on contemporary life. However, the new face of terrorism and the political and cultural issues it has raised urge a consideration of how colonialism continues to haunt responses of aggression and resistance within this new context. (1)

Since the collapse of the Ottoman Empire, the borders drawn by colonial powers have been placed under scrutiny with every conflict in the region, and with every conflict, there are efforts to reimagine geography to better fit an imaginary peoplehood associated with clear territorial boundaries. As writers in the diaspora, expressing themselves in English, the novelists I have discussed seek to find a space for their texts amid already existing narratives in the West about 'the Middle East'. It is in this context that Ferial Ghazoul argues that 'Arab writers who write in English, French, and Italian are no longer seen as traitors opting out of their own culture and into the culture of the (ex-)colonisers, but as cultural ambassadors who are able to voice a previously silenced point of view' (121–2). Being at a temporal and geographical distance from the past they reimagine, Anglophone Arab writers leverage the sentiments of nostalgia, the need to turn back to yearned-for pasts, to intervene in narratives about the Middle East, and to grapple with the spectres of colonialism and ideological narratives of loss that continue to animate present conflicts. These novels problematize appeals to tradition, whether by highlighting patriarchal oppression, underlining the privileged position of the intellectual elite or complicating the idea of a single national culture. It is this complexity that Yasin recognizes in Mahjoub's *Travelling with Djinns*: '[o]ur history was never going to be a straightforward linear narrative but rather a series of contortions, disjointed incidents, haphazard circumstances that eventually led down to us' (63). However, it is difficult to entirely dismiss the nostalgic mode that frames the depiction of the anti-colonial nationalist era in these novels, and how this nostalgic mode is interlinked with the possibility of alternative forms of nationalism. As Partha Chatterjee asks (in response to Benedict Anderson's notion of imagined communities): 'if nationalisms in the rest of the world have to choose their imagined community from certain modular forms already made available to them by Europe and America' then 'what do they have left to imagine?' (*Nation* 5). The nostalgic narratives that I have examined in this chapter are an imaginative return to the moment of the formation of nationalist movements, inviting the reader to consider the 'spectres of what might have been' (Žižek 86).

Chapter 3

NATIONAL HISTORIES AND FAMILY NARRATIVES

HISHAM MATAR, LEILA ABOULELA AND RANDA JARRAR

In Mohja Kahf's bildungsroman *The Girl in the Tangerine Scarf* (2006), a novel about a Syrian family that flees the Ba'athist dictatorship to resettle in America, we are introduced to Khadra and Eyad, who are learning Arabic with the 'Arabic readers that their parents made relatives send from Syria every year'. The books feature the ideal Father and Mother, from the Assad regime's perspective: '[s]ee Father and Mother. Father is brave. Mother reads a letter from Father at the front. Father wore a Syrian Army uniform and Mother never wore hijab.' These images are presented in 'secular Ba'athist textbooks, with a picture of the Syrian president, Hafez Asad [*sic*], in the front'. Khadra notices that 'the first thing [her] parents did was tear that page out and throw it away' before 'they set to teaching the children Arabic' (121). The irony here is that the same books intended to inculcate a new generation into accepting the regime's pan-Arab socialist ideology are used by the protagonist's parents, opponents of the regime, to teach their children Arabic and keep them attached to Syria as 'the homeland'. The scene highlights the interconnections and contradictions between the family and the nation state, where the family is both a legitimating metaphor of the nation and subordinated to state ideology. Kahf's bildungsroman follows the maturing protagonist's changing world view through the transformation of her relationship with her family and her country of origin, initially seen only 'through the inherited lenses of her parent's memory' (268). Nationalist sentiment is entangled with familial relationships through the transmission of stories about the homeland. The overlap of home and nation involves a coalescence of childhood, the family home and the homeland as three predominant sites of nostalgia.

This chapter examines how nostalgically framed scenes of childhood, home and family, usually associated with belonging, cohesion and stability, involve the same dynamics that shore up nationalist discourse, with its legitimating metaphors of the nation-as-family and the homeland-as-home. The family is a crucial site for the formation, instilling and enacting of national identity. Rather than being a private space secluded from the public sphere, '[h]ome reflects and resembles the nation' and is both a 'target and mirror of the marketplace, as central and centering as any institution in the public realm' (Strehle 1). The nationalist project is based on the idea that 'the family of the nation overrides and replaces the individual's family but evokes similarly strong loyalties and vivid attachments' (Smith 79). However, the break-up of family ties undoes idealized conceptualizations of home. Personal disillusionment with family stability maps the disintegration and instability of the familial unit onto the disintegration of the nation, questioning the extent to which the nation and family can function as stable anchors.

In this chapter, I focus on novels by Hisham Matar, Leila Aboulela and Randa Jarrar, exploring the ramifications of the complex intertwining of the political and the personal in the postcolonial nation state, from state violence to the displacement directly linked to that violence. The novels I will discuss depict the effects of political struggles on families living through national upheavals, an intrusion of political violence into the familial realm which disintegrates the distinction between public and private, the instabilities in the family mirroring the failures of the national project. Structurally, the novels move between then and there (the country of origin) and here and now (in exile). The back and forth, along with the self-reflexive commentary by a mature protagonist on the experiences of their younger self, embeds the reimagining of the past into the narrative. As the novels are narrated from the vantage point of being outside the homeland, this perspective highlights how life in diaspora remains linked to the turbulence 'back home', reflecting the enduring relevance of the homeland as well as how exiles continue to be affected by the turmoil of violent postcolonial histories. The traumatic violence that comes to define the homeland is experienced at the level of the family, and the novels follow the maturing protagonists' growing awareness of the implications of that violence for themselves. The novels share the theme of disillusionment in the degeneration of the national project, reworking the trope of nostalgia for the homeland to explore the narrative of the utopian nation that never came to be.

In texts which foreground the traumas of intra-national violence and the fractured subjectivities of diaspora, nostalgia for the homeland necessarily involves the reconstruction of national narratives. In a discussion of Anglophone Lebanese literature, Hout points to the destabilization of national coherence in such narratives, which she argues

> evince a degree of nostalgia in the very fact of having been published. Nationalism, defined in psycho-social terms as devotion to one's own nation, assumes the sense of personal as well as communal belonging when it derives from some kind of conformity or continuity. If so, how does nationalist sentiment suffer or change when such conformity and/or continuity are neither possible nor perhaps even desirable? (*Post-War* 24)

The investment in the nation is not simply the result of a longing for a homeland that confers belonging but involves a critical mapping of the conditions of that belonging in the context of war and state violence. Anglophone Arab writers make use of nostalgic narratives as a way of reimagining the histories that shape the nation, intervening in and contributing to national narratives despite their diasporic distance. Exploring the connections between home and homeland, family and nation, they imaginatively bridge the geographical and linguistic rifts that complicate national belonging. Yet in examining the legacies of violent histories elided in official nationalist discourse they also highlight the constructed notion of the nation-as-family. Their reimaginings of national narratives are thus fraught with ambivalence, intertwining nostalgia for the homeland with a sense of estrangement from that homeland. The desire to fondly remember childhood, home, and family from the vantage point of diaspora is inextricable from the traumatic remembering of the violence that instigates displacement. Nostalgic tropes thus counter-intuitively complicate the idealized nationalist vision, as the writers depict the primary sites of nostalgia, the family, the home and childhood, first within a traditionally nostalgic frame, and then trace the development of a more complex view of the politically unstable homeland from the perspective of exile.

Discussing the representation of the familial, personal sphere in relation to nationalist struggles reopens the theoretical debates set in motion by Frederic Jameson's famous contention that '[a]ll third-world texts are necessarily [. . .] allegorical' (69). As Qin Wang argues, Jameson's essay remains relevant even in 'a world whose historico-political situation is dramatically different from the time when it was originally written' (655). Jameson's argument continues to be brought up in postcolonial studies and critiqued for confining this mode to a homogenized 'Third World' and for the notion that 'the telling of the individual story [. . .] cannot but ultimately involve the whole laborious telling of the experience of the collectivity itself' (86). As Wang points out, there are similarities between this taking on of collective value and the 'minor literature' coined by Gilles Deleuze and Félix Guattari where

> cramped space forces each individual intrigue to connect immediately to politics. The individual concern thus becomes all the more necessary, indispensable, magnified, because a whole other story is vibrating within it. In this way, the family triangle connects to other triangles – commercial, economic, bureaucratic, juridical – that determine its values. (17)

Deleuze and Guattari mention the 'third world' here, suggesting that the 'minor no longer designates specific literatures but the revolutionary conditions for every literature' within established literature, where the writer finds 'his own point of underdevelopment, his own patois, his own third world, his own desert' (17). The metaphorical use of the third world parts ways with Jameson's more literal idea of the third world. Yet, in 'Who's Afraid of the National Allegory?' Imre Szeman suggests that it is precisely the insistence on different sociopolitical conditions that makes Jameson's argument convincing. Rather than making aesthetic judgements, the argument involves thinking through different modes of public intrusion into the private space, mystified in some contexts, and overt in others, demanding a corresponding political intensity.[1] The novels that I will discuss in this chapter dramatize this intrusion, and the interrelationship of the nation and the private sphere of home, through representing the family as the conflict site for the political campaigns and ideological narratives shaping nationhood.

In the rhetorical invocation of citizenship as belonging, community is imagined through the sites of family and home. As Anne McClintock writes, '[n]ations are frequently figured through the iconography of familial and domestic space. The term 'nation' derives from *natio*: to be born' (*Imperial Leather* 357). Tracing the development and use of the metaphor of nation-as-family, McClintock notes that it 'offered a single genesis narrative for national history'. However, at the same time, 'the family as an institution became void of history and excluded from national power. The family became [. . .] both the organising figure for national history and its antithesis' (*Dangerous Liaisons* 91). The state presents power imbalances and subordination as natural power dynamics that are ostensibly inescapable even in the social unit of the family, which is at once a legitimating model and a depoliticized structure. In what follows, I will briefly discuss the background for the novels examined in this chapter in relation to what Suad Joseph describes as the 'metaphorical and lived similarities between political and kinship systems' in the Arab world (347). The deployment of familial metaphors for the nation in Arabic literature realizes the ambivalent relation that McClintock cites: the family both charges nostalgic sentiment for the utopian homeland and extends political critique of the neocolonial state.

Nostalgia and the neopatriarchy

The authors of the novels discussed in this chapter are of one generation, born between 1960 and 1970, an era that witnessed the declining popularity of pan-Arab ideologies due to repressive policies, inter-Arab rivalries, defeat in the 1967 Arab-Israeli war and the breakdown of unification attempts.[2] This period was marked by the tension between state sovereignty and *waṭaniyya* (nationalism based on territory) on the one hand, and pan-Arabism and *qawmīyya* (nationalism based on 'peoplehood'), on the other hand. P. R. Kumaraswamy notes that most countries in the region have suffered from problems over forming national identities: '[m]ore than three quarters of a century after the disintegration of the Ottoman Empire, from which most of them emerged, these states have been unable to define, project and maintain a national identity that is both inclusive and representative' (63).[3] Arab nationalism offered one overarching narrative that sought to impose unity on a discordant region, and thus, as Adeed Dawisha has pointed out, when 'Arab Nationalism dominated the political and psychological landscape, it suffered little from its authoritarian proclivity' (306). However, in the wake of the demise of Nasserist nationalism, the Islamist wave that followed was fuelled by growing resentment at the repressive policies of Arab states. The failure of the Nasserist project meant that touting 'national interest' in order to justify anti-democratic policies was less convincing.[4]

It is in this context that Hisham Sharabi, in his influential work *Neopatriarchy*, discusses the central feature of the modern Arab state as 'the dominance of the

Father (patriarch), the centre around which the national and natural family are organised' (7). Sharabi uses the term 'neopatriarchy' to refer to a society where 'material modernisation [. . .] only served to remodel and reorganise patriarchal structures and relations and to reinforce them by giving them "modern" forms and appearances' (4). Though Sharabi's work was first published in 1988 and analyses autocratic political regimes during the Cold War era, as Suad Joseph has pointed out, 'images of the Arab state as a family writ large are seemingly ubiquitous' even today. The cultivation and manipulation of the idea of the 'national family' through utilizing the 'metaphor of state leader as father' involves a naturalization of power imbalances that depends on an acceptance of patriarchal authority and the centrality of patrilineage (S. Joseph 348).[5]

There are however problems with turning this analysis into a cultural explanation about authority structures in society. In an explanation of the 'Saddam syndrome' for example, Ghada Karmi is quoted as arguing that 'the main problem is that a system of authority is reproduced in the Arab family' (qtd. in Aly 83). Ramy Aly rightly notes that what makes this argument problematic is 'the implied particularity and integrity of these values across time, place and context', which suggests that 'the solution [. . .] is the imposition or adoption of a true or loyal European modernity in the Arab world' (84). Though the notion of a replication of power structures offers an understandable framework, the social and political circumstances that shore up authoritarian structures in the region complicate the analogy between authoritarian structures in the family and nation along cultural lines. As Nazih Ayubi notes in *Overstating the Arab State* (1995), the emergence of pan-Arabism as a source of coherent identity was set against Turkish nationalism, European colonialism and Zionism, an effort to integrate the Arab world which deviated from its goals of unification to legitimating illiberal and authoritarian regimes.

It is notable that the representations of nationalist movements in Arabic literature are often figured through this narrative of the failures of decolonization, which is reinterpreted as a failure to continue a family history of resistance. For example, in Jabra Ibrahim Jabra's novel *al-Baḥth ʿan Walīd Masʿūd* (1978, *The Search for Walid Masoud*, 2000), the apolitical Amer, who 'refuses to look back at the past, to his country's history' relates the trajectories of national history to a patrilineal heritage:

> [t]o him all history started with his grandfather, when he was fighting the Ottomans during the last years of the nineteenth century, then continued with the British occupation of Iraq, when his father distinguished himself as a national fighter, sustained by the dream that every time he was jailed or placed under house arrest his country came closer to the day of liberation. But liberation remained a dream. From the time Amer crossed over into his forties, he felt his immediate history had been severed from him. (146)

In this passage, Amer's identification with the nation is dependent upon what Diane King calls 'lineal masculinity' where 'collective memory is masculinized and codified as male achievement transmitted through patrilines' (328). While his patrilineal forebears work towards nationalist goals, Amer's severance from this heritage, living 'for the present, for the present alone' reflects awareness of his failure to continue their nationalist legacy (*The Search for Walid Masoud* 146). Amer's sense of severance, looking back on what seem to be the futile struggles of previous generations, is the theme of the novel as a whole, the premise of which is the search for Walid, a Palestinian political activist and writer who is the symbol for nationalist struggle in the contemporary age. As Samah Selim suggests, the text 'initiate[s] a journey through the psychic and political landscape of a quixotic Arab modernity that is, like the novel's central character, intensely present and yet irretrievably lost' (89). In so far as there is a resolution to this quest, the novel follows the trajectory of the relationship between Walid and Wisal, who ultimately leaves her comfortable life to join the Palestinian resistance, upholding the cherished ideals of sacrifice for the sake of the nation.

Jamal Mahjoub raises the nostalgia that stems from this generational sense of disconnection as a shared dilemma in an interview with actor Alexander Siddig, where they discuss what 'link[s] the two of us, both born in the 1960s, the children of Sudanese fathers and English mothers'. In this conversation, Siddig describes his character Ibn Khaldun in the British drama series *Spooks* as 'trying to take a snapshot of this guy before he disappears. He was my father. He was your father. He was the father of all the generations that had a liberal upbringing' ('Accidental Arab'). Agreeing with this characterization, Mahjoub adds:

> He's also the archetype of old Arab nationalism, the intelligentsia who became marginalised, the technocrats of Nasser's early ambitions. But they were deemed a threat, and the West feared them. So did Nasser, who imprisoned them. They left a void that was eventually filled by political Islam. ('Accidental Arab')

Both Siddig and Mahjoub mourn the 'disappearance' of the nationalist generation and attempt in their work to represent them. The disappearance of a generation for whom commitment to a nationalist cause was possible thus represents the shift from the national framework to coming to terms with the failures of the dreams of national liberation.

Just as national narratives involve a paralleling of patriarchal authority and leadership, the 'master national narrative [. . .] assigns Woman a fixed role as an historical metaphor' (Fayad 148). Mona Fayad argues that '[w]ithin the twentieth-century Arab literary tradition, Woman as historical metaphor is most commonly represented through the allegory of mother/earth/country' (148). Like the father/leader parallel, the mother/land trope is an ambivalent one. The metaphor is used both to express nostalgia for the homeland and to express a rejection of history and the home. For example, consider Moroccan novelist Mohammed Berrada's *Luʻbat al-Nisyān* (1987, *The Game of Forgetting*, 1997), which begins: '[i]n the Beginning was the Mother' (15). The main character in the novel, Hadi, is a leftist journalist suffering from a midlife crisis, disillusioned by the deteriorating political situation in Morocco, and devastated on a personal level by the death of his mother, Lala

Lghalya. Hadi's mother is referred to as 'indispensable, like salt in food' (17) and represented in terms that depict her as a repository of memory, 'the roots of a tree extending far beyond this old house' (20). The mother comes to represent the longed-for homeland. In contrast, as Miriam Cooke has discussed, the negative image of the mother can work as a rejection of tradition where 'the mother's body must be erased because it reifies the persistence of tradition and of a patriarchal system' (152). For example, in Muhammad Abi Samra's novel, *al-Rajul al-sābiq* (The Former Man, 1995), the mother is rejected as embodying a culture that is out of place in the contemporary world. The protagonist is a Lebanese émigré who returns to visit his native Beirut, addressing his mother in terms that link her to a nation he sees as out of step with modernity: 'I began to see you as old [...] as old as fashions and objects being used at a time and a world not their own' (qtd. in El Enany 147).

In these novels, the mother is either the symbol of the failed utopian national project, or the symbol of an ageing impoverished culture that is out of place in the contemporary world. In this sense, both the positive and the negative connotations of the nation are bound up with the mother – on the one hand, the nation is identified with a maternal nurturing role, and on the other hand, with failure and stagnation. The mother–child bond becomes a potent symbol of ambivalent attachment to the nation. So, in Samar Attar's *Līnā: Lawḥat fatāh Dimashqīyya* (1982, *Lina: A Portrait of A Damascene Girl*, 1994), the protagonist Lina links her conflicted feelings for her mother and for her country, describing Syria as 'a cat eating its own children' (168). Through this image of infanticide, Lina articulates the lack of future in her country. Inverting the mother–child analogy, Palestinian poet Salim Jubran writes, '[j]ust as a mother loves her disfigured child, so do I love my own beloved, my country' (qtd. in Allen 210). The representations of the country as a cannibalistic mother and as a disfigured child are mirror images of each other – they use the emotional attachment between mother and child to convey the depths of the conflicted relationship for the nation. Both images reflect an ambivalent and critical nostalgia for the nation that could have been.

The Iraqi poet Saadi Youssef encapsulates this nostalgia for the failed national project in 'A Desperate Poem', in the lines '[t]he country we love was finished / before it was even born / The country we did not love has claimed / the blood left in our veins' (71). Here, Youssef depicts the postcolonial nation as a vampiric force, while the longed-for country remains unborn. These lines capture the ambivalence and the volatility of nationalism as, in Richard Werbner's words, 'at once positive and negative for the project of human emancipation and liberation' (92). Werbner suggests that despite 'often cruelly violent moments within twentieth-century nation-state building' national narratives remain 'energised by a myth of being prior to the postcolonial nation state, of carrying forward primordial identities' (92). The exile's relationship to the nation negotiates this tension between the exclusionary processes and erasures that are a component of nationalist movements, and the attachment to nationhood that is fundamental to articulations of community, ethnicity and identity.

The experience of dislocation does not necessarily weaken the connection to the native place but rather suffuses that connection with nostalgia and loss. Said describes exile as being 'predicated on the existence of, love for, and bond with, one's native place; what is true of all exile is not that home and love of home are lost, but that loss is inherent in the very existence of both' (*Reflections* 185). Having asserted nationalism's 'essential association with exile', Said raises a series of questions about this association:

> [h]ow, then, does one surmount the loneliness of exile without falling into the encompassing and thumping language of national pride, collective sentiments, group passions? What is there worth saving and holding on to between the extremes of exile on the one hand, and the often bloody-minded affirmations of nationalism on the other? Do nationalism and exile have any intrinsic attributes? Are they simply two conflicting varieties of paranoia? (*Reflections* 177)

Though Said concludes that these questions are unanswerable, he points to the consequences of exiles being 'cut off from their roots, their land, their past' as an inevitable disruption of a monolithically defined national identity: 'there is certainly nothing about nationalism's public and all-inclusive ambitions that touches the core of the exile's predicament. Because exile, unlike nationalism, is fundamentally a discontinuous state of being' (*Reflections* 177). As we will see, this discontinuous state informs the representation of the nation in Anglophone Arab literature. The narratives discussed here feature protagonists who look back on the failures of the nationalist ideals of their parents' generation, from a life outside the homeland. They combine yearning for a utopian homeland with dramatizing the impacts of the 'bloody-minded affirmations of nationalism' (177). Exploring the triangulated relationship between nationalism, family and nostalgia, the novels critique the failures of the postcolonial nation from the vantage point of diaspora and exile. In this context, nostalgia is leveraged to showcase the discontinuities between the emancipatory national project and the violence of nationalist ideologies that constitute the citizen as powerless subject.

The difficulty of writing the history of a 'broken' nation is a central question in Arabic literature. As Elias Khoury puts it in his novel *Mamlakat al-Ghurabā'* (1992, *Kingdom of Strangers*, 1996): '[w]e find stories tossed in the streets of our memory and the alleys of our imagination. How can we bring them together, to impose order on a land in which all order has been smashed to pieces?' (84). For the Libyan novelist Hisham Matar, the question he grapples with is 'how do you tell the story or the reality of existing in this very peculiar political atmosphere?' ('Reluctant Spokesman'). This chapter will explore Matar's question through examining how the imbrications of childhood, home and nation open up an exploration of complicated histories that have led to displacements and dislocations, where the nostalgic framing only amplifies the lack of resolution.

Hisham Matar's In the Country of Men *and* Anatomy of a Disappearance

In Hisham Matar's debut novel *In the Country of Men* ([2006], 2007), the protagonist Suleiman recalls the summer of 1979 in Libya, when his father was arrested for dissident activity. Christopher Micklethwait notes that the novel 'exposes and critiques the mechanisms of state power in a violent hyper-vigilant postcolonial dictatorship' through the child narrator's perspective on the surveillance, show trials and public executions of a police state (174). Along similar lines, Nouri Gana has argued that Matar's novels convey 'the power of the state apparatuses to penetrate the lives of Libyans and extend its rule over them with their own consent and collaboration' (20). This pervasive surveillance, and the fear it provokes, is established in an early scene in *In the Country of Men* where a restaurant owner demonstrates his loyalty to the dictator by 'chant[ing], loud enough for all the restaurant to hear, "long live the Guide" toward a large mural he had had a couple of art students paint at one end of the restaurant' (18). Suleiman is aware that this is intended as a performance for a particular audience: 'if the restaurant had a table of revolutionary committee men or Mokhabarat, people we called antennae, he chanted El Fateh, El Fateh, El Fateh, punching the air with his fist' (19). The restaurant owner's actions dramatize the 'fear of being watched, of becoming an object of knowledge in the state's disciplining of the citizenry' which forces citizens 'to comply with and reproduce affectations of loyalty and subservience to the regime' (Micklethwait 175). This scene is paralleled later on in the novel, when Suleiman watches as Moosa, one of his father's friends, hangs up a portrait of Gaddafi in the family reception room to ward off suspicion: '[t]he benefactor, the father of the nation, the guide [. . .] He punched his fist, chanting El Fateh, El Fateh, El Fateh' (160-1). In identifying the dictator as '[t]he benefactor, the father of the nation' Moosa mocks the regime's assumption of paternal authority to justify its autocratic reign. Yet, like the restaurant owner who makes a performance of saluting the mural of the Guide in his restaurant, Moosa ensures that there is a large portrait of Gaddafi in Suleiman's home – notably, this portrait of the Guide replaces the smaller portrait of Suleiman's father, Faraj. The scene thus dramatizes the antagonistic parallels between the father and the 'benefactor, the father of the nation' through the perspective of Suleiman and his evolution into a participant in a culture of betrayal (160).

The novel charts Suleiman's loss of innocence as he betrays his best friend, and later informs on his father to the friendly security man patrolling outside the family home. Rather than being framed as a condemnable action, Suleiman's betrayal is represented as though it was inevitable, as a development which draws him into the system governing the country, 'the country of men' signifying not only the opposite of a country of law, but also Suleiman's induction into a society where men are both beneficiaries of and victimized by the patriarchal autocratic system.

The novel opens with Suleiman's conflicted relationship with his mother, which is described in paradoxical terms as 'an intimacy' and as 'the innermost memory I have of love', even though Suleiman later recognizes that in this relationship '[t]here was anger, there was pity, even the dark warm embrace of hate' (21). Especially in the beginning of the novel, as Robert F. Worth points out in his review, the focus is on 'the claustrophobic intimacy of an only child's intense bond with his desperately lonely mother' (Worth).[6] This bond is intensified by Suleiman's confusion about what is happening around him, from his mother's alcohol addiction disguised as illness to his father's secret dissident activities. The interrelated levels of claustrophobic home and nation are related through the euphemisms Suleiman's parents employ in an attempt to create an illusion of a normal family, euphemisms which mirror the discourse of a stable and secure homeland that cares for its citizens. The charade of a happy home is however placed under tension by the mother's storytelling. Suleiman recalls: 'though I feared those nights when we were alone and she was ill, I never wanted her to stop talking. Her story was mine too, it bound us, turned us into one.' Asserting 'her story was mine too', Suleiman constructs an identity based on his mother's past, even as Najwa is revising his understanding of that past and shattering his illusions about the family as refuge: '[t]he only things that mattered were in the past. And what mattered the most in the past was how she and Baba came to be married, that "black day" as she called it' (21). Suleiman learns that his mother was forced into a hastily arranged marriage after her family discovers an innocent high school romance. Already in the opening pages, when Najwa tells Suleiman '[o]ne day, you'll be a man and take me away', we see Suleiman's interpellation into the 'Country of Men' (12).

The overlap between home and homeland often 'reveals its deeper affiliation with the public realm, as a patriarchal space where power relations vital to the nation and culture are negotiated' (Strehle 1). In Matar's novel, the opening pages introduce us to a close-knit relationship between a mother and son which is shaped by the absent father's presence. It is Najwa's resentment at her marriage which fuels her 'unpredictability and her urgent stories' (21) and associate her in Suleiman's mind with a figure of resistance: '[s]he never started the story from the beginning; like Scheherazade she didn't move in a straight line' (11). In a study on childhood in Arabic autobiography, Tetz Rooke argues that, given the parallel between patriarchal family and autocratic government, it is unsurprising that 'a successful challenge of repressive family rules reflects a collective dream of a freer and more equal society' (237). Through making his parallel then, Matar offers us a familiar framework through which to connect the storyteller as a resistance figure, both within the family and in society. Crucially however, Najwa rejects this comparison with Scheherazade and refuses the compromise the storyteller makes at the end of her tales: 'your heroine's boldness was to ask to be allowed [. . .] [t]o live' (16). It is at this point that Najwa connects the powerlessness of living in a dictatorship with her own circumscribed life. Despite her non-conformist views, she constantly reiterates that '[h]ere it's either silence or exile, walk by the wall or leave' (52). Her resignation, both politically and in private life, is linked to her resentment of Scheherazade as a figure who is represented as 'accepting – always accepting – a life forced upon her' (86).

Through the linking of Najwa and Scheherazade, Matar highlights the parallels between oppression on the level of the family and the nation, where the mother's forbidden stories seem to be an attempt to inoculate Suleiman against the pervasive logic of submission to the heads of households and countries. Despite the fact that Najwa herself is unable to escape this logic, she constantly expresses her desire to escape even the framework of the homeland which she feels perpetuates a subjugation to authority: 'let me see the clouds above my country [. . .] I want to look down and see it a distant map, reduced to lines, reduced to an idea' (95). In taking this stance, Najwa expressly stands against her husband Faraj's nationalist activism and his dissident politics, which she depicts as a dangerous megalomania, stating that 'Faraj can fly after his dreams all he wants but not me, I won't follow' (96). Najwa disparages dissidents, depicting them as irresponsible 'children playing with fire' (95) and specifically critiques her husband's 'crazy dreams' (80). At the same time, perhaps in order to ensure Suleiman's safety, she insists on him understanding the consequences of political dissidence by watching the regime's propaganda, including televised executions. While his father Faraj attempts to shield him – '[h]e shouldn't see this' – Najwa insists, '[i]t's his country too' (33). The complex motivations of Najwa and her conflicted relationship to her homeland allows Matar to undercut the national narrative that 'assigns Woman a fixed role as an historical metaphor' to instead explore the conflicted responses navigating life governed by repression on the familial and national level (Fayad 148).

Despite Najwa's best efforts, Suleiman gradually becomes enmeshed in Faraj's political activities in ways she cannot control. When Suleiman watches the televised interrogation of Ustath Rashid, his father's close friend, he hears a question about his father, and reflects that '[i]t was strange to hear Baba's name on television'. The regime's knowledge of his family is further underscored when he is directly named in his father's *kunīa*[7] as '[t]he voice reread the name, this time inserting "Bu Suleiman" into Baba's name, which [. . .] made [Suleiman] feel implicated, dragged by [his] name into something [he] knew nothing about' (114). Later, Faraj is imprisoned, and, when he is released, Suleiman is initially unable to recognize him due to the effects of torture on his face. This traumatic moment is compounded by Suleiman's eventual realization that the reason Faraj is released is because he has confessed and given the names of his co-conspirators. In fact, the debate between Suleiman and Najwa over whether Scheherazade is 'a coward who accepted slavery over death' (14) or 'a brave woman who [. . .] gained her freedom through inventing tales' (15) is played out in the choices made by the two dissidents represented in the novel: Rashid, who does not betray his friend and is executed, and Faraj who cooperates and is released. Neither choice is represented as the right one. There is no heroism, only horror, in Rashid's execution in the national basketball stadium, while Faraj loses his friends and his business after he is released from prison, and lives with his betrayal of his own ideals. The older narrator who looks back on these events understands this, but through the retrospective narration we also feel the confusion the younger Suleiman feels in witnessing these events. Interweaving scenes of a child playing with neighbours and picking fruit from the mulberry tree with scenes of a child watching televised interrogations confuses nostalgically framed memories with extreme violence and terror. The effect highlights the extent to which childhood memories and nostalgic conceptions of family are not only interrupted by but can be constituted through an awareness of the entanglements of the political and the personal, and the violence intrinsic in state power.

The extent of state power on the family is made visible through the disciplining of dissidents as though they are children. When Ustath Rashid is arrested and interrogated on national television, Suleiman notes that 'he looked like a schoolboy in detention' (113), and when he is sentenced to be hanged, Suleiman is discomfited by the fact that 'he didn't cry honourably, he cried like a baby' (185). The descriptions of the infantilization of the adults around Suleiman form a narrative of lost innocence. In one especially poignant scene, Suleiman's mother Najwa is described in child-like terms when she asks for help from a neighbour who is the wife of 'an Antenna, a man of the Mokhabarat'. The wife reassures Najwa by relating a story that presents the Guide in a fatherly light, asking a would-be assassin why he would attempt to kill him: '[w]hen [the assassin] was caught, the Guide sat with him and asked, "why did you want to kill me, my son?"' (160–1). In this scene, the paternalistic reassurance that makes clear that the dictator alone can offer mercy lays bare the power dynamics of the nation-as-family. The wife's story leaves Najwa looking 'astonished, hopeful, ridiculously naïve' in Suleiman's eyes, as much a 'ridiculous child' as he recognizes himself to be when he looks back on his childhood need for a 'steady and unchangeable concern. In a time of blood and tears [. . .] I was the ridiculous child craving concern' (168). Here an anxiety emerges that nostalgia is itself an infantilizing or regressive emotion. However, this anxiety does not banish the nostalgic mood. On one hand, Matar underscores the connection between the family and the homeland in terms of the expectation of security and stability, and on the other, his writing shows how the home and the homeland can be the most 'unhomely' places, leaving the focalizing character feeling, as Suleiman does after watching the execution of Ustath Rashid, 'as if at any moment the rug could be pulled from beneath my feet' (198). The fact that the various traumatic incidents in this novel are not given in a linear narrative form but as disjointed parts break up the narrative in the same way that the protagonist's present keeps being disrupted by the past.

In the Country of Men traces the disillusionment with nationalist discourse related to the idea of the nation-as-family, which ultimately ends with a disavowal of nationalist ideology. Here there is a correlation between physically leaving the homeland and letting go of the past, which is an intrinsic part of narrating the history of the nation from the vantage point of exile. Towards the end of the novel, Suleiman's parents decide to send him away to Egypt 'to thrive away from the madness' (228). However, having failed to return to complete his military service, Suleiman then becomes 'an evader', his escape from the nation itself becoming a problem (231). Citing the terminology of Gaddafi's regime, which labelled dissidents abroad as *kilāb ḍālla* (stray dogs), Suleiman rhetorically wonders '[w]hy does our country long for us so savagely? What could we possible give her that hasn't already been taken?' (231). This juxtaposition of 'longing' and 'savagery' captures Suleiman's conflicted feelings of nostalgia for a homeland that has inflicted suffering on his family. In this context, the gendered cultural logic ('her') is complicated, the theme of longing for a nurturing motherland undercut when cast in malevolent terms.[8]

At the end of Matar's *In the Country of Men*, we re-encounter Suleiman in exile, having resigned himself to never returning to his homeland. We read that it is 'astonishing' to Suleiman 'how free [he] came to feel from Libya'. He concludes that '[n]ationalism is as thin as a thread, perhaps that's why many feel it must be anxiously guarded' (230). This might be taken as a conscious form of 'unwriting' the nation, in Rosemary George's terms, where she suggests that 'immigration [. . .] unwrites nation and national projects because it flagrantly displays a rejection of one national space for another more desirable location, albeit with some luggage carried over' (186). Despite this declaration of being freed from nationalism however, Suleiman describes an 'an ever-present absence' which leaves him feeling 'like an orphan not entirely certain of what he has missed or gained through his unchosen loss' (233). As Said puts it, though exile is 'strangely compelling to think about, it is terrible to experience', since its 'essential sadness can never be surmounted' (*Reflections* 173). The change that Suleiman undergoes is one where the strength of nationalist feeling fades yet remains as an ambivalent feeling of loss. The political violence that in part prevents return to the homeland simultaneously prevents the unwriting of the nation, since that violence plays itself out at the level of the home. The structure of *In the Country of Men*, retrospectively narrated from the older Suleiman's perspective, draws the reader to anticipate some resolution. However, the end offers little sense of closure, as we leave Suleiman in exile, without fully understanding how his life has changed. Matar's novel is ultimately about the limbo and the pathos of failing to live up to a nationalist legacy, the difficulty of fully comprehending national realities from the vantage point of diaspora.

In the Country of Men was published in 2006, in the years following Libya's rehabilitation on the international stage. In his review of the novel, David Dabydeen reflects on the connection between the novel's message and the mood at the time to 'move beyond' the history of animosity:

> 'People should not forget the past, they should move beyond it,' Blair said of his visit to Tripoli. It is this platitude that Hisham Matar, a Libyan exile, confronts in his debut novel, which chooses to remember the brutality of Libya under Gaddafi. (Dabydeen)

In 'choosing to remember' and depicting the brutality of autocratic regimes, Matar is concerned with the possibility of providing an account that is able to convey the traumas of nationalist violence, which plays out at the level of a self-reflexive interrogation of how to tell the story of the nation. Matar's works have been described as 'autobiographical novels' which feature an 'indexicality of Libya and its history' (Harlow 444). Yet the attempt to write such a history fails in the novels themselves, which instead focus on the destruction of efforts to write down alternative national histories. For example, Suleiman recalls that his uncle Khaled had written a text 'before he went off to America' which 'took him seven years to write and [. . .] read like a long poem, telling the history of our country'. However, this endeavour has a farcical end; when Khaled returns from America, he finds that his writings 'had been devoured by the family's chickens' (146). This story echoes in a comedic tone another scene of destroyed writing, where the family burns the books and writings of Suleiman's father to keep the texts from the secret police. Suleiman witnesses this scene of burning, a deliberate forgetting for survival, and decides to save one of the books from the fire. As the reader might anticipate, the saved book returns at the end of the novel, when Suleiman learns that his father is again sent to prison in part because of his own earlier act of rebellion: 'after fifteen years [...] Baba decided to take his book with him one day and read from it to his fellow factory workers [...] the book I had rescued from the fire' (236). In later life, when Suleiman considers his father's actions, he wonders: 'had he managed to delude himself that he could still change things? Had he come to prefer death over slavery, unlike my Scheherazade, refusing to live under the sword?' (237). This question is connected to Suleiman's earlier comparison of his mother's storytelling and his uncle's written poetry: 'How well could he, Uncle Khaled, the "great poet" as Baba called him, write under Shahrayar's sword? What would come out? Could he make music, could he sing? Scheherazade did, night after night [...] It's one thing not to fear death, another to sing under its sword' (66). There is a self-reflexive element to this question, as Scheherazade here is invoked initially as a figure of resistance and later as someone accepting subordination. This shift follows the trajectory of the novel into a form of mourning for the nation that is now the object of nostalgic narrative. The rendering of the homeland is thus ambivalent and contradictory, represented both as an idealized space with emancipatory potential and as a narrow and claustrophobic site of violence and control.

Like *In the Country of Men*, Matar's second novel, *Anatomy of a Disappearance* (2011), centres on the relationship between father and son in the context of political struggle and efforts to further national liberation. Significantly, in *Anatomy of a Disappearance* the family's homeland is unnamed, allowing Matar to superimpose, via metonym, the persistence of oppressive dictatorships across the region.[9] At the beginning of this novel, the young narrator Nuri el-Alfi lives with his father Kamal, an 'ex-minister and leading dissident' in exile in Egypt (106). Exploring similar themes to Matar's first novel but focused more closely on the father–son relationship, this second novel is also a coming-of-age story about a son's struggle for intimacy, but that struggle is in this case extended indefinitely following the father's abduction and disappearance. At the novel's conclusion, Nuri has returned from England to Egypt, and in the final lines, is trying on his father's clothes, and then replacing them to await his return: '[t]his might still fit him. I returned it to its place' (246). These lines capture the condition of being suspended in the past, in the limbo that is the psychological shadow of a disappearance, without the finality of bereavement. Metaphorically, this suspension of temporality, the inability to come to terms with an undetermined fate, extends to the exile's relationship to the lost homeland, the unhealable rift that makes belonging always contingent, and which inspires a nostalgia for a time before this severance.

In a way similar to Suleiman's discovery of his father's activism, Nuri becomes aware of Kamal's political activities by 'search[ing] the indexes' of his father's books: '[i]t was not until [he] encountered [his] father's name – Kamal Pasha el-Alfi – that [he] realised what [he] was looking for.' Again, the father's name represents the intersection of political and personal. In both scenes, histories of violence intrude suddenly into the protagonist's life: as Nuri reflects, '[he] read these things about [his] father before [he] could understand what they meant' (26). Reading about his father's political activities, Nuri images himself fulfilling the same roles: 'I, too, wanted secret meetings in Geneva, allies in Paris with whom I had watched history march and worked to change its course' (90).[10] While this romanticized idea of espionage and being an agent of historical change highlights Nuri's childishness, it also paints the nostalgia of childhood with the patina of violence and threat. From the start of the novel, Nuri contrasts his father's nationalist sense of purpose with his own unsettled identity. When Kamal's friend Taleb tells Nuri 'he wanted someone to inherit it all', Nuri understands the significance of the word 'inheritance' as it presents the obligation towards a political cause in terms of a familial legacy (*Anatomy* 62). The dynamic of inheritance presents the national project in familial terms, giving an emotional impact to the ambivalence felt towards the nation. Having failed to commit himself politically, Nuri describes feeling 'guilty [. . .] at having lost [his father], not knowing how to find him or take his place. Every day I let my father down' (108). This sense of betrayal of the father's nationalist work ties in with the discussion of patrilineage here. The ambivalence about taking the father's place becomes a political indictment as well as a personal failure.

Discussing his second novel, Matar notes that he is 'fascinated with the structure of the family [. . .] One of the questions that *Anatomy of a Disappearance* is asking is, is it possible to ever know your parent [. . .] But also [. . .] how do you tell the story or the reality of existing in this very peculiar political atmosphere?' Both Matar's novels explore familial bonds in a context where, as he puts it, 'private life is infiltrated regularly by these regimes' ('Reluctant Spokesman').[11] In other words, Matar's novels might be said to explore what Homi Bhabha describes as the 'unhomely' intrusion where 'the intimate recesses of the domestic space become sites for history's most intricate invasions' and where 'the border between home and world becomes confused; and, uncannily, the private and the public become part of each other, forcing upon us a vision that is as divided as it is disorienting' ('The World and the Home' 141). The unhomely is a term Bhabha derives from Freud's notion of *unheimlich*, 'the name for everything that ought to have remained secret and hidden but has come to light' (Freud 224). However, Bhabha redefines it slightly in order to speak to 'the estranging sense of the relocation of the home and the world in an unhallowed place' (141). In *Anatomy of a Disappearance*, the violent intrusion of the state into the home reveals the contingency of a protected private sphere and the beguiling illusion of an all-inclusive national project.

In a way similar to Matar's first novel, the permeability of the home is dramatized through Nuri witnessing his parents arguing, when Nuri's mother Ihsan raises an objection to the idea that Nuri should 'inherit' Kamal's project:

'Don't transfer the weight of the past onto your son,' she once told him.
'You can't live outside history,' he argued. 'We have nothing to be ashamed of. On the contrary.'

After a long pause she responded, 'Who said anything about shame? It's longing that I want to spare him. Longing and the burden of your hopes.' (26)

In this early scene, Matar stages the choice of either therapeutic forgetting or traumatic remembering, capturing the dilemma that will haunt Nuri for the remainder of the novel. The parental dynamics here are slightly different than the first novel, in that Ihsan seeks to protect her son by pushing against Kamal's efforts to educate him, rather than insisting he understand what is happening. In fact, Nuri recalls that his mother shielded him from the father's 'secret work'. However, the outcome is similar, in that in this novel too the dissident father's 'daydreaming' is experienced as out of joint with his parental role, Nuri feeling 'as if [Kamal] were the boy obliged to share a meal with adults, as if he were the son and I the father' (8). Matar explores the discrepancies between the utopian project to reform the nation and everyday reality through these familial dynamics, allowing us to reflect on the costs to political activism. Nuri is aware, for example, that Ihsan has suffered due to Kamal's work: 'Mother looked better in photographs taken before I was born. I do not mean simply younger but altogether brighter [. . .] her eyes anticipating more joy' (35). The conflict between Nuri's parents regarding the extent to which he should be involved in Kamal's politics is an aspect of their ideological differences, including their religious beliefs. Nuri remembers that before Ihsan's death Kamal had seen religion as unhelpful to the nationalist project and 'often greeted Mother's references to the divine with irritated sarcasm' (7). Later however, when Kamal begins to become more religious, Nuri resents his father's encroachment on 'Mother's territory' (27).[12] The differences in Nuri's parents' approach to faith and religion cements the ideological conflict at the level of both home and nation, inextricable from the failures of the nationalist project.

Matar depicts the disillusionment with nationalist structures metaphorically through the disintegration of the family unit, undercutting the notion of singular cultural origins through revealing an entangled and complex familial history. *Anatomy of a Disappearance* is on one level the story of three mothers, offering 'an anatomy of love, of Nuri's melancholy love for his dead mother; the filial love for his family's devoted housekeeper Naima; and the dangerous love for his stepmother Mona' (Gurría-Quintana). The most dramatic turning point in the novel is arguably not the father's mysterious disappearance, but the revelation that Naima is Nuri's birth mother.[13] If nation-as-family is based on the notion 'that the nation, like the family, has a single point of origin', the revelation of mistaken origins and unclear lineages undermines that analogy (Puri 133). Significantly, the period of Naima's arrival into the family is narrated together with the repercussions of the event that exiles them: '[e]ighteen months after my parents employed Naima, our king was dragged to the courtyard of the palace and shot in the head.' This one sentence, we later understand, conjoins the beginning of the unhomely 'secret' in the family (the fact that Naima is Nuri's mother) and the violence that prevents them from returning home. The nostalgic narrative that would seek to affirm connection to the homeland is here undercut by the realities and discontinuities of exile, by the recognition of the geographic and linguistic rifts which themselves inspire nostalgia.

Matar's autobiographical work, *The Return: Fathers, Sons and the Land in Between* (2016), narrates his return to Libya following the 2011 uprising, seeking to find out more about the abduction and disappearance of his own father, Jaballa Matar, a dissident disappeared by the secret service and not heard from since the mid-1990s.[14] Though Matar has argued that his novels are not autobiographical, the themes that repeat in his fictional texts are clearly related to his own experiences, the triad of fathers, sons, and 'the land in between' examined in his non-fiction writing. However, I would argue that it also relates more broadly to a generation in exile, mourning the passing of an earlier generation's progressive dreams. In both of Matar's novels, the protagonists' conflicted relationship with their dissident fathers is accompanied by the recognition that they are unable to continue their nationalist work. Despite their differences, both novels contrast an idealized notion of nation-as-family, which is often deployed as a way to confer legitimacy on political collectives, against the realities of violence that extend from the state into the home. The child-protagonists become the focus of reader empathy, where the figure of the 'disappeared' father and the trauma of that disappearance represent a loss of innocence and an awakening to the depredations of the state.

In an article written shortly after the publication of his first novel, *In the Country of Men* (2007), Hisham Matar asks: '[h]ow can one write under the weight of inconclusive grief?' ('Inconclusive'). The question relates to the author's inability to mourn his father, but also speaks to the 'inconclusive' nature of the past given ongoing political violence which leads to an inability to 'move on' from the past and from an attachment to the homeland. Elsewhere, Matar writes of his 'silent condemnation of those fellow-exiles who wished to assimilate – which is to say [his] bloody-minded commitment to rootlessness' as '[his] feeble act of fidelity to the old country' or perhaps 'to the young boy [he] was' when he left the country ('The Return'). In this paradoxical statement that presents rootlessness as an act of fidelity to childhood and to country, to be rootless is not (only) a position of hybridity, but rather is refigured as a refusal to abandon the past, as an investment in the 'old country' that was once a homeland, or perhaps in a younger self. This statement simultaneously asserts connection and acknowledges that a return is not possible, gesturing towards commitment as it undertakes a disavowal of belonging.

Leila Aboulela's *Minaret*

Sudanese British novelist Leila Aboulela was born and educated in Khartoum and has since lived in Scotland and Dubai. She has published a number of short stories as well as novels, beginning with her debut novel *The Translator* in 1999. This first novel sketches some of the themes Aboulela returns to throughout her work. The protagonist, Sammar, is a widow who is attempting to begin her life anew. The novel connects Sammar's psychological journey to the kindling of a romantic relationship with the professor she works for as the eponymous translator. The main conflict in the novel turns on Sammar's attempts to convince the professor to convert to Islam so they can marry, moving the narrative forward through a familiar romance plot but also using the themes of religious conversion to explore Sammar's own spiritual reawakening and newfound purpose. Given the themes which recur in her works, Aboulela's novels are typically discussed in relation to Islamism, faith-based identity and gender politics, dimensions that I will also partly address in my discussion. However, Aboulela's novels, in particular her second novel *Minaret*, are also deeply concerned with the failures of nationalist politics and the legacies of the postcolonial state's formation.

Minaret follows the protagonist Najwa's transformation from her privileged life in Khartoum to her family's exile, after the president Jaafar al-Nimeiry is ousted in a coup.[15] As Mike Phillips suggests, '[t]he story of Najwa's fall unfolds with the deliberate inevitability of a morality tale, but in the process Aboulela describes the uncertainty and terror of the country's westernised elite in the 80s' ('Faith Healing'). The coup brings the protagonist's privileged life to a sudden end, resulting in the arrest of her father, known as 'Mr Ten Per Cent' for his corruption (8). In contrast to Matar's work, in this novel the protagonist is implicated not in dissidence but in her father's corrupt politics. Najwa is forced to confront the reality of her father's ill-gained wealth when she meets with another university student, the Marxist Anwar, who believes that '[l]andowning families, capitalists, the aristocracy [. . .] were to blame [. . .] for the mess our country was in' (11). Following the coup, the family is forced into exile in London, and Najwa replaces her father's nationalist politics with a transnational religious identity, turning towards the multi-ethnic community at her mosque. In this case borrowing elements of conversion narrative rather than the marriage plot of her first novel, Aboulela uses the trajectory of spirituality to frame Najwa's journey towards finding solace in a depoliticized religious narrative.

In a way similar to the scenes of recognition in Matar's novels, Najwa's sense of implication in her father's crimes is dramatized in a central scene where her surname becomes an accusation:

> [Anwar] was explicit now, using my father's name – my surname [. . .] that was my name in the direct accusation of my father. That was my name that made everyone laugh. I was an aristocrat, yes, from my mother's side, with a long history of acres of land and support for the British and hotels in the capital and bank accounts aboard. And if all that wasn't bad enough, my father stood accused of corruption. (38)

The father–daughter relationship in Aboulela's novel differs from the father–son dynamics in Matar's novels, relating not to a failure to live up to the father's work but to shame at his implication in corruption. Aboulela is also more interested in Najwa's negotiation of her exile than in examining the anxiety of inheriting parental legacies. However, in both cases, the protagonists experience political suppression, corruption and war through the direct impact on their family – in particular, their implication in the political activities or betrayals of their fathers. In *Minaret*, the reasons for exile are first hinted at with this moment of public shaming which puts the protagonist on the path to disillusionment and rejection of her father's politics. Aboulela is concerned with dramatizing the guilt by association that in part motivates Najwa's later rejection of nationalist frameworks. Initially, Najwa is oblivious to the not-so-hidden 'secret' of her father's corruption and is primarily concerned about the family's position in society, 'liv[ing] at a certain standard' (35). However, like in Matar's novels where the protagonists realize that they are indirectly implicated in dissident activities, Najwa's awareness that she is publicly connected to her father's corruption involves a sudden uncovering of secrets that come to light and destabilize the idea of the secure, private sphere of home. In Bhabha's terms, '[t]he home does not remain the domain of domestic life, nor does the world simply become its social or historical counterpart. The unhomely is the shock of recognition of the world-in-the-home, the-home-in-the-world' ('The World and the Home' 141). The shock of recognition in this moment of shaming complicates any formulation of home through a nostalgic lens.

Following her father's execution and the family's exile, the disintegration of the family is represented as a fall from grace which 'seemed to have no end, as if we would fall and fall for eternity'. As Najwa reflects '[they] became unfamiliar to each other simply because [they] had not seen each other fall before' (61). The family's fall structures *Minaret*, splitting Najwa's life into before and after the coup, between her life as a privileged teenager raised in a secular family in Sudan, and her life as a practising Muslim working as a maid/nanny for Arab families in London. The family once used to holiday in London, the same city they flee to as exiles. Aboulela sensitively explores the impact of such a catastrophe on the family, and in this case in particular on Najwa's mother. Although the protagonist sees her mother as a self-assured woman who would 'rise to whatever the situation demanded' (19) after the family's exile, Najwa sees her mother fall apart, 'sometimes crying for no reason, muttering to herself in the middle of the night' (56). When the family receives a call from the exiled president, Najwa's mother is unable to challenge him: '"[i]t's all his fault," she said afterwards, "it's all his fault." But on the phone, she had been [. . .] respectful in the same way she always had been with His Excellency' (59). The failure of her mother to take a stand leads to Najwa having conflicted emotions about their relationship, though she continues to take care of her mother through the long illness that leads to her death. Aboulela resists romanticizing exile or representing the mother-figure as someone able to nurture love for the homeland. Instead, Najwa is left alone with her responsibilities, towards not only her mother but also her twin brother Omar, who soon becomes involved in a life of crime and drugs.

Aboulela dwells on the mutilations of involuntary exile contrasted to the family's previously privileged freedom to travel. It is only after her father's execution that Najwa looks back on her life of privilege with shame, recalling herself and Omar as 'children from hot Khartoum coming to London every summer – walking into an ice-skating rink in Queensway as if they had every right to be there. Money did that. Money gave [them] rights' (94). Nostalgia for this privileged childhood is interrelated to nostalgia for the homeland throughout the novel, as for example when Najwa feels an affinity to 'princesses in exile':

> I cut out the pictures of princesses in exile: daughters of the Shah, daughters of the late King of Egypt, the descendants of the Ottoman Sultan. They were all floating in Europe knowing they were royal, but it didn't matter, it didn't matter anymore. (178)

Though in the opening pages Najwa claims that she does 'not brood or look back' except when 'a shift makes [her] remember', much of the novel is in fact concerned with her 'look[ing] back' at her life in Khartoum (1). So, for example, she feels close to a Sudanese employer because she 'needed to sit within range of her nostalgia' (143). The comforting space that nostalgia offers is offset against her feeling of alienation, unlike the 'Muslims girls who have been born and brought up in Britain' who 'strike [her] as being very British, very much at home in London' (77). To find her own way to be at home in London, Najwa eventually turns to the mosque, making being Muslim her primary identity, replacing a national identity that maps onto origins and roots with a religious identity that is derived from dress and practice.

As in her first novel, Aboulela hangs her exploration of these themes onto a romance plot, in this case Najwa's romantic relationship with Tamer, the much younger son of her employer. Though this plot does not develop much over the course of the novel, their scenes become moments of reflecting on their experiences of being in-between identities. Since Tamer shares not only Najwa's experiences of dislocation but also her finding faith as an answer to alienation, the two share what Boym calls 'diasporic intimacy', which stems from shared histories of displacement (252–3). Like Najwa, who increasingly turns away from a national identity, Tamer's mother describes him as 'Sudanese in name only' (71). This statement captures the hierarchy between the homeland and the diaspora, where processes of acculturation are seen to delegitimize the claim to an 'authentic' national identity. When Tamer explains to Najwa his confused sense of his identity, he states:

> My mother is Egyptian. I've lived everywhere except in Sudan: Oman, Cairo, here. My education is Western and that makes me feel that I am Western. My English is stronger than my Arabic. So I guess, no, I don't feel very Sudanese, though I would like to be. (*Minaret* 110)

The qualifications in this passage, and the final comment on wishing to be Sudanese though being unable to claim that identity, demonstrates how diaspora can be seen as 'the bastard child of the nation – disavowed, inauthentic, illegitimate, an impoverished imitation of the originary culture' (Gopinath 317). Aboulela presents both Tamer and Najwa's turn to religion as an alternative form of affective belonging to offset this lack of national identity. Living elsewhere, being educated differently and, importantly, being linguistically more competent in English translates, for Tamer, into the conclusion that he is not 'very Sudanese'. However, this does not

3. National Histories and Family Narratives

resolve the problem of defining identity, and the ongoing importance of the past. As Najwa puts it, 'I try to forget the past, to move on, but I'm not good at it. I'm not European' (118). In both these statements, 'Sudanese in name only' and 'not European', Tamer and Najwa's sense of self is based on the negation of an identity that leaves them feeling distanced from Sudan but unable to 'forget the past'.

The inability to forget underlines the problem with 'the therapeutic approach to history' which 'seeks to effect a premature closure to political crises [...] that admit of no such easy resolutions'. The argument has been made that such a 'global cure' is 'not so much an abolition of the past but its integration into wider, "normalising" narratives of the kind found in advanced European or Anglo-American societies' (Gibbons, Kirby and Cronin 91). Such normalizing narratives would suggest that the problems of the past are in the past and looking back on them in the present should be framed in terms of remembrance or reconciliation. However, in the novels that I have discussed thus far, such normalizing narratives would elide the ongoing impact of political crises. It is precisely because the instability is ongoing that moving on becomes difficult; as Najwa reflects, to build a future she feels she must at least understand 'how it would feel to have [...] a stable country':

> [a] place where we could make future plans and it wouldn't matter who the government was – they wouldn't mess up our day-to-day lives. A country that was a familiar, reassuring background, a static landscape on which to paint dreams. A country we could leave at any time, return to at any time and it would be there for us, solid, waiting. (165)

There is an irony to Najwa's subsequent comment that growing up she had a 'fractured country but not a broken home' – though she goes on to explain this, pointing out 'my parents didn't divorce', the separation of the family, their exile, the months of waiting for a verdict on the trial, and finally the father's execution all demonstrate the interrelationship of the fractured country and the broken home (165). Envying how others live their lives, 'how [their life] moves forward' with 'no fragmentation, nothing stunted', Najwa describes her own experience as repetitive: 'I circle back, I regress; the past doesn't let go' (118). She experiences her mode of nostalgia as one which 'constantly closes down the horizons of becoming by pulling back everything to a single point of origin' (Papastergiadis 14). The affective longing for belonging can morph into the fixity of a particular kind of nostalgia which seeks to 'go back in time', as Najwa does in Aboulela's novel, as an outright rejection of the present.

Najwa is not the only character depicted as struggling to come to terms with exile and make a place for herself in the new society. For Anwar, a Marxist student in Khartoum who flees the country after an Islamist coup and seeks asylum in London, 'the bitter reality of Sudan' becomes an obsession driving the myth of return. At least initially, he insists that '[i]f the government fell today [he] would go back tomorrow' (109). Najwa reflects on how this condition of always awaiting return transforms Anwar's life: '[f]or him [...] London was temporary, exotic. His life was on hold, he was constantly waiting to go back and take up his rightful place' (76). As the narrative focuses more on Najwa's life in London, it becomes clear that the instability of 'back home' is inextricable from the current lives that the immigrants lead. In one scene where Najwa and Anwar walk through London, they express their envy of people in the crowd they see as having a 'stable country':

> In Queensway, in High Street Kensington, we would watch the English, the Gulf Arabs, the Spanish, Japanese, Malaysian, Americans and wonder how it would feel to have, like them, a stable country [...] That was why we were here: governments fell and coups were staged and that was why we were here. (174)

The repetition of the reminder 'that was why we were here' suggests the extent to which the conflict back home continues to shape the lives of immigrants whose imagined return hinges on political change: nostalgia is interrelated with the traumatic inability to 'to forget the past, to move on' (*Minaret* 118). The impact of the instability 'back home' flows through the narrative, as for example when Najwa's uncle Samir ruthlessly cuts his ties to his homeland: '[i]t's called immigrating. I've had it up to here with incompetence and instability' (124). Similarly, while Anwar initially puts his life on hold, seeing himself as awaiting return to the homeland, we follow his gradual transformation as he finds himself tempering his antiimperialist stance as an asylum seeker in London:

> [h]e used English words more and more, was less sharp in his criticism of the West. And this was the same Anwar who had led student demonstrations against the IMF and burnt the American flag. I did not dare ask him if he felt his antiimperialist convictions contradicted seeking political asylum in London. (156)

Having once attributed responsibility for the wrongs of the world to the global forces of imperialism and capitalism, Anwar comes to enjoy the anonymity of life in London, telling Najwa: 'here no one knows our background, no one knows whose daughter you are, no one knows my politics. We are both niggers, equals' (157). While there is an obvious irony to this juxtaposition of terms, it represents Anwar's movement away from the preoccupation with the specific political circumstances of his country to a broader identification with marginality in the metropolitan centre, which he suggests here is potentially empowering.

In contexts marked by ongoing political instability, nostalgic modes of identification must grapple with the nebulousness and precariousness of home not only in the diaspora but also in the 'homeland' itself. Najwa and Anwar are described as having 'bonded watching the Gulf War on TV' (229), activating a different kind of collective identity. In fact, Najwa notes that 'there was a sense of anti-climax now that the war was over [...] the news left us unfulfilled' (229). This curious description of war as 'fulfilling' suggests the subsuming of private grief into a political conflict that involves a heightened sense of community and justifies a withdrawal from the dominant culture. The centrality of the Gulf War for the protagonists is a result of the disturbing rupture that the war represents in the immigrant narrative of integration. Writing about the Arab community in Britain in 1992, Camillia El Solh argues that the war activated more dynamic understandings of collectivity and community (236). Paul Tabar similarly notes that '[a]lthough political tensions have always brought the question of loyalties and identities to the fore, very few world historical events have been as immediate and intense as the Gulf War was for Arab communities in the diaspora' (271). Reflecting on this formative experience for Arab diaspora, Fadia Faqir has described her own reaction to the war as an experience that disconnected her from society: 'you become so embittered and anguished over seeing yourself mutilated every day on screen that you build a castle around your immigrant heart and refuse to have anything to do with the host society' ('Stories' 59). The therapeutic approach to history assumes a degree of closure, and a process of mourning and memorialization. However, such narratives are contingent, based on what Judith Butler calls the differential 'grievability' of lives and the framing of violence (*Precarious Life*). Here, the description of watching the war as 'seeing yourself' claims the other as the self, while the metaphor of 'build[ing] a castle' involves constructing a protective, but also self-enclosing, space. Faqir describes withdrawal from the larger society with a metaphor that draws the borders of belonging as close as possible, yet claims strangers as part of the self.[16] Watching the war from a distance, on the television screen, emphasizes the disconnections from both home and the host society, as Faqir refers to it here. For Aboulela's protagonist, watching the start of the Iraqi invasion of Kuwait on television is a formative moment, shifting her self-conception from that of a privileged Sudanese teenager who holidays in London to a refugee from an unstable region.[17] This change gives her an acute sense of inferiority, described in visceral, disturbing language which reflects an internalization of racist discourse:

> for the first time in my life, I disliked London and envied the English, so unperturbed and grounded, never displaced, never confused. For the first time, I was conscious of my shitty-coloured skin next to their placid paleness. (174)

The war becomes another factor which furthers the protagonist's split sense of herself, divided between here and now and then and there, 'the Najwa who danced at the American Club disco in Khartoum' and 'Najwa, the maid Lamya hired by walking into the Central Mosque one afternoon' (111). This parallel between spaces highlights the fact that both the club and the mosque represent another cultural world, the club an enclave of Westernization in Sudan, the mosque in London offering an alternative connection to the homeland. The plot of the novel follows a movement towards creating new forms of attachments in exile, and in particular the connections the protagonist develops at the mosque, which is represented as an orientating structure: 'we never get lost because we see the minaret of the mosque and head home towards it' (118). The use of 'we' captures Najwa's transition from an alienated individual to a sense of belonging, replacing national frames with a transnational religious identity.

As I have mentioned earlier, the shift away from national frameworks towards transnational religion is a recurring theme in Aboulela's writing. Waïl Hassan describes Aboulela's novels as grounded in 'the Islamic resurgence that has attempted to fill the void left by the failure of Arab secular ideologies of modernity' (*Immigrant Narratives* 181). In an analysis of Aboulela's first novel *The Translator*, and its allusions to Tayeb Saleh's novel, *Season of Migration to the North* ([1969], 1991), Waïl Hassan concludes that

> whereas [Saleh's] are narratives of failure (of the national project, of the colonial bourgeoisie, of postcolonial intellectuals, of secular Arab ideologies of modernity), [Aboulela's] are narratives of redemption and fulfilment through Islam. (*Immigrant Narratives* 183)

In *Minaret*, Aboulela's Islamist-leaning discourse is similarly couched in the framework of a transnational Islam that dislocates itself not only from the national but also from the political. Aboulela spends some time elaborating this depoliticized notion of faith through the conversations between Najwa and Tamer. Having grown up outside Sudan, Tamer states: 'I guess being a Muslim is my identity.' Najwa too comes to share Tamer's sense of distance from national identity: 'things changed for me when I left Khartoum [...] now, like you, I just think of myself as a Muslim,' acknowledging that 'even while living here in London, [she has] changed' (110). Exchanging the stories leading to the formation of their identity politics, Tamer and Najwa come to express a faith-based identity. The wording of 'just [...] as a Muslim' and 'I guess being a Muslim' suggests both uncertainty and that the characters find a reassuring simplicity in their new identification.

In discussing her own religious identity, Aboulela describes faith as providing solace and identity across borders: 'I can carry [religion] with me wherever I go, whereas the other things can easily be taken away from me' ('Keep the Faith'). This portrayal of a transportable religion is reflected in *Minaret*, where Najwa finds a multinational group of friends in the central mosque in London, a community which represents a broader shift within Muslim diaspora. Katy Gardner describes this shift as the transformation of 'an Islam based around localised cultures and moulded to the culture and geography of the homelands' to 'an international Islam of Muslims from many difference countries and cultures' (Gardner 225). Through emphasizing the disengagement of Islam from particular national contexts, Aboulela portrays religion as a comfortable space to construct a transnational identity. The religious characters in *Minaret* in fact explicitly state their dissatisfaction with the politicization of faith. Religion becomes a space of retreat from the political problems they face in relation to both Britain and Sudan.[18] As Tamer notes, he resents the fact that 'unless you're political people think you're not a strong Muslim', and throughout the novel both he and Najwa defend their religious space against political engagements (117).

At various points, the religious characters reiterate their attitude of determinedly apolitical religiosity, as Najwa does when debating with the politically engaged Anwar. When Anwar points out the effects of Islamist fundamentalism on Sudan, Najwa seeks to turn the discussion to the private sphere, to the religious practice of her friends. Elsewhere in the novel, she expresses the wish that she and Tamer could 'go back in time. A time of horses and tents; swords and raids. We are both too simple for this time and place' (255). This nostalgia for a 'simpler' time connects to a perverse valuing of belonging over a 'modern' freedom, as Najwa describes her 'distorted desires' of being a 'concubine, like something out of the Arabian Nights, with life-long security and a sense of belonging' instead of 'settl[ing] for freedom in this modern time' (215). The intertwining of alienation and nostalgia here problematically highlights the escapist turn to an idealized past. As Waïl Hassan argues, Najwa's attitude represents a 'nostalgia for an idealized Arab past paradoxically and unreflectively conceived in Orientalist terms' (197). It is the consoling narrative of this idealized past that draws Najwa to her apolitical form of religion, in order to create a new narrative of belonging.

This connection between nostalgia and belonging is a theme Aboulela returns to often in her writing. For example, in her short story 'The Museum', the protagonist visits a museum to see 'sunlight and photographs of the Nile, something to appease her homesickness, a comfort, a message'. However, she soon realizes that 'the messages were not for her, not for anyone like her' (*Coloured Lights* 102–3). There is an interesting contrast here between the nostalgia for home and the notion of a global cultural heritage, which involves seeing beyond the local issues to view history from a more global perspective, but through a cosmopolitan framework which is not always experienced as inclusive. In *Minaret*, it is the mosque rather than the museum that becomes a place Najwa goes to in order to soothe her nostalgia. At the start of Najwa's religious journey, her new friends give her books to read, which feel familiar, 'as if [she] had known all this before and somehow, along the way, forgotten it' (240). In the following passage, Najwa articulates the attraction of an ideology that seems to hold the answers to her question:

> Refresh my memory. Teach me something old. Shock me. Comfort me. Tell me what will happen in the future, what happened in the past. Explain to me. Explain to me why I am here, what am I doing. Explain to me why I came down in the world. Was it natural, was it curable? (240)

As this passage suggests, religion is seen as offering a coherent narrative, the conversion narrative presented as an unambiguous spiritual awakening, a healing force. For Najwa the 'bits and pieces' of religion 'make [her] feel solid' (98). Elsewhere, she describes 'all the splinters inside her coming together' (66). The very apolitical nature of her faith provides a sense of completeness to a fractured subjectivity. While Anwar sees religion as being responsible for the conflict in Sudan, Najwa delinks the political realities of the nation from her construction of coherence around faith.

At the end of *Minaret*, Najwa is preparing to go on a pilgrimage to Mecca, having decided that her only community and identity is that of a Muslim. Some reviewers have picked up on the novel's confessional tone and the elements it borrows from spiritual autobiography to argue that the narrative arc ends on a rediscovering of self through faith. Mike Phillips for example has described the novel as tracing 'Najwa journey's from pride and confusion to humility and peace' ('Faith Healing'). The theme of atonement is one that Aboulela has commented on, expressing her view that 'Najwa will overcome the guilt [. . .] it will be the Hajj that will be the final stage in her process of completely getting over the past and becoming a new person' (Aboulela, 'Interview'). However, this attempt to become a new person through the pilgrimage represents a perfect example of the tensions between freedom from the constraints of imposed narratives and the re-entrenchment of identity politics. Moreover, the pilgrimage is not an event that occurs within the timeframe of the novel. Instead, the promise of the 'final stage' which will enable Najwa to get over the past remains an unfulfilled plan. Rather than ending with 'humility and peace', the last words of the novel are a dream, or rather a nightmare, of the destruction of the family home in Sudan, where Najwa dreams of being a child and waking up to find her parent's room 'in ruins' (276). The dream begins with Najwa imagining herself as a child surrounded by her parents 'sure that they love me' – a dream that captures the security of her childhood. However, in the dream her parent's room is 'dark and cluttered, all the possessions that distinguish us in ruins' (276). Here, the ruined family home becomes a microcosm for the ruined nation, the physical decline of the familiar space capturing the sense of loss and alienation from the homeland.

The description of the ruin of familiar and familial spaces is a recurrent theme in the writing of Anglophone Arab writers. In an essay on growing up in Khartoum, Jamal Mahjoub describes the changing landscape of his childhood neighbourhood: 'the old villas have been ripped down [. . .] The streets frequently flood as the old drainage system, installed by the British back in the 1930s, falters under the pressure and the dirty water bubbles up from the ground' ('Rumble on the Nile'). In *Cairo, My City, Our Revolution*, Ahdaf Soueif describes her feeling that the 'disintegration' of Cairo is a purposeful act: 'the city was disintegrating. Partly through neglect and partly, we felt, on purpose [. . .] Nothing was maintained or mended. Old houses were torn down and monstrous towers built in their place' (34). The physical structures of old buildings, whether torn down or disintegrating, become the ruins of the past in the present (as with the archaeological traces discussed in Chapter 1), and symbolically capture the metaphorical ruin of the nation. Coming at the end of Aboulela's novel, the scene of the parental room in ruins suggests the novel does not ultimately arrive at a fixed, stable subjectivity but rather undermines the idea of home as the space which can provide stability. Though Aboulela unambiguously represents faith as a source of strength and healing for the fractures of exile, the novel ends on a scene of destruction that demonstrates the unhealable rift of dislocation, and to some extent, the fictional nature of a coherent sense of self.

Randa Jarrar's A Map of Home

Randa Jarrar is an American writer of Palestinian and Egyptian heritage, born in Chicago and raised in Kuwait, Egypt and the United States. Her debut novel *A Map of Home* is a semi-autobiographical coming-of-age story, which Jarrar has described as a 'fictionalization of mostly my grappling with my loyalty to my parents and culture' (Beirut39). *A Map of Home* is narrated by Nidali Ammar, beginning with the protagonist's birth to her leaving home to fulfil her ambition of becoming a writer. The protagonist's mixed background, similar to Jarrar's own, complicates identifying any one location as home, as Nidali reflects early on: 'Mama is an Egyptian, her mother was a Greek, my father is a Palestinian [...] I was Egyptian and Palestinian. I was Greek and American' (8). In addition to this multi-ethnic heritage, the Ammar family is constantly on the move, and Nidali's identity comes to be defined by her peripatetic life. The novel is structured in three parts following the family's travels to and through places where their presence proves temporary or insecure. In the first part, the family moves from the United States, where Nidali is born, to Kuwait, where her Palestinian father is employed as an architect. In the second part, the family is forced to flee Kuwait during the Gulf War, when Palestinians become unwelcome. They move to Egypt, where they live in the family's summer house in Alexandria, their accommodation reflecting the temporariness of their stay. In the final part, they move back to the United States, to Texas, where they live in a trailer, the mobile home concretely symbolizing not having a permanent home and the constant mobility of their lives. These multiple dislocations speak to the complications of creating a single 'map of home', which in turn complicates any one-dimensional notion of the nostalgia for home.

Discussion of the novel has focused on Jarrar's use of humour, and particularly on the protagonist's feminist rebelliousness and frank sexuality. Critics have identified a subversive potential in reworking mainstream American readers' assumptions, including through the disruption of 'normative productions of the Muslim female body' which gives the novel 'substantial feminist cultural value' (El Gendy 14). While the portrayal of the protagonist's father Waheed as controlling and abusive might be understood to reinforce stereotypes, Jarrar's humour is seen to offset this danger: 'the mainstream U.S. reader may not be able to stereotype if he or she were too busy laughing at the text's witty portrayal of very human characters' (Bujupaj 200). The critical emphasis on Nidali's irreverence and rebelliousness is often cast against Waheed's more stereotypical nostalgia for Palestine. For example, Alghaberi argues that 'Waheed's view of home is romantic, idealist, nostalgic, while his daughter is pragmatic in perceiving and constructing the idea of home' (3). Similarly, Nancy El Gendy argues that 'Nidali actively resists tragedy and victimization in favour of survival', and that Nidali 'shift[s] the narrative from a tragic obsession with the homelessness of exilic Palestinians' (9). However, the celebratory attitude towards the individualistic attitude of the protagonist as distinct from her father's attitude may overlook the extent to which Nidali herself experiences a range of nostalgic emotions, while her parents at times approach nostalgic politics with scepticism. Pitting the protagonist against an older generation's romanticism elides the complex and at times contradictory attitudes which both Nidali's father Waheed and her mother Fairuza express over the course of the novel. In fact, all the characters – not only Nidali – negotiate the complications of identity formation in ways which move between the nostalgic perspective and the rejection of being bound to and shaped by collective understandings of home and nationhood, seeking to negotiate between an individualist quest for freedom and loyalty to family and nation.

Nidali's tense relationship with her parents is intertwined with her ambivalent sense of belonging. Early on in the novel, Nidali remembers how as a child she had 'no memories about where I belonged'. She reflects that her history is shaped by her parents: '[w]e were a family with a short history then; my parents were making my memories. It must be strange to be a parent, to be like a filmmaker who is always on, always rolling one memory or another for your child' (287). This passage speaks to the creative aspect of reconstructing belonging in the context of displacement, but it is also an early moment which captures Nidali's ability to empathize with her parents' experience. She recognizes that the family's 'short history' is a consequence of violent dislocation from place, a result of Waheed's statelessness as a Palestinian, unable to re-enter Palestine after the 1967 war. That the family name Ammar literally means builder is a reflection on what it means to make a home while being unable to settle in one place, which adds a symbolic resonance to Waheed's giving up of his poetry to work as an architect, speaking to the implicit connection between the physical construction of home and the artist's ability to construct memories 'like a film maker'.

In the first chapter, Nidali remembers how her father would tell her that '[o]ur people carry the homeland in their souls', and how this metaphor 'forced me to have compassion for Baba, who, obviously, had an extremely heavy soul to drag around' (9). The glorification of Palestine is central: 'Baba [. . .] explained to me that the reason his homeland was in constant turmoil was that it stood in the centre of the world' (223). However, even as a child, Nidali is sceptical of this claim of Palestine as central: '[o]n the map, sure, it was in the centre, but [. . .] Didn't he know that any point could be the world's centre?' (223). However, this patronizing attitude towards her father's attachment to Palestine gives way later to a recognition that when her father 'dictated history', his attempts to pass on a narrative stems more from a sense of loss than pride, a way for him to grapple with the fact that he 'didn't really know who he was or where he belonged' (37). Waheed's stories are born from a need to inculcate in his daughter Nidali a sense of attachment to a homeland, and in that sense, he seems to match the stereotype of the melancholic and nostalgic Palestinian longing for home. As an artist, he takes on the identity of the exile, changing his name from Saeed (happy) to Waheed (alone/lonely). However, as the novel unfolds, we realize that like Nidali herself Waheed vacillates between his nostalgia and the recognition of identity as changeable in a way that does not follow a linear progression.

This shift in mode is represented in two scenes about the map of Palestine. In the first, Waheed teaches his daughter to draw Palestine through 'trac[ing] the map and draw[ing] it over and over again', in an attempt to fix the map in her memory. Later, when Nidali draws the map from memory, her father informs her that in fact the idea of maps is more complicated than they might appear: '[t]hat map is from a certain year [. . .] There's no telling where home starts and where it ends' (193). It is this recognition of mutability which allows Nidali to create her own map of home by erasing the lines, creating 'a blank page' as the boundary-less map within which she can locate herself. It is, then, the seemingly nostalgic Waheed that reiterates what Nidali learns from others, such as her grandfather, who remind her that 'when it comes to maps, accuracy is always a question of where you stand' (189). Once Nidali understands the relativity of any map of home, she is able to reflect on how she is 'not half something and half another' but rather 'whole, a circle', allowing her to erase the lines that determine what it means to belong (58). The father–daughter relationship is then more complex than that of a nostalgic, conservative father and a pragmatic, rebellious daughter: both characters are conflicted about where they belong, though the ways they grapple with this uncertainty about home increasingly diverge.

As I have mentioned, much of the discussion of the novel has focused on Waheed's controlling and patriarchal behaviour in contrast to Nidali's bid for liberation. The conflict between father and daughter is a central theme from the opening pages, where Waheed first names his daughter Nidal, a boy's name meaning 'struggle', before adding the feminizing and possessive 'I' at the end, an anecdote that captures his contradictory desire for her to have the freedom of a man, to be educated and independent, and his patriarchal notions of sexual freedom. However, what has often been overlooked is the extent to which Waheed's past life impacts his controlling behaviour, as he recalls his sisters marrying and leaving the house, 'each one more miserable than the last' (5). Waheed is determined that his daughter will be educated, telling her that '[t]o be free, you must be educated' (24), while also seeking to use her to fulfil his own frustrated aspirations, asking her to '[w]rite poetry like [he] used to do' (65). His control of Nidali is not disconnected from patriarchal attitudes but proves increasingly related to his need for her to inherit, and to write, the stories he passes on. He explicitly states that he wishes for Nidali to inhabit those stories as an alternative home, suggesting the possibility of home being more than the physical territory that can be mapped: 'I lost my home', Baba said [. . .] 'and I gained an education [. . .] which later became my home. That can also happen for you' (106).

Waheed himself is unable to fully inhabit this imaginary home of writing, as we see when Nidali expresses an interest to 'hear [Waheed's] stories', and he decides that he should write a memoir and have her write it down. However, Waheed is never able to go beyond the title of his memoir, and so Nidali sits in silence, waiting to receive his stories, 'look[ing] down at the blank page' (109). The blank page of Waheed's untold stories, his inability to record his life, becomes the inverse of Nidali's freeing blank map, when she experiences a liberation through erasing the borders and 'survey[ing] what remained: a blank page' (193). While Nidali's blank page is an escape from the confining lines of identity, the blank page for Waheed (the empty page of his would-be memoir) is an intimidating, silencing space. Nidali recognizes that her father has 'hundreds of twisting anecdotes and witty lines [. . .] stor[ed] [. . .] in his head' but also that 'he could never let [the stories] go' (109). Again, this silence leads her to empathize with him: '[w]hen I saw that Baba was afraid, I felt sorry for him' (109). Waheed's failure to become a writer becomes redirected into his controlling behaviour, limiting Nidali's freedom in order to mollify his own frustrations with himself. In other words, he uses patriarchy and conservative ideas about the need to protect his daughter from Western corruption in order to disguise his own powerlessness and the silencing he experiences.

Jarrar explores this use of conservatism as a defence further through Waheed's efforts to control Nidali's mother, Fairuza. Since Waheed resents his wife's investment in her piano-playing, he appeals to religion to prevent this behaviour. Nidali sees through this disguising of vulnerability, noting that her father was simply 'unwilling to just admit that he was afraid of losing Mama to the piano' and therefore 'declared that it was un-Islamic to bring pianos into the house and play music all day'. In other words, Waheed's patriarchal behaviour is strategic, a pragmatic's retreat to conservative attitudes, performing the role of the patriarch. Meanwhile, Fairuza too deploys performative forms of resistance, in her case appealing to pre-Islamic traditions. As Nidali reports, Fairuza registers her objection to the trailer home in Texas by borrowing a truck and 'turn[ing] the trailer around so that instead of facing west, it now faces east. And when [Waheed] comes home, he – a poet who reveres pre-Islamic poetry – will remember how Jahilia's women turned their tents around when they wanted to divorce their husbands' (250). Both Fairuza and Waheed knowingly deploy tradition in their embattled marriage, using religion and culture to stake their claims to an authentic selfhood in lieu of other forms of belonging.

Jarrar humorously uses the nuclear family to speak to national politics, through analogies which liken family disagreements to battles and wars. For example, at one point Nidali comments that '[s]eldom in Mama-Baba history had victory been so efficient or so visibly decisive in so short a span of time' (72). Linda Maloul points to the disjunction between the comedy and the war imagery here, suggesting that 'Nidali is psychologically scarred by her parents' continuous fights' (191). While these scenes help the reader to understand Nidali's desire to escape her family, we also sense her empathy for the failures of her parents' relationship, and how, on a more serious and wistful note, 'their art had failed them [. . .] their love for each other had failed them' (111). The family violence the protagonist records speaks to the connections between private and public, between domestic violence and the violence the family experiences through war and displacement. There is a nostalgic aspect to Nidali's contrasting of the stories she has heard of Waheed and Fairuza's earlier relationship, and their present reality. She recalls, for example, how Waheed had once written a poem that became famous, and how 'although most people saw the poem's repeatedly addressed beloved as the Arab world, the beloved was really my mama' (36). During his time as poet, Waheed's personal life is assumed to be subsumed by politics, while later, as a failed artist, his politics subsumes his family life, embedded in the very names of his children, first in Nidali, my struggle, but also in his son's name, Gamal, named after the Egyptian pan-Arabist leader Gamal Abdulnasser.

Once the Gulf War breaks out, the Ammar family leaves Kuwait for Egypt, and then on to the United States. There is a tension in this part of the novel between the need for self-invention and the idea of a 'new home' as a betrayal, since as Waheed expresses it, he has 'never had one' (200). Nidali shares his unease, though in her case it is a sense of anxiety about rooting herself in a new place once more: 'I did not want [...] to work at feeling at home again, to lose that home again, then have to start all over again' (207). Once in the United States, she finds herself at once 'missing a hundred different things from "home," and [...] starting to forget [...] where home really was' (221). In this part of the novel, Waheed and Nidali are contrasted against Fairuza, who represents the ability to move on, or at least to make the attempt to adjust to her new surroundings. Nidali recognizes that her mother is adjusting better than she herself could: 'I sat and watched her, jealous of how easily she seemed to root herself here. Me, I felt splintered, like the end of a snapped off tree branch' (231). This attitude of separation from the past carries forward into Fairuza's support for her daughter's autonomy against her husband. In one passage, Fairuza exclaims: '[e]nough [...] Let the child go, she's suffocating here' (234–5). Later, when Nidali tells her parents that she wants to leave to go to a college, it is Fairuza who repeats 'Khalas, Waheed. Let her go' (280). As with the previous novels I have discussed, this moment of parental disagreement reveals opposed views about how far children should bear the burdens of history or be urged to look towards the future. Yet Fairuza is not entirely happy to forget the past: for all her flexibility and her support for letting go, it is Fairuza, we learn at the end, who has kept all of her daughter's writings throughout the years, telling her that '[y]ou must keep all this for posterity. I want you to write' and insisting that she should remember her family and her past through her writing: '[d]on't you ever, ever, in your life, umrik, ever, ever . . . ever forget us' (289). A strategic forgetting, in Fairuza's logic, can be necessary in order to move forward with life, but entirely leaving the past and the family behind spells an unforgivable betrayal and abandonment.

The novel's most dramatic moment of mapping nation and family onto one another involves connecting Palestinian homelessness with the patriarchal notions of family honour. In a deeply ironic moment, when Waheed declares '[m]y daughter [. . .] will not leave my house', Nidali points out the painful truth: '[b]ut we haven't even built it yet' (280). In this exchange, Nidali scores a vicious point against her father by emphasizing Waheed's failure to offer his family stability over the years. Though Waheed's second name is Ammar, one who builds, and though he is an architect by profession, he has been unable to build his family a home or offer them stability and security. This painful moment juxtaposes the dishonour of a daughter leaving home and a Palestinian exile having no home.

The themes of homelessness and shame which blend the national and family story come to a head towards the end of the novel where, in a section narrated in a distancing third-person voice rather than the first person, Nidali describes elliptically how she reports her father's abuse to the police. The passage is fraught with her awareness of the racism her father may face as a result of her actions, her recognition that 'daughters in America can teach their parents lessons. Cops in America don't like Arabs and they definitely don't like Arabs who hit their teenage daughters and chase them around the house with knives' (249). It is sharply ironic that it is Nidali, finally, who forecloses the Ammar family's dream of having their own home, since her reporting on Waheed means that her father will have a criminal record and find it difficult to buy a house. In the end, Nidali becomes one more figure controlling Waheed's ability to finally settle down somewhere. Jarrar's story of the multiple dislocations of the Ammar family, of the destruction of the national and family home, ends by returning us to the early pages of the novel, and the truth of Waheed's statement about the realities of being Palestinian, needing to 'carry the homeland' so that 'you will always have it in your heart' (9). In this novel, the nostalgia for home involves more than the sanitized longing for a lost geographical territory – it coexists with the recognition that the map is mutable, that the borders are unfixed and that home exits in multiple ways, including in the memory and the imagination.

The writer representing the homeland from afar puts together a narrative that is fractured and distorted by the experiences of dislocation. As Rushdie puts it, the writer who imagines the homeland 'tries to reflect the world' but 'is obliged to deal in broken mirrors, some of whose fragments have been irretrievably lost' (9). In their writing, Matar, Aboulela and Jarrar oscillate between then and there and here and now to reconstruct national history from a spatial and temporal distance. They focus strategically on the site of the home and the family, the legitimating metaphor of the nation, to problematize the national narrative. As I have described, family and nation are knitted together in nationalist discourse across ideological divides, and in ways embedded in literary tradition. For example, at the conclusion of his trial in 2011, former Egyptian president Husni Mubarak recited a famous line of poetry, a line ironically long entrenched in Arab dissident discourse, which I translate as follows: 'my country, however unjust to me is dear/and my family, though they think ill of me, are noble.'[19] In expressing love and loyalty for country and family while simultaneously indicting their injustice, the juxtapositions of this line capture the paradoxes of alienated nationalism that are a feature of contemporary literature in the Arab world. The novels I have discussed in this chapter reflect on the impact and consequences of this alienated nationalism, examining national identity and history through the narrative of families caught up in the private violence of patriarchy and the state violence of dictatorship.

Paraphrasing Bhabha, Said notes that '[n]ations themselves are narrations' (*Culture and Imperialism* xiii). The novels I have discussed in this chapter are testimonies to how this narrative is continuously created, and how the violence of the state can be erased not only by the national narrative but also by global politics. The upheavals within the family cause the protagonists to undergo a process of attempting to establish their identity and construct their sense of self, always having to return to the inherited narrative of their parents' political engagements. The protagonists' politics emerge as they witness the reach of the state into the home. Their disenchantment from the nationalist cause however remains in tension with an ongoing attachment to the homeland as they become implicated in the political events that shape both nation and family. The tension between the love for home/homeland and the suffering that it inflicts runs through the novels, where longing for a stable country that conforms to the ideals of home is cast against the political realities witnessed from afar. The inextricable connection between the 'fractured country' and the 'broken home' becomes the basis for a reorientation away from the homeland as another false narrative similar to a nostalgic view of the family. The writers embed a self-reflexivity in the protagonists' reflections on the realities of the state and the family which they do not fully understand as immature witnesses. The novels showcase the 'unhomely' intrusions that collapse the illusion of a private sphere, even as they subordinate official narrative to personal history. Through these negotiations of narratives about nationhood and family, Anglophone Arab writers rewrite the plot of the national story to include the violence excluded from official representations of the national imagination. In doing so, they leverage various forms of nostalgic impulse to critique reductive narratives of family and nation and to bear witness to the complex vibrancy and violence of nationalist logic.

Chapter 4

REIMAGINING BELONGING IN THE DIASPORA

ROBIN YASSIN-KASSAB, SELMA DABBAGH AND RAWI HAGE

Jamal Mahjoub's *Travelling with Djinns* (2003), as the title suggests, is a novel about a journey. In a central passage early on, the narrator describes the motivation for his road trip, representing it as a quest, 'searching for the heart' of Europe, which he describes as '[his] dark continent'. Here and elsewhere in the novel, Mahjoub writes back to narratives of colonial adventurers searching for the 'dark heart' of Africa, using the same language of exploration and adventure in relation to the dislocations of postcolonial migrancy (59). The novel blends elements of the road novel and Sufi mystic narratives, emphasizing 'the importance of movement, of insight gained through motion' (11). While this trope subverts the assumed naturalness of the link between identity and territory, the novel is as concerned with dramatizing the events that lead to displacement. The title captures this dynamic tension between a literal 'moving on', and the extent to which the past not only haunts but also produces the present. At the centre of the novel is the realization that there is no home to 'run away to'. As Said puts it, '[t]he pathos of exile is in the loss of contact with the solidity and the satisfaction of earth: homecoming is out of the question' (*Reflections* 142). Mahjoub's narrator describes himself as someone who has 'two passports and quite a variety of other documents to identify [him]'; yet, his papers only 'tell the world where [he has] been, but not who [he is], nor where [he is] going to' (5). An unsettled life transgresses the territorial confinement of identity. The dislocations of such a life disrupt the taken-for-granted connections that structure conventional theories of social identity. In the absence of deriving identity from location, nostalgia for the homeland is a crucial component in forming the bonds of community and belonging in diaspora.

In a speech given in 1997, Mahjoub describes the 'new global distribution of Sudanese' in the wake of the 1989 coup as having created 'a global dislocated country, a society spread across the boundaries of the world's nations' ('The Writer and Globalism'). The identification of the Sudanese diaspora as a 'dislocated country' extends the commitment to 'the homeland' into a deterritorialization of belonging. Dennis Walder argues that the 'scope for multiple forms of identity within and beyond the nation-state' creates an 'increasing lack of certainty or finality about home as a place of origin, undermining nostalgia as a phenomenon of positive identification and affiliations even while it is more widely and profoundly felt' (49). The disconnection of identity and place necessitates the reimagining of belonging, both problematizing and strategically utilizing nostalgic modes and narratives to negotiate and mediate these new understandings of belonging outside the homeland.

In this chapter, I examine the role of nostalgia in relation to representations of diaspora in Robin Yassin-Kassab's *Road from Damascus*, Selma Dabbagh's *Out of It*, and Rawi Hage's *The Cockroach*. In each case, diaspora is both the subject of the work and the condition out of which the novel is written. Taking the mobility and displacements of immigrant subjects as their theme, these novels unfold as a drama of choice about identification and belonging in diaspora. Martin Genetsch argues that 'the central concern for many who feel themselves uprooted is how to make life in the diaspora "liveable"' (vi). Dramatizing just that process of making life 'liveable', the writers explore different strategies to negotiate belonging in the diaspora, from assimilation to exilic nationalism to turning to faith and religion. Ultimately, the narrative arc leads the protagonists to the realization that a location that can be identified as home can no longer be 'the goal of the voyages of self-discovery and self-identification' (Gurr 18). Nevertheless, nostalgic attachments are shown to be strategic invocations that produce a sense of home. That is, the search for ways to make life in diaspora liveable is not about the desire to find or return home, but rather to produce new modes of belonging beyond the naturalized link between identity and territory, to undertake what Khachig Tölölyan describes as the movement 'from exilic nationalism to diasporic transnationalism' (25). This shift acknowledges the consequences of disconnection from the native place, which according to Said involve the impossibility of return:

> [e]xile [...] is restlessness, movement, constantly being unsettled, and unsettling others. You cannot go back to some earlier or perhaps more stable condition of being at home; and, alas, you can never fully arrive, be at one with your new home or situation. (53)

On the one hand, the impossibility of return implies the pre-existence of a centre from which exile occurs, and the irrevocable nature of the displacements that result from that movement. On the other hand, the recognition that 'you can never fully arrive' challenges the notion of being a citizen of the world, adapting to any location. This contradiction is similar to the tensions described in Avtar Brah's concepts of 'desire for home' and 'homing desire'. As Brah puts it, home is 'a mythic place of desire in the diasporic imagination' (192). Yet she stresses that homing desire 'is not the same as the desire for a "homeland"' (197). The tension between seeking a stable sense of identity and seeking to escape the policed boundaries of identity 'places the discourse of home and dispersion in creative tension, inscribing a homing desire while simultaneously critiquing discourses of fixed origins' (Brah 192–3). It is the shift between the desire for home and the recognition of its mythic and elusive quality that I will explore in this chapter. I argue that the texts examined negotiate different modes of belonging, exploring the tension between communitarian and universalist frameworks in the diaspora, as well as between national narratives as a powerful force shaping identity in immigrant spaces and the development of transnational modes of belonging, negotiating different forms of nostalgic attachment.

Nostalgia and dislocation

The pervasive use of the term 'diaspora' has rendered the concept somewhat ambiguous in recent years, a conceptual drift that has led some critics to argue that the term is becoming increasingly meaningless. The metaphorical and vague use of the term lends particular force to Avtar Brah's argument that we cannot allow 'location to easily dissolve out of focus' (201). Foregrounding location necessitates focusing on the circumstances of displacement. The formations of Arab diasporas in North America, South America, Australia and Europe have widely different histories – there are few commonalities between, for example, the Levantine migration to the Americas in the early twentieth century and the postcolonial context of North African communities in France. In this context, it is telling that Zahia Salhi asks: '[b]eyond the pressures of conflict and polarisation, is there specificity to the literature and art of Arab diaspora?' (54). As already discussed in the introduction, it is not my intention to argue for a specific and recognizable tradition of the Anglophone Arab novel. I would thus refocus Salhi's question to ask what role nostalgic narratives play in literature by Arab diaspora writers, given the 'pressures of conflict and polarisation' which they confront.

A central aspect of Arab diaspora in recent decades has been the over-determining nature of Islam as an identity and the conflation between Islam and Arabness. This has been a recurring topic, particular in the United States, where the majority of the Arab American community is Christian. The slippage around the terms Arab/Muslim has led to some efforts to distinguish between the two. In a study on Arab-British activists, for example, discussing Islam becoming the primary marker of identity, Caroline Nagel and Lynn Staeheli show that while activists acknowledge that 'Arabness is culturally bound up with Islam', they try to promote an Arab identity which is separate from 'a British Muslim identity, which, they argue publicises, and politicises religious affiliation' (107–8). These parallel and sometimes intersecting identities were institutionalized over the past couple of decades in reaction to global politics. Investigating this conflation in *Britain's First Muslims: Portrait of an Arab Community* (2010), Fred Halliday argues that it is only since 1990 that 'it became more common to talk of a "Muslim community" in Britain, of "Islam in Britain" and of "British Muslims"' rather than referring to communities in ethnic or geographic terms (ix). This shift, he maintains, emerged in part following the campaign against Rushdie's *The Satanic Verses* in 1989 and the Gulf War in 1990–1 (xvi).

Conflicts and pressures have been central to the formation of an Arab diaspora discourse, particularly in the satellite era, where transnational television channels and the internet increasingly connected people in a politicized cultural sphere. In the introduction to *Anthūlūjiyā al-adab al-'Arabī al-mahjarī al-mu'āṣir* (Anthology of Contemporary Arabic Diaspora Literature, 2004), Lutfi Haddad notes that this transnational media is part of a different contemporary experience of diaspora. He contrasts previous generations of Arab exiles with the present practices of those living outside the region, connected with and frequently returning to visit relatives 'back home'. Along the same lines, Dalia Abdelhady suggests that 'the myth of return is no longer meaningful, even as a rhetorical device, since moving back and forth is relatively easy' (177). However, though the actual physical journey might have become easier in some cases, the notion of home in conditions of forced migration does not always allow for such ease of movement. As Laura Huttunen puts it, 'there are [. . .] some circumstances in people's lives when "homes" in their universalistic taken-for-grantedness become problematised [. . .] where is home, or what is home, in a situation where one's home is shattered by a violent war and one is forced into exile?' (177). Where displacement is inextricable from the political, cultural and social turbulent upheavals of the region, the homeland no longer functions as the idealized space keeping the myth of return alive. In such circumstances, memory work becomes a struggle to make sense of crises. These themes of memory, exile and the impasse of political crises intertwine in Anglophone Arab writing. For example, in Moroccan-American writer Anouar Majid's novella *Si Yussef*, the eponymous storyteller insists that 'memory is not the past, no; it is the present struggling with the past' (59–60). The novel is simultaneously concerned with critiquing the disabling nostalgia that leaves the protagonist 'suspended in a paralysis' and dramatizing the present conditions that drives the impulse 'to recapture the past, a past that has retreated in anger and shame' (34). To address 'the present struggling with the past' is thus to examine both literal and metaphorical forms of distance from the homeland and the present, and to acknowledge the multifaceted role of nostalgia in the reconstitution of history and belonging (*Si Yussef* 60).

Return and its impossibility is a recurrent theme in the contemporary corpus of Arabic literature that deals with life in the diaspora. Consider Halim Barakat's *Crane* (2008, *Ṭā'ir al-ḥawm*, 1997), an autobiographical novel where the unnamed narrator looks back on his childhood in a village in Syria before describing his experiences as a student in the US in the 1960s. *Crane* is the story of an Arab intellectual in exile, unable to call any place home yet unable to find affirmation in a state of hybrid in-betweeness. As the narrator puts it: 'I tried in vain to convince myself that "I am constantly changing" as opposed to Arabs who say "I am what I was" and Americans who claim "I am what I am"' (21). These phrases yoke attitudes to identities in a somewhat stereotypical fashion. Nevertheless, the transition the narrator seeks to make is clear. To understand identity as continually shifting, the focus must be moved from the territorial frame of identity to understanding subjectivity as unfolding continually. In contrast to a 'settled' sense of selfhood, the protagonist becomes aware of the performative nature of identity as he experiences life abroad: '[l]ike others I relived my own culture by eating kibbeh, tabouleh, hummus and ful and by dancing the dabka' (49–50). The narrator returns repeatedly to the contrast between the instability 'back home', and the stability of being 'suspended' in diaspora, a variant of the insight that, as André Aciman puts it, 'exiles can be supremely mobile, and they can be totally dislodged from their original orbit, but in this jittery state of transience, they are thoroughly stationary' (13). The narrator constantly reflects on the dispersion of the family: 'it's a mystery to me what took them to Australia. Latif now lives in Germany and Salwa in El Paso, Texas. Why are families so scattered?' (65). The strain this 'dispersion' puts on family ties is a constant concern for the character, reaching a critical point when he reflects that his daughter is unable to speak Arabic with her dying grandmother.

The novel as a whole explores the re-centring from geography to language as a cornerstone of identity. This shift is dramatized in a problematic, racialized encounter early on in the novel where the narrator is greeted by a stranger who guesses his identity before identifying him as Muslim: 'I suddenly noticed a black man coming straight toward me [. . .] "Alsalaamu alaykum!" he said [. . .] I felt an enormous sense of relief' (25). Although Barakat himself is Greek Orthodox, his fictional narrator in this semi-autobiographical text feels 'relief' following the interpellation by this friendly and racialized 'other' who confers recognition upon him. In this scene, the link between identity and geography is reconfigured to a connection between identity and religion, as a transnational Islam is invoked. This moment is presented as one of rehabilitation – the protagonist not only is moved out of the anonymity of a passer-by in a multicultural metropolitan city but also is moved from the position of the marginalized minority to a privileged position in relation to language. In other words, in recognizing the words 'Alsalaamu alaykum!' the narrator is for a moment no longer a foreigner, who, as Derrida puts it in relation to the concept of hospitality, has 'to ask for hospitality in a language which by definition is not his own' (*Of Hospitality* 15). The 'enormous sense of relief' he feels speaks to the depth of alienation experienced by those constantly in the position of asking for hospitality (25).

Anglophone works by Arab writers also address the repercussions of *ghurba*, both in terms of metaphorical and literal exile, reflecting on what Hout describes the exile's 'state of cognitive and emotional dissonance, whether generated by war and/or political/sectarian division in one's own nation or induced by physical uprootedness abroad' (*Post-War* 25). However, the fact of writing in English adds to the disruption of any sense of natural connection between territory and identity. Speaking of Lebanese fiction in both languages, Hout describes one of the 'significant points of distinction' between Anglophone Arab and Arabic-language writers in the following terms: 'most Arabic-language Lebanese writers, whether they emigrated [. . .] or not, still largely deal with internal exile as a psycho-social or a political phenomenon without addressing lives in the diaspora as such' (4). I would expand Hout's point here to make the case that Arabic fiction, even when the subject is literal exile rather than internal, tends to be more focused on the homeland and the character's relationship with it than with the country of exile. While Arabic-language authors have a particular level of language skill and connection with their literary tradition, Arab writers who write in English tend to be more focused on representing ways of creating liveable lives in the new countries of settlement, and therefore reflect on the dangers of nostalgia as paralysis in the context of displacement and exile.

Robin Yassin-Kassab's Road from Damascus

Robin Yassin-Kassab is a British-Syrian writer who was born in London and grew up in England and Scotland. He co-authored *Burning Country: Syrians in Revolution and War* (2016) with Leila al-Shami and has been a prolific commentator on Syria since the 2011 uprising. His debut novel *The Road from Damascus*, as the title suggests, has elements of spiritual biography, tracing the protagonist Sami Traifi's ideological transformation from nationalism to what he describes as a 'contingent faith' in Islam (348). Critics have approached this novel as part of a corpus of Muslim fiction, or as Naseem Aumeerally describes it, the 'emerging genre, referred to as "Muslim writing"' which 'has functioned as a powerful and creative platform [. . .] to chart the diverse, complex and provisional cartographies of Muslim identities' (3). Aumeerally mentions *The Road from Damascus* as well as Aboulela's *Minaret* as part of this genre. Along similar lines, Claire Chambers's reading of the novel furthers her broader argument that 'British-resident authors of Muslim heritage share certain preoccupations' (119). C. E. Rashid has also explored the novel's nuanced exploration of 'British Islam' in the context of literary responses to the Rushdie affair, arguing that 'this novel of transformation performs a new British-Islamic discourse in order to unpick the recently constructed opposition of Islam and literature' (98). While the British Muslim narrative is an important aspect of the novel, in what follows, I will focus more closely on the novel's interrogation of Arab nationalism from the perspective of diaspora. I argue that Yassin-Kassab's novel unfolds as a series of ideological disillusionments that chart the protagonist's confrontation with the failure of nationalist politics. While the values Sami's Ba'thist father espoused seem increasingly problematic, his mother's and later his wife's narrative of a transnational *umma*, or global Islamic community, has its own complications. Inviting the reader to follow the protagonist's successive disenchantment from various ideologies, Yassin-Kassab poses the question of how one might find alternatives beyond restrictive dichotomies, highlighting the inadequacies of political vision in the Arab world today.

The Road from Damascus follows the British-born protagonist Sami, who as the novel opens has abandoned his failing marriage and his doctoral thesis on Arabic literature to visit his parents' home city of Damascus. Though the novel is set in 2001, we are drawn back, through Sami's quest to better understand his family history, to the Hama uprising in 1982, when Sami's father supported the Syrian Ba'athist dictatorship in its attempt to stamp out efforts at rebellion by the Muslim Brotherhood. Over the course of the novel, Sami learns the extent of Mustafa's involvement, which includes reporting his brother-in-law Faris to the authorities, leading to Faris's two-decade long imprisonment. Early on, Sami realizes that 'there was a secret here which [he] alone had not penetrated' though it takes him the course of the novel to understand the full story of his father's betrayal and its repercussions (5). It is the gradual discovery of this secret which provides the impetus for Sami's disillusionment with his father's ideology of pan-Arabism and sustains the narrative tension in the novel.

The opening pages of the novel introduce us to Sami 'searching for breath in the smothered heart of Damascus, home of his ancestors, the former city of streams and orchards' (1), aiming to 'reconnect with his roots':

> He'd been here for a month, in order to (he listed): reconnect with his roots, remember who he was, find an idea. And the tourist stuff too: to bathe in the wellsprings of the original city, the oldest continuously inhabited city on earth. A city that had briefly ruled the world. Where jasmine and honeyed tobacco scented the evening air. Where Ibn Arabi wrote his last mystical poetry, where Nizar Qabbani wrote 'Bread, Hashish, and Moon.' (1)[1]

The nostalgic mode in these opening pages is already somewhat ambivalent, if not ironic, with the description of the scent of 'jasmine and honeyed tobacco' vying with the comment on 'smothered' air. Already in the opening pages, Sami is aware that his longed-for homeland is, in fact, a 'cacophonous country' (2). He recognizes the exclusionary practices that are constitutive of nationalist discourse, imagining a future Syria with where '[t]he wrong identity would end you at the intersection. Dead for wearing a cross. Dead for wearing a hijab. Dead for Ali's sword swinging from your car mirror' (7). The violence elided in nationalism's promise of inclusion is made evident to Sami when he visits his maternal aunt Fadya in Damascus and begins to learn of his uncle's story, as an anonymized, exemplary tale, 'the story of a man in this country' (5). Faris is described as one of many long-term prisoners who, when they are finally released, find their homes have changed: '[s]ome came out but found everyone dead. Some found their homes, but the key wouldn't fit the door. There were strangers inside' (8). Imagining this scene, Sami is reminded of

> Palestinian families in the refugee camps, and their useless keys sometimes brought out of a cabinet to show to a guest, sometimes hooked on a nail in the reception room, thicker and heavier than keys of today. The image extended. Entire countries and pasts: houses without keys. (8)

That Sami relates the image of returning political prisoners locked out of their homes to the 'useless keys' of Palestinian refugees is significant, as it highlights a broader association of personal exile and estrangement with collective exile and a lost homeland. Metaphorically, Palestine becomes every Arab nation 'finished/before it was even born' in Saadi Youssef's words (71). The pervasive image of the house as nation has its own particular symbolism in this context, where the keys and ownership papers of Palestinian refugees became the icons of a failure to return.[2] This metaphorical value explains the appropriation of the iconic keys, symbolizing being locked out of the homeland. Sami's description of '[e]ntire countries and pasts' as 'houses without keys' mirrors the overlap between the 'exclusion [. . .] from the nation' and 'exile from history', which Lorenzo Casini sees as characterizing modern Arab literature; a doubled alienation which 'takes the form of the impossibility for the characters to be active actors' and where it is not 'possible to project one's existence towards any imaginable future' (7). Keys in this context are a symbol of memory, which, as Palestinian writer Talal Alyan explains, is

> a self-prescribed stabiliser [. . .] [o]ur grasping of the past should be understood not only as an act of resistance but also one of centring. Without it, we would surrender ourselves to more than physical occupation and exile; we would be displaced from ourselves. ('Nakba')

This description of memory as a stabilizing force, which prevents psychological displacement, suggests there is more to the nostalgic clinging to memory than futile sentimentality. Here nostalgia is understood to be a 'self-prescribed' palliative which is both a form of resistance and a form of locating oneself in a situation of dislocation.

Although Sami hopes to feel that he has returned to his roots in visiting Damascus, he soon realizes that the past itself is constantly under erasure in this ancient city. When Sami sees Ottoman homes being torn down, he reflects on how the removal of the walls allows him to see the 'hitherto private squares of paint' rendering 'borderless' what had been divided into public and private, allowing him to see into the home, to take in the history that is being destroyed as 'white dust motes swirled thickly. History refusing gravity' (2). The phrasing in this last comment recalls Said's criticism of the 'astonishing sense of weightlessness with regard to the gravity of history' (*Culture and Imperialism* 303). The destruction of historical buildings captures Yassin-Kassab's concern with the ramifications of such deliberate, institutionalized forgetting and erasure, and the impact of intentional erasures sharpen the political potential of nostalgia, rendering it a trenchant form of refusing to move on.

Upon his return to London, Sami comes increasingly to doubt the validity of his father's ideology. The tensions inherent to the nationalist narrative are framed primarily through the father–son relationship, exploring the masculinism with which the idea of nationalism is forged in Sami's 'realisation that the condition of being an Arab was impotence [. . .] not the idea he'd inherited' (90). The framing of failure in an entirely masculinist model, the anxiety of 'impotence' in Sami's words is a recurring rhetorical trope in Arab discourse. The Lebanese poet and writer Etel Adnan for example speaks of a region 'castrated by underdevelopment and occupation' (12). In his indictment of nostalgia for the golden age, Samir Kassir speaks of 'the feeling of impotence' which is 'coupled with a civic powerlessness [. . .] all the more overwhelming because the Arab unconscious filters it through nostalgia for a forgotten but still fantasised-about glory' (27–8). Nostalgic narratives offer a redemptive fantasy that relieves these feelings of impotence and failure. The loss of one inherited set of political ideals leads to a search for alternative forms of belonging, as Sami begins to contrast his own identity struggles with the paths taken by others around him, including his wife Muntaha, who decides to wear the hijab and define herself as a British Muslim, and the path taken by his brother-in-law Ammar, who shifts from hip hop to an Islamist-inflected 'know-nothing political posturing' (Jaggi, 'Beyond Belief'). Sami's father-in-law Marwan, meanwhile, once a secular nationalist poet imprisoned by Saddam Hussein's regime, seeks out places where he can connect with those who share his background 'on the wide-ranging circuits of Arab London' (79). The different trajectories of these characters take the protagonist, and the reader, on a journey through a variety of modes of belonging, which are at first embraced and then discarded in an effort to fashion a stable identity in exile.

A range of strategic uses of nostalgia are exemplified in the story of Marwan, who once 'believed he was a model citizen of the new Iraq' (70). Marwan initially willingly restricts himself to the 'innocuous fare' of 'laudatory hymns to the city, the nation, to brotherhood and other abstractions', nationalist poetry which ascribes to the ideas of progress: '[h]e lovingly ornamented the present and future, and also conjured the dusty provincial town he'd grown out of, representative of the primitive past' (70). As a poet, Marwan employs nostalgia to create a superficial homogeneity that becomes the national myth. After he is imprisoned, however, Marwan's nostalgic nationalism is transfigured, in what Yassin-Kassab suggests is a common story for 'that generation of Arabs [. . .] they were secularist and internationalist, and now they're conservative and vaguely Islamist' (Jackson). In his new community, amid other exiles, he discovers a new, performative form of nostalgia, where a rhetoric of return is a way to signal one's sense of being in exile, even when it is impossible: '[m]ost of them talked of going home, even the Palestinians from disappeared villages' (80). Marwan joins in, presenting himself not as a former political prisoner but as a temporary expatriate, 'a mild critic of his country's regime, but a patriot', pretending to want to return to Iraq to disguise the story of his imprisonment. Like the other exiles, he 'preserve[s] the survivalist suspicion' which keep him from giving his opinions about politics (80). Here, Yassin-Kassab's representation of diaspora life reveals the inextricability of political instability 'back home' and modes of making life liveable in the diaspora. Nostalgia for the homeland is a survivalist performance, intertwined with anxieties that subsume political criticism. The exiles' unwillingness to commit themselves politically allows them to avoid confronting the difficulty of return. Expressing an unqualified longing for the past is here a pretence, overlaying the more complex position of yearning that recognizes the impossibility of return.

The idea of nostalgic attachment as performance is a reoccurring one in the novel. One reviewer remarks that the characters 'whether religious or agnostic [. . .] have the commonality of an angry alienation' (Athanasiadis), yet Yassin-Kassab often seems as interested in creative adaptation as in the consequences of alienation, exploring, for example, how Sami's invents traditions to reconnect 'with what he now described as his heritage' (14) through 'a transplanted nationalism in which the significance of signs had swivelled away from their original focus' (13). Sami seeks to come to 'amicable terms with his appearance. He was an Arab, was all' (14). The timeless identity of 'an Arab' here elides the variety of identities in Syria that Sami is aware of but knows he does not have to consider when performing his Arabness in a metropolis like London. In wearing a keffiyeh for example, Sami recognizes that 'a member of his class in Syria would never wear one. Wouldn't be seen dead in one. But this wasn't Syria' (13). He can then knowingly appropriate the keffiyehs of the 'farmers and labourers' as markers of his ethnic identity and as a way of claiming for himself an association to the intifada. That is, he can create a link back to the homeland through markers of authenticity that he knows are inauthentic. In fact, Sami sometimes wears his scarf 'actually in a Kurdish style', ironically using a cultural marker that he knows would identify him as non-Arab in the region (and from a minority suppressed by the pan-Arab ideology his father supports) to mark himself as Arab. The choices a younger Sami makes to identify and perform as an Arab in multicultural London follows the logic of the pan-Arabist ideology he inherited in that it deliberately erases class and ethnic differences in Syria. In these negotiations of identity, Yassin-Kassab explores how a second-generation, British-Syrian identity is constructed. As an older Sami recognizes, his performance of identity owed much to a youth culture of '[s]triking poses, claiming allegiances' including a 'recycling of third world meanings' (13). The nostalgic attachments to the 'homeland' are ambivalent, seeking to perform Arabness while being distanced from the power imbalances of national structures.

Sami is not alone in performing this 'transplanted' form of nationalism. Hasna, another character who flees her homeland to London and who later becomes Marwan's wife, is described as 'building a shrine to Iraq [. . .] representing her sacrifice in an iconography of lost bliss' using 'traditional craftwork items she'd never been interested in before' (81). At first glance, this seems to capture the uncritical romanticizing of the nation, a concrete example of how 'displacement is more likely to produce immobile memories', as Julia Creet describes in her discussion of the crucial role memory plays in the context of migration (10). However, Hasna's sudden interest in the traditional, like Sami's transplanted nationalism, is a reminder that identity relies on performance, a reproduction of what is deemed authentic as a strategy to create a sense of belonging. Both use material artefacts as part of what Karim Haiderali Karim describes as '[re]creat[ing] home by instilling [. . .] resonance into the spaces they occupy [. . .] with their languages, customs, art forms, arrangements of objects and ideas' (10). In each case, the characters are aware of their fabrications in reproducing authenticity as a strategy to create a sense of belonging. Through exploring these strategic uses of nostalgia, the novel leads the reader to question the parameters of integration as either an aspiration or as a failure to hold on to traditional attachments, offering a critique of such reductive categories.

While Sami is experimenting with performing Arabness, his wife Muntaha begins to come to terms with the reality that '[n]obody anywhere lives in smooth connection to the past' (86). Her recognition that '[e]verybody changes and disperses' (235) repositions her family's exile as part of the inevitable fluctuations of identity, her focus having shifted away from the territorial frame of identity. Yet she also performs a form of authenticity, putting on hijab 'to feel and look more like a Muslim woman' (99). At this point in the novel, there is a widening gulf between the increasingly religious Muntaha and the nationalist, secular Sami. Muntaha, in pointing out to Sami that '[n]obody talks about the Arabs anymore', highlights the anachronism of Sami's clinging to a receding Arabism (98), while for Sami, his wife's religiousness is similarly outmoded: 'the long childhood of a people' (60). Muntaha finally separates herself from Sami's talk of 'the Arab nation' by stating 'I'm British anyway. I'm a British Muslim' (98). This yoking of her religious affiliation to her adopted country becomes a way of rejecting Sami's pan-Arabist politics, detaching herself from this context and inscribing herself instead into a multicultural Britain. A consciously personal form of religion, Muntaha's faith is clearly defined as a spiritual expression rather than a dogmatic or political creed, perhaps resonating with what Asef Bayat and others have described as a post-Islamist trend, tending towards a re-secularization of religion which limits its political role. Yassin-Kassab's exploration of the divergent paths Sami and Muntaha take thus becomes an enquiry into the different conceptualizations of what it means to be Arab and/or Muslim in Britain.

Muntaha's depoliticized faith is contrasted to that of her brother Ammar, whose strident narrative of political grievance is inflected by Islamist discourse. Sami is initially drawn in by Ammar's self-fashioning, from playing Dungeons & Dragons to becoming a wannabe gangster and then eventually 'gravitat[ing] toward political Islam' as 'an ideology that voices his frustrations far more eloquently than Public Enemy and the Five Percenters' (Athanasiadis). This 'capacity for self-definition' is, according to Sami, a form of 'immigrant strength. When you're uprooted, you get to plant yourself in a new location. You have a kind of choice' (218). That choice is however irrevocably shaped by personal experience. As Sami goes on to reflect, Ammar's 'nationalist option had been shut down in his distant boyhood when people calling themselves Arabists shattered the al-Haj family. History had squashed the possibility of Arabism' (218). Here we see Yassin-Kassab's tracing of the consequences of history on the pathways taken to make life liveable in the diaspora. In Ammar's case, the injustices experienced by his family fuels his rhetoric of victimization, but from the perspective of the *umma*, the global Islamic community: 'Palestine, brother. Iraq. Crusader bases all over the Gulf, on holy soil [. . .] Hindus desecrating mosques in Kashmir. Oppression all over the *umma*. But we waking up now. Palestine's the start of it. Soon there'll be a world intifada' (265). Identifying himself with a broader cause, Ammar finds solace in a shared story of suffering and victimization that in and of itself frames belonging within the transnational *umma*.

After joining Ammar's group, Sami similarly sees the group's members through the lens of the violent histories shaping their present:

> [t]he mosques of his childhood stretched out beyond this one like a hall of mirrors diminishing into the infinite. And the screams of Syrian detention chambers [. . .] echoed around the basement walls. The histories of these others too weighed down the present. The Arabs, the Indo-Pakistanis, the Irishman, the African. From what tortures had their father fled? Over which jagged topographies of pain? (223)

While Sami understands how adopting a group identity helps this group to resolve their uncertainties, he soon realizes the continuity between Mustafa's secular fundamentalism, which supports the nation state at all costs, and Ammar's militant Islamism, which makes religious identity the superseding, mobilizing force. There is a contradictory quality to Ammar's rhetoric, which depends upon his audience's identification with 'our people', a narrowing of identity to the allegiance under attack, insisting on the primacy of religious identity and the suppression of other forms of affiliation. Like Aboulela, whose work is discussed in the previous chapter, Yassin-Kassab explores the role of religion in establishing a sense of connection to the past and to the homeland. Aboulela's characters are determinedly apolitical, while Yassin-Kassab's novel dramatizes the jihadist appropriation of nationalist causes, but both writers interrogate the relationship between nostalgia and alienation, between diaspora identities and the collective identity conferred by religion. In both cases, there is a process of conversion in which the belonging afforded by religion eclipses the emotional attachment to the homeland.

Eventually, Sami becomes as disillusioned and repulsed by Ammar's Islamist politics as he was by his secular father's apologetics for the Ba'ath regime. This second disenchantment becomes clear in the climactic event represented towards the end of the novel, the attacks of 9/11. Reactions to the live coverage of the attacks capture the characters' different political positions. First, Ammar attempts to convince the others that it is 'something to restore a man's pride' that 'the heart of America' now 'looks like Gaza [...] Looks like Baghdad' (316). Responding to this provocation, Muntaha is represented as the corrective voice, taking an 'academic tone' as well as a religious one, in her admonishment of her brother (316). For Sami, having abandoned the nationalist framework that made sense of the world, witnessing the attack crystallizes his ideological confusion: 'What was happening? Sami couldn't tell. He had no scale to measure the event. Nothing inherited from [his father] Mustafa. No nationalist way of judging. No Qabbani verses to help him' (315). Lacking his previously self-assured perspective, Sami vacillates between the feeling that this is an attack against 'the empire', realizing the extent of the death and destruction, and the awareness that 'there'll be wars if Muslims did it' (318).

The immediate impact of the attacks becomes apparent when, having been previously apprehended for drug use, Sami is arrested after he is caught leaving the mosque because his religiosity is deemed suspicious. As Jaggi puts it, 'the police conclude he has a false identity, since the pious beardie and the coked-up dissolute cannot be one and the same' ('Beyond Belief'). In a novel so concerned with exploring different modes of belonging, the suspicion around Sami's transformation, the belief that he is not himself, perfectly illustrates both the experimentations that are part of performing identity, and the inflexible boundaries that are set up around religious and national belonging.

For a disillusioned Sami, an identity based on faith does offer one solution to the anxieties about identity in a multicultural society. This shift to a transnational faith is captured in a central yet brief moment when Sami is greeted by a passer-by: 'As-salaamu alaikum! A grinning skullcapped black man of Sami's age had spied him for a brother and passed on. An instant of fraternity' (224). For Sami, this brief encounter presents an alternative 'exclusion boundary' which, unlike the boundary between Sami and British society, 'split open to absorb him' at least for the very brief moment of exchanging the Arabic greeting (244). The scene is remarkably similar to the passage I discussed earlier from Halim Barakat's novel. In both texts, this telling and problematic interracial moment is presented as one of rehabilitation, where the interpellation by this friendly 'other' confers recognition through an Islamic, Arabic greeting. As a transnational Islam is invoked through these pointedly interracial encounters, both protagonists comment on the importance of the moment of positive identification, a temporary break in the anonymity of being a passer-by in the multicultural metropole.

Though these moments of encounter might seem to represent a transnational mode of identification, they are predicated on the centrality of the Arabic language. From the position of the marginalized minority, the protagonists take on a more privileged position in relation to language, to Arabic as the language of the Qur'an. Importantly, soon after this scene, Sami begins to reconsider the importance of language as a focal point of identity, expressing his envy of Muntaha's closeness to Arabic in terms of religion, as proof that she is '[c]onnected. Using her mother tongue. Her *lughhat al umm*. In Arabic *umm* means mother and also origin and basis. Amma, meaning to lead a prayer, derives from the same root, as does *umma*, meaning the nation or the Islamic community' (323). Sami is drawn to the ontological coherency of the Arabic terms and the potential this connection to origin offers for achieving a sense of belonging. The inclusion of Arabic words, tracing the etymological connection between *umm*, mother, and *umma*, (religious) nation, link linguistic competence to a more grounded sense of religious community. The root for '[u]mma, meaning the nation' makes it, as Mona Fayad has pointed out, an 'abstract feminization of *al-umm*, the mother' (Fayad 6). The connections made between etymology and origins, nationhood and belonging, are implicitly contrasted against the discontinuities, the geographic and linguistic rifts, of exile. It is the precariousness of exile that makes the promised cultural intelligibility of the *umma* appealing here. Tellingly, Sami's reconciliation with Muntaha is based on recognizing that her relationship with 'her people, her ancestors, didn't mean trouble', since it circumvents the 'trouble' of failed nationalist politics (323). The narrative arc makes clear that this ideological shift, the recognition of the appeal of the *umma*, is a matter of a need for connection, linked to a post-national discourse about creating community across territorial boundaries.

Whereas within the nation, religion is one of a number of factors constituting belonging, the dislocation from territory (and, to a certain extent, from language) in the diaspora means religion becomes more central to the construction of collective identity. Sami's spiritual journey reveals the interrelationship of alienation and the coherent answers provided by religious ideology. His turn to religion is in part to seek an answer to the question of his father's betrayal, which continues to haunt him – a question which reformulates the 'what went wrong?' question that haunts nostalgic discourse. When Sami puts this question to his mother, Nur explains Mustafa's single-minded belief in the pan-Arab narrative by stating that Mustafa 'had dreams' about what this ideology could accomplish:

> He thought it was only a matter of time until everyone would work in an office, productive eight-hour days, and go home in the evening to read novels or go to the cinema to watch art films. He thought everyone would own a car and a house to fit a nuclear family [. . .] Progress, so-called [. . .] they made the country a prison to do it [. . .] He thought there'd be one Arab nation. One Arab nation from the Ocean to the Gulf. What we have now is everything but. We have everything smaller and everything bigger. Little sects and ethnicities, little nationalisms and big Islamism. But no Arab nation. (340)

In the phrase '[w]hat we have now is everything but' the nation, Nur emphasizes the failure of Mustafa's project as an ideology that demands conformity. In the repetition of 'he thought', and the fact that Nur 'veer[s] from he to they, from Mustafa to the Ba'ath Party', we get a sense of the overlap of resentment at the equivalence of nation and family (340). In both cases, the same repressive functions to conform are at work. The danger which is expounded here is the cost of repressing the flaws and fissures in history, an inflexibility which stands in contrast to the negotiations of belonging Yassin-Kassab dramatizes in this novel.

Throughout *Road from Damascus*, nostalgia offers a frame to deal with the sense that 'the past is a nightmare determining the present and the present is empty' (246). Yassin-Kassab's exploration of the divergent paths the characters take becomes an enquiry into the spectrum between the perspective of the migrant whose main focus is backwards to the country of origin and the perspective of the migrant who seeks to build a life in the host country. The attachment to the past is represented sympathetically, even as the characters also face the realization that '[t]he roots are shallow and mythical, we all come from everywhere at once, and we are floating creatures' (38). For example, Muntaha realizes that there is little to be gained from an inflexible attachment to the past, since the connection to that past is always tenuous, and often a pretext for control: 'Only the shape of tradition remains, only folkloric stuff for tourists. Only oppression justifying itself as tradition' (86). She comes to the same realization when she looks back on her father's life as an immigrant and recognizes that 'Marwan was nothing special. Everybody migrates. Everybody changes and disperses' (235). Exploring the complex relationship between territory and identity, including the inevitable multiplicity and fluctuations of identity, Yassin-Kassab subverts the notion that, as James Clifford puts it, '[d]welling [. . .] [is] the local ground of collective life, travel a supplement; roots always precede routes'. Instead, the journey reveals that practices of displacement can 'emerge as constitutive of cultural meaning rather than as their simple transfer or extension' (3). The notion of a history bound to origins and roots is replaced with the routes that the characters have traversed, playing out an ambivalence in the ways belonging is enacted differently in relation to nostalgic attachments to the homeland and the past.

Sami aspires to reach a state of equilibrium in relation to his scattered narratives of identity, believing Muntaha has found a balance in 'accepting her past [and being] hopeful for the future' (323). Finally, however, having acknowledged the inevitable break with the past does not entirely resolve the search for belonging.

The novel ultimately draws to an end without offering a clear resolution, leaving us with Sami confronting his inability to define who he is:

> For what is he now? Not much anymore. Not Mustafa's son, nor Marwan's son-in-law, not an academic. Not a member of the eternal Arab nation. So what, then? He's Nur's son. Muntaha's husband. But to define himself as other people's attributes – it isn't much. (340)

There is no sense of resolution to the question 'what is he now?' There is no alternative ideology for Sami, only an ambivalence about how he might define himself, and how he might position himself in relation to the idea of the nation. Undercutting the stability of nationalism might ease the restrictive trappings of belonging, but it raises the question of whether such a divestment from the frameworks of collective identity simply represents a turn away and escape from the complex issues of postcolonial nationhood.

In this novel published in 2008, Yassin-Kassab imagines a Syria embroiled in a civil war, having his protagonist reflect, prophetically as it turns out, that '[t]hat's what it could be like, very easily' (7). In the foreword to the translation of *Madīḥ al-karāhiya* (2006, *In Praise of Hatred*, 2012), a novel by Syrian writer Khaled Khalifa set during the civil strife in the 1980s, Yassin-Kassab writes: '[g]lancing from Khalifa's novel to internet updates, it seems that nothing has changed since the eighties [. . .] It's as if Syria is locked in a recurrent curse' (xiii). Yassin-Kassab suggests the challenge Khalifa faced in writing his novel was 'how to represent recent Syrian history, which has often been stranger and more terrible than fiction' (xii). This challenge is also, perhaps, the difficulty Yassin-Kassab faced himself in writing his novel, exploring how the lives of Syrians in the diaspora remain haunted by the unresolved traumas of the homeland.

Selma Dabbagh's Out of It

Selma Dabbagh is a Palestinian British lawyer and human rights activist, as well as being among a growing number of Anglophone Palestinian writers such as Jarrar, Susan Abulhawa and Naomi Shihab Nye, whose literary outputs explore the collective and personal experiences of dispossession and displacement. In interviews, Dabbagh has been careful to stress that she wishes to resist 'definitions that limit [her] potential or define [her] destiny according to that which [she] was born with or into'. She writes that she is 'not as Palestinian as others are, nor as much of a refugee', but also notes that she shares commonalities with Palestinian experiences, in particular the experience of repeated dislocation, writing wryly, '[m]y list goes like this: Scotland, England, Saudi Arabia, Kuwait, France, Egypt, West Bank, Bahrain.' Her writing, Dabbagh asserts, is 'influenced by the dispersal and disintegration of Palestinian lives by an increasingly unsympathetic world order' ('Dispersal').

These concerns shape the plots of Dabbagh's debut novel *Out of It* (2011), which represents a story of transnational Palestinians grappling with ideas of nationalism, identity, resistance, and family. The novel follows the Mujaheds, who at the beginning have returned to Gaza with their family, having lived abroad in Switzerland as part of the 'Outside Leadership' of the PLO after the Oslo accords. As in Jarrar's novel (discussed in Chapter 3), Dabbagh represents the transitory nature of Palestinian diaspora through movements reflected in the structure of the text, which is split into five parts, the titles of which orient the different sections around specific geographic areas: 'Gazan Skies', 'London Views', 'Gulf Interiors', 'London Crowds' and 'The Gazan Sea'. The movement through these locations captures the cyclical, perpetual movements of the protagonists who are unable to achieve stability or find home in the locations they move between. The title inscribes a line of flight, however with the ambiguity of the 'it' there is no clarity about what that escape entails.

In an interview about her novel, Dabbagh describes the idea behind it as that of tracing the consequences of dispersion in the wake of conflict and understanding the forms of political identity in diaspora. She suggests that '[t]he Mujahed family members reflect different responses to the modern Palestinian experience defined by exile and internal displacement' ('New Texts'). Elsewhere, she describes how her novel explores 'the range of responses of characters to their sense of political engagement' ('Focusing on Dispersal'). In a way similar to Mahjoub and Aboulela's novels, Dabbagh dramatizes the conflict within one family, where each sibling forms differing allegiances in the context of 'contrasts in the political world between the Palestinian leadership who had returned from exile and the growing Islamic movement' (Moore, 'A Conversation'). Some find belonging in religious identity, others in nationalist ideology; some take the new country to be their home and others take on the narrative of the clash of civilisations. As Yassin-Kassab notes in his review of the novel, Dabbagh explores 'the increasingly violent internal competition between the religious parties and the corrupt Palestinian Authority' where 'each family member aims, in some way or other, to escape their predicament' ('Out of It'). The idea of being 'out of it' thus comes to represent different things for each of the characters.

Dabbagh has been careful to highlight the particularity of her own experience of Gaza. When she explains her decision to set her novel in part in Gaza, she remarks that she did so because 'it represented the extremity of the Palestinian situation'; however, she also acknowledges that since she has not lived there she 'could not write a graphic, socio-realistic depiction of Gaza' and therefore created her own 'conflate[d]' space from accounts of Gaza as well as accounts of 'the siege of Beirut in 1982 or [. . .] Iraq after 2003' (Moore, 'A Conversation' 327). This idea of conflating geographies which have been under siege and occupation is reminiscent of Radwa Ashour's explanation, discussed in the introduction, that she found correlatives between her 'experience of the bombing of Baghdad, a bombing which brought with it the 1967 bombing of Sinai, the 1982 bombing of Beirut, and the persistent bombing of Southern Lebanon' ('Eyewitness' 94). In addition to drawing empathic connections between places and experiences, this layering allows the writers a certain creative licence. Dabbagh acknowledges that '[her] Gaza [...] might be unreal to the people of Gaza but [...] [its] blurred reality [...] allowed [her] to stress the fictive nature of [her] story' (Moore, 'A Conversation' 327). The Gaza Dabbagh writes is her own creation, responding to the needs of the story she wishes to tell about the dislocations of Palestinian experience, and the need for memory work in response to this dispersal.

The blurred lines between fiction and fact are explored in the novel through the character of Sabri, the eldest son of the family, who spends his time attempting to write a history of Palestinian resistance focusing on the intifada. Before the narrative begins, we are told that Sabri had survived an Israeli attack that killed his wife and baby son and cost him his legs. Now using a wheelchair, Sabri (whose name symbolically links to 'patience') relies on his mother for help and deals with the impatience of his younger siblings. Described as a 'middle manager character with [. . .] a broad dome of a head that was becoming increasingly visible', Sabri attempts to escape this limited situation by assuming the role of chronicler (25). In other words, Sabri becomes a stand-in for the Palestinian writer, attempting to record a difficult history. Atef Abu Saif writes that literature has been an avenue for Palestinians to remember, 'the faithful scribe of history, events, and tragedies, of the details of their displacement and refugeedom' (ix). Sabri in this sense represents the urgency of archiving stories about the past for the needs of the present, to explore the personal stories that are lacking in the official narratives of struggle and resistance. In a way similar to the unearthing of family secrets in the work of Matar and Aboulela discussed in the previous chapter, Sabri's research allows him to find evidence that his mother had a role in the resistance that worked to undermine the Organization, a hidden history that contributes to his parent's divorce. Through this realization, Sabri confronts the extent to which the home is a site of national struggle, not a space secluded from the violence of the conflict.

Over the course of the novel, Sabri's writing shifts through the generations, moving from 'documents concerning his mother' to the intifada, the 'history of an uprising that he had lived through' (40). Claire Gallien notes that the narrator 'quotes lengthy extracts from Sabri's doctoral dissertation on the first intifada', an aspect of the novel which 'could be read as inserted for the instruction of Western readers still unfamiliar with the Palestinian/Israeli conflict' (61). Dabbagh is clearly conscious of this sort of exposition as a literary problem, noting in an interview that '[i]t breaks the spell of the writing [. . .] to have characters explaining their circumstances' (Moore, 'A Conversation' 327). In her novel, she attempts to balance between historical accounts and personal narratives, having Sabri reflect at length on the difficulties of narrating a history so entangled with his personal life, realizing that '[h]e was this history right from the beginning' and that '[h]is proximity to the subject matter was what made it unsettling' (40). Even as Sami is obsessed with preserving Palestinian history, he is unsettled by the past, and even resentful of its intrusions into his daily life. Sabri is in particular overwhelmed by memories of his wife Lana, who he senses is 'everywhere': '[h]is past with her kept coming back to him in these random flashes of memory where he could see himself, as an unwitting protagonist in an art-house movie of spliced film' (41). The representation of nostalgia here is self-consciously mediated, representing Sabri as a character in a film, in a way which speaks to his inability to connect with the object of his nostalgia. Representing Sabry's grappling with loss, Dabbagh negotiates between opposed concepts of memory. On the one hand, Sabri experiences the entropy of elusive memory which only becomes more elusive with every effort to grasp it: '[t]he more he thought of [Lana's] face, the more it faded' (42). On the other hand, even clear memories are acknowledged to be deceptive; for example, he realizes that one particular memory of his wife 'for all its clarity [. . .] was a scam [. . .] a fabrication' (85). Between these two ways of relating to memory, struggling to recall the past and confronting the deception of recollection, he is left grappling with how to distance himself from the reality he has lived through. Once Sabri arrives at the point where he has to record an era of history that he remembers, he is no longer able to see himself as the archivist, the historian. Instead, Sabri discovers what Umberto Eco calls 'the harmfulness of the study of history' and confronts '[t]he sense that the past is restricting, smothering, blackmailing us' (Rosso 2). Sabri attempts to write the authoritative account which would provide the uninitiated reader with the necessary context for the conflict, but keeps confronting the unreliability of his nostalgic recollections. He castigates his own memory as fraudulent and harmful, a feeling ultimately encapsulated in his bitter statement '[t]o hell with memory' (85).

While Sabri's understanding of resistance struggles with the difficulty of preserving history, for Jibril, Sabri's father, the way 'out of it' is to cling to the pastness of the past, insisting to himself that '[t]here was nothing he could do, anyway. It was all in the past' (161). This attitude allows him to protect himself against the charges that come with having been part of 'the Organization,' which opens him up to the excoriation of fellow Palestinians resentful of the privileges his position granted him: '[s]o, your children went to school in Switzerland, did they? And us? [. . .] where's our five per cent? Lost it in the casinos of Monaco, did you? While our families rot in the refugee camps? Bravo my friend, bravo!' (161). Similar outpourings of sarcastic invective occur elsewhere in the novel, for example when a bulletproof car blocks a narrow street, giving the crowd an opportunity to pour out their scorn on their leadership: 'Negotiated us away in exchange for that car, did you? So you can move it up and down the one kilometre of Gaza you liberated, did you? Bravo! Bravo' (47). The similarity of the language and syntax in these passages suggests that Dabbagh wants to give her readers a sense of the deep resentment harboured by Palestinians and Gazans in particular against their leadership, highlighting their struggle not only against occupation but also against the prevailing regimes, between excoriating 'the outside leadership, on the basis of its corruption, and condemn[ing] the Islamic alternative on the basis of its social conservatism' (79). Jibril's compromised position, as part of the Palestinian leadership, lays the groundwork to help the reader understand the need to find different modes of relating to Palestinian identity outside the official forms which have proved ineffectual, another version of the need to locate ways 'out of it'.

The novel focuses on Jibril's twin children, Iman and Rashid, who have contrasting views on their duty to Palestine. For Iman, returning to Gaza involves not only geographical relocation but also an opportunity for the reclamation of identity, attempting to negotiate sometimes conflicting nationalist and religious frameworks of resistance. Having returned to Gaza from Switzerland, Iman turns to nativist rhetoric that yokes identity to territory and demands civic engagement: '[t]his was their lot, their country, their place in the world. This was what she had come back for and it was for her to find a meaningful role within it' (18). Iman wants to stay in Gaza out of a sense of nationalist duty; what she seeks to 'get out' of, in this sense, is being an outsider. Needing someone to reassure her that '[y]ou were right to come back to Palestine. You do have a role here' (13), she eventually finds that role through affiliating herself with Islamist movements. Iman's attraction to the coherence provided by religious ideological narratives is both sympathetically dramatized and complicated by the recognition of the limitations and dangers of such narratives. As with Aboulela's representation of the attraction of religion, discussed in the previous chapter, there are elements of conversion narrative to these sections of Dabbagh's novel, though Iman's religious identity relates to her desire to belong to a resistance movement upon her return rather than a sense of loneliness in diaspora. Initially, Iman asserts that 'the religious lot gave her the creeps' (19), but she changes her mind when an Israeli bombing leads to the death of one of her students, and she comes to feel that '[d]eaths of children changed everything. Resistance movements started with dead children' (71). Dabbagh notes that her intention was to consider 'what it meant for individuals to have to, even at a quotidian level, constantly weigh up the competing demands of the cause and their society, on the one hand, and their own personal wishes or desires on the other' ('New Texts'). Thus, Iman is represented as having 'a kind of choice' in her response to the realities of Gaza, even as that choice is circumscribed (218). Eventually, Iman becomes too involved and is warned that she should leave Gaza, once again finding herself 'out of it'. Her repeated dislocations from Gaza result in a sense of suspension in diaspora. Through an exploration of Iman's jittery and transient connection to Gaza and to Palestine as a homeland under erasure, Dabbagh explores how the failures of nationalist and religious programmes heighten the contradictory sense of stationary displacement in the Palestinian context.

In contrast to Iman, her twin Rashid seeks to escape Gaza, having various ways 'out of it', from marijuana to his visa documents for London, which he calls his 'certificates of release' (14). Rashid (at least from his sister Iman's perspective) 'just prostrated himself before anything Western' (71), and in that sense functions to provide a contrasting attitude, focused not on finding ways to belong in Gaza but simply to escape. Despite Rashid's seeming wish to be consigned to a present lacking any emotional attachment to the past, a form of historical amnesia, demands are made of him to conform to expectations of Palestinian resistance, in particular the expectation that he should be invested in Palestinian history and the legacy of the Nakba. Once he arrives in London, we again have passages which seem to be included to, as Gallien puts it, 'update the reader on the history of the conflict' (61). This explanatory material includes a conversation Rashid has with his professor, who, it transpires, was a member of the Mandate Police in Palestine. This direct connection to Palestinian history proves difficult for Rashid to relate and listen to, an inability to map the features of the past onto the present which is symbolically captured in his attempt 'to find in Myres' face the features of the past', realizing that 'it can be as hard with some old people, as it is with some babies, to tell what or where a face has come from, and where it will be going' (129).

Rashid is repeatedly reminded that he must remain engaged in activism because what is happening around him is 'a war' (30, 160). For example, his girlfriend Lisa, who is involved in Palestinian activism, repeatedly advises him to 'think of alternatives to just Getting Out [. . .] it's not really something that you can just escape from. It's part of you, part of your family' (30). Through Rashid's attempts to escape this burden of expectation, Dabbagh explores how displacement engenders complex and conflicted narratives of resentment and guilt. For Rashid, the inability to locate himself presents a recurring challenge, his conflicted sense of attachment to and displacement from Palestine crippling any ready-made national identifications. That he 'never knew where to start' in discussing Palestinian history makes him realize that the question '[w]here is it that you're from?' is a problematic one, 'a question requiring a simple tick when he really needed to write an essay' (135). Here the inability to respond to a seemingly simple question involves recognizing the difficulty of giving a complete account. As Judith Butler points out, 'the very terms by which we give an account, by which we make ourselves intelligible to ourselves and to others, are not of our making' (21). Dabbagh's characters confront the need to account for the national and religious conflicts that shape their lives as they alternate between attempting to extricate themselves from or locate themselves within recognizable narratives.

Once he leaves for London, Rashid feels, at least initially, that he has been freed from the constraints of being Palestinian and Gazan: 'there was no Gaza anymore. He was out' (119). At this point, Rashid seeks to imagine a life without such a burden, 'wonder[ing] what he would have done if Palestine had played no part in his life' (126). His attempts to escape, to be 'out of' the ambiguous 'it', are however ultimately blocked by confrontations with stratifications that remain alive and well, forms of inequality that ensure that life is experienced differently due to factors that shape the supposedly fluid nature of identity. He is soon drawn back to thinking about what he has left behind, out of a combined sense of nostalgia, guilt and estrangement. In one scene, he reflects on 'the otherness of the passengers' in the London underground, realizing that they are marked by '[t]heir darkness, for they all were, without exception, washed up there like him'. The recognition that 'they are not from here' forces him to ask the question: 'what of their national duties? What of his? Pulling him out of any comfort zone presented to him, pushing him out into a conflicted world where he had no place' (120). The political and historical obstacles which hinder Rashid's path 'out of it' become incontrovertible when he is arrested because he is assumed to be a wanted Palestinian political activist. Though the case of mistaken identity is resolved, his arrest sparks the realization for the apolitical Rashid that, however much he wishes to free himself from his Palestinian identity, that identity will always accompany him. Ultimately, the comforting notion of a common humanity and a liberating cosmopolitan identity fails, as Rashid recognizes that he is unable to find a place for himself in either the 'comfort zone' of London or the 'conflicted world' of Gaza. In the final pages, he returns to Gaza, still imagining the possibility of 'flying above it all, up, over, out of it all' (308).

Dabbagh investigates the contradictory desire for belonging and for freedom from obligation in a context where nostalgia is seen as necessary fuel for preserving history and maintaining the Palestinian struggle, as a 'national duty' as Rashid puts it (120). The three siblings in Dabbagh's novel attempt in different ways to expand the limitations of Gaza's besieged reality, from Sabri's writing of history, which intertwines personal and political nostalgia, to Iman's determination to find home in resistance, to Rashid's desire to escape the boundaries of national duty altogether. The Mujaheds' physical return to Gaza from their privileged lives in Switzerland does not translate into creating a sense of being *at home*, a feeling which, Dabbagh seems to suggest, is impossible in the context of ongoing occupation and blockade. Rather, the characters struggle with contradictory impulses to return to and to escape Palestine. In her discussion of Gazan writing, Gallien writes that fiction not only 'expose[s] the violence and suffering of Gazan life under siege' but also 'challenges territorial fragmentation by transgressing the colonial map imposed by Israel and by defining counter-geographies' (57). Dabbagh's *Out of It* stages precisely this desire to challenge the enforced borders maintained by occupation as well as the impediments to such challenges, weaving a narrative that moves between Gaza, the Gulf and London, in which the characters are transnationally mobile and yet paradoxically stationary.

In an interview in which she is asked about the value of literature, Dabbagh lists what storytelling can do, including: 'to bear witness/reclaim history; to provide solace [. . .] to recognize heroism that is generally unsung [. . .] to create beauty; to interrogate societal values; and to positively visualize the future' (Moore, 'A Conversation' 329). The verbs that Dabbagh uses, 'provide, create, visualize', situate literature as generative, representing rather than reflecting. In a context where the Palestinian narrative of the Nakba is often relegated to history (eliding the ongoing processes of dispossession), this production of meaning speaks to the need to provide 'an imaginative (re)construction of the past in response to current needs', insisting that narratives which continue to move us remain relevant and real, rather than being nostalgic remnants we must go beyond (Neumann 334).

Rawi Hage's Cockroach

Rawi Hage is a Lebanese Canadian novelist who has published four novels to date. Hage's fiction deals with the Lebanese civil war and the experience of being an immigrant. *Cockroach* is his second and perhaps most successful novel so far. The novel's unnamed protagonist is an immigrant from a Middle Eastern country living in Montreal who describes himself as a cockroach. This self-description blurs the boundaries between the literal and the symbolic, from scenes of the protagonist's seeming transfiguration into a cockroach to his identification with the insects infesting his home. The symbolic meaning associated with the insect shifts between the dehumanizing discourse of immigrants as vermin to the cockroach as a symbol of survival; as the protagonist is warned by a Jehovah's Witness early on that after the apocalypse, '[o]nly the cockroaches shall survive to rule the earth' (7). The novel is structured as a series of episodic scenes of daily life, including the protagonist's interactions with fellow immigrants, his romantic feelings for an Iranian woman called Shohreh, his work as a busboy at a restaurant, and his flirtations with the restaurant owner's daughter. The novel, mostly composed of episodic scenes, is given a sense of linearity through the structuring device of weekly therapy sessions which are imposed on the protagonist following a suicide attempt. It is through these scenes that the reader gains some insights into the protagonist's past, filtered through his unreliable re-narration of his life to his therapist Genevieve. The tensions between the return to the past during the therapy sessions and the protagonist's moment-by-moment daily life lays the ground for the novel's exploration of the implications of forgetting and remembering as strategies for immigrant survival.

Much of the critical attention the novel has received has focused on Hage's use of the cockroach image to alter the contours of the immigrant narrative. Given the familiarity of the man-as-cockroach image, reviewers frequently describe the novel as a rewriting of Kafka's *The Metamorphosis*, though Hage himself has disavowed the comparison, stating that 'Kafka doesn't and can't have a monopoly on acts of metamorphosis' ('From the Ground Up'). The cockroach becomes a reflection of the immigrant narrator's awareness of his subaltern status. In Gillian Bright's argument, the novel 'operates as a parable for the return of the shameful repressed' (71), while Wisam Abdul-Jabbar argues that Hage's protagonist 'introjects the vermin as a representation of internalized antagonism' (168). However, even as the novel explores the consequences of immigrant self-hatred, the decidedly unlikeable protagonist is far from a victim, breaking into the homes of strangers who provoke him, as well as the homes of his therapist and his friends, turning their intrusions into his life into a physical invasion of their privacy. Lisa Marchi argues that, in opposition to the 'good immigrant' narrative, the novel dramatizes how 'the protagonist slowly liberates himself [. . .] neutralizing the forces that want to discipline, correct, and convert his supposedly deviant body into a good migrant and ultimately a happy Canadian citizen' (52). Marchi argues that Hage's immigrant novel counters two dominant narratives, both the 'negative image of the melancholic migrant' and the 'shiny representation of the successful immigrant who finds comfort and fulfilment in his/her new homeland' (50). Other critics have also emphasized that the protagonist's refusal to assimilate is no indication of nostalgic inclinations. Hout argues that the protagonist in *Cockroach* 'clearly has no interest in acclimatising to mainstream Canadian culture – but nor is he keen on flaunting his origins' (170). Similarly, Libin finds that the narrator assumes a position between nostalgia and assimilation, expressing 'disdain for backward looking' yet refusing the 'headlong rush into assimilation and embrace of Western ideologies' (83). In these readings, the protagonist is understood as inhabiting an in-between position, rejecting both the narrative of the immigrant dream and the nostalgic longing for home.

While the protagonist expresses a vehement rejection of nostalgic sentiment, the notion of inhabiting an in-between space between nostalgia and assimilation is hardly celebrated in the novel itself. In fact, the protagonist is particularly scornful of those he describes as 'lost mutts' who 'can't decide what breed they belong to', caught between their past identities and their new realities (144). He describes these lost souls as 'welfare dogs' who 'sprinkle traces of their lives here and there for no reason except to have the illusion of marking territory and holding vanishing places' (144). Here, the protagonist excoriates the attempt to simultaneously hold on to the past while clinging to the 'illusion of marking territory' as a failed and contradictory strategy. The dehumanizing image of immigrants as dogs 'marking territory' stands in contrast to the image of the immigrant as cockroach, which is reclaimed from the discourse of the immigrant vermin to represent a liberating underground identity and freedom from territoriality. Notably, when the protagonist feels that he is failing in this quest, he imagines the cockroach patronizingly addressing him as '[d]ear child' and castigating him for returning to past trauma: '[l]et's not open wounds and recite the past,' in contradistinction to the therapeutic model of working through and empathetic listening (202). At this point in the novel, it becomes clear that the protagonist might aspire to but does not necessarily achieve the cockroach's survivalist ethos as a model for the creation of a new life in diaspora.

In the opening pages of the novel, we are introduced to the protagonist's association with the cockroach. Soon after, the protagonist explains his attempted suicide as a reaction to 'the oppressive power in the world that I can neither participate in nor control' (4–5). His powerlessness is captured in his constant reflections on the intertwined sense of isolation and invisibility in the snowy landscape of Montreal. He notes the insubstantial and self-isolating nature of those he passes, in 'the silenced ears, plugged with wool and headbands, and the floating coats passing by in ghostly shapes'. He asks: 'How did I end up trapped in a constantly shivering carcass, walking in a frozen city with wet cotton falling on me all the time?' (9). Lisa Marchi argues that *Cockroach* is 'exemplary of recent Arab diasporic literature that counters the negative image of the melancholic migrant, as a subject fatally trapped within a deeply hurting past and paralyzed by nostalgic grief' (50). These scenes of being trapped in a frozen world however resonate with a long tradition of Arabic literature in which the cold becomes a metaphorical language to speak precisely of the paralysing nature of *ghurba*, estrangement from the homeland, often cast in nostalgic terms. Johanna Sellman has discussed how 'empty forests, barren snowy landscapes, and fantastical arctic vistas' are recurring tropes in representations of Europe in post-Cold War Arabic literature (6). In Hage's novel, the cold weather is personified as a hostile host, barely tolerating the protagonist's presence: 'if you ask why the inhumane temperature, the universe will answer you with tight lips and a cold tone and tell you to go back where you came from if you do not like it here' (193). Here, through shifting to second person, Hage invites the reader to step into the protagonist's reality, facing the 'inhumane' natural cold as well as the 'cold tone' of the society, the uncertainty of migrant existence.

The protagonist is certainly disparaging of nostalgia as an attitude. He is scathing in his description of Montreal itself as a deeply nostalgic place, as reflected in the '[p]hotos of la campagne rustique, le Québec du nord des Amériques, depicting cozy snowy winters and smoking chimneys [. . .] pasted on every travel agent's door' (27). Hage has discussed French Canadian reality in terms of the 'complex existence' of a minority, noting that to behave as a minority means that '[t]here is always this sense of being under threat, fear of extinction of your language of race' which triggers 'almost instinctive [. . .] reactions from nationalism to favouritism to a sense of superiority mixed with inferiority' (Ray 13). In Hage's novel, the nostalgic notion of 'le Québec du nord des Amériques' implicitly connects the French Canadians to the immigrants 'marking territory', both performing an instinctive retreat into essentialized identities, which highlights the problems with a progressive wholesome narrative of welcome, integration and shared humanity (27).

Through the fragmentary episodes of the protagonist's daily life, we witness his interactions with fellow immigrants, including an Algerian man he calls the professor. The protagonist describes this character as a 'charlatan' who sits in the café telling stories about his past 'for the free coffee and to bum cigarettes from those nostalgic souls' (116). Here, nostalgia is manipulated for social power (in the same way as the protagonist manipulates others through tales of trauma and the exotic), yet manipulation does not necessarily contradict with the genuine depth of nostalgic emotion. The protagonist becomes a witness to the professor's profoundly nostalgic existence when he breaks into his home to find 'a bunch of knick-knacks, objects he must have kept from his stay in Paris' as well as documents and papers in 'an old green suitcase' that makes the protagonist imagine 'departing trains, trench coats, and a beautiful woman in a head scarf and pointy shoes waiting on a platform' (150). This imagery is drawn from a romanticized and anachronistic idea of the journey, where the professor plays the role of 'an intellectual revolutionary' and 'a sixties-era Third World lady-tourist-chaser' (150). The image of the exile is then juxtaposed with the reality of the professor's experience as an immigrant, the insecure need for evidence that is suggested in the bundles of documents labelled 'Immigration' and 'Torture'. The protagonist is later moved to scornful pity for the 'poor naïf professor' whose journey is so deeply out of sync with contemporary immigration realities. Later, the protagonist will describe the professor as 'the lost exile [. . .] a goner, a little lost imposter, a lonely spy walking out into the cold of the world' (298). The tone is pitying as well as scornful, highlighting the levels of complexity in the relationship between the two characters. When the protagonist burns one of the professor's letters, he is burning the idealized images he associates with the professor, 'the Mediterranean shores, the fancy resorts' (186). This destructive act is seemingly motivated by the protagonist's avowed rejection of nostalgia, yet the language here suggests that this anti-nostalgic antagonistic attitude shields him from the complex confrontation with empathy and jealousy. The tone with which he speaks of the professor intertwines disdain and sympathy.

The tension between forgetting the past and longing for connection is exemplified in the protagonist's relationship with the Iranian musician Reza, referred to early on as 'the Middle Eastern hunchback', as though he is an embodiment of a regional posture of lament (11). Notably, in the very opening lines of the novel, the protagonist describes his 'bizarre mix of emotions and instinct' in the presence of women by likening himself to 'a hunchback in the presence of schoolgirls' (3). Reza becomes an unwelcome reminder of the protagonist's own reality. As with the professor, the protagonist expresses scorn for Reza's nostalgic moods, when '[h]e either gave me long monologues about Persia and the greatness of its history, or [. . .] re-enacted the tears of his mother, whom he will never see again before she dies because, as he claims, he is an unfortunate exile' (11). The protagonist distances himself from witnessing Reza's vulnerability by speaking about its performative nature, through the reference to monologues and to re-enacting tears, and through the distancing aside 'he claims'. Later, the protagonist will cynically use his relationship to Reza in order to regain favour with the leftist crowd that once bought drugs from him, showing them the santour, the instrument Reza plays, and referring to the musician's traumatic experiences. Libin suggests that throughout Hage's novel the 'émigrés want to relegate their traumas to the past and convert them into cultural currency to use in transactions with liberal Canadians, transactions guaranteed to reiterate the hierarchy between guest and host' (86). In the case of the relationship between the protagonist and Reza, this manipulation is not only employed as a strategy against liberal Canadians, but also serves to protect the protagonist from empathizing with Reza. Like the protagonist's burning of the professor's letters, the game distances the protagonist from confronting the reality of Reza's 're-enacted' tears or being expected to respond with empathy. With both the professor and Reza, the protagonist employs cynical defence mechanisms to avoid confronting or grappling with their nostalgic emotions.

The cynical use of trauma in *Cockroach* explores the tensions between the ideal of cosmopolitan openness with its notion of exchange between cultures and a reality dominated by one-way influence that entrenches inequalities. As Leela Gandhi describes, '[o]ur conception of the "political" or "ethical" is in many ways hopelessly circumscribed by the secular, rational calculations which underscore the movement of modern European thought – from Europe "out" into the (post)colonial world' (116). Through the interactions between the therapist and the protagonist, and between the protagonist and his bourgeoisie victims, Hage explores how trauma discourse always functions within certain power relations. The protagonist is aware of how migrants must grapple with the contradictory emotions of resentment and gratitude, in a context where Western liberal democracies provide the beacon of progress and human rights for the disenfranchised. It is in this context that the protagonist speaks disdainfully of 'the industry of tears', as a cultural resource which is always used and manipulated. He goes on to describe the liquid as a mysterious source of power:

> The ancient Phoenicians [. . .] gathered their tears and buried them underground. Their whole kingdom floated above small glasses of tears before their boats hit the seas. I wondered why all cultures demand tears. The industry of tears! Tears must be seen then buried. Even Genevieve wanted my tears! (143)

The reference to the ancient Phoenicians recalls Reza's 're-enacted' tears as an exile lamenting his mother and the greatness of Persia at once. The image of a kingdom afloat on glasses of tears and of the boats hitting the seas is a suggestive one in the context of immigrants fleeing the traumatic experiences of war and persecution in their homeland. Referring to his therapist Genevieve's demand for his tears, the protagonist clearly understands the role he should play as the grateful immigrant who, in order to express his gratitude, should be seen to be in tears at the traumas he has suffered. Yet there is an element of bathos to this passage, as the protagonist goes on to refer to tears as a physical liquid produced by the body which can be caused by emotions other than sorrow, imagining himself collecting and labelling 'tears from laughter, tears from spicy food, tears from pain, tears from nostalgic memories, tears from broken hearts, tears from poverty' (143). Again, we have at once an awareness of and a distancing from confronting the depth of emotions associated with leave-taking and with the experience of estrangement. Tears from 'nostalgic memories' are rendered banal to some extent, their power stripped, through being associated with other types of tears.

In his therapy sessions, the protagonist shifts between an obtuse reticence and an antagonistic game where he plays with the expectations of both Genevieve and the reader, clearly deriving some amusement from these manipulations. For example, when he is asked what his mother was like, he pretends to misunderstand the question and simply describes her physical features. Later, he speaks casually of violence in his household, while exhibiting an awareness of the traumatic framing Genevieve might impose on these events. He insists on speaking about the everyday, rather than specifying a singular traumatic event that must be worked through. His testimony, in its matter of fact tone, resists the framework of a traumatic narrative, and instead increasingly pushes the therapist to a pragmatic approach, until she ultimately reveals her judgemental attitude, pointing to the laziness of immigrants and their wasting of taxpayer money.

Much of the critical discussion of these therapy sections associate the reader with the therapist and see the protagonist's recalcitrant attitude as a refutation of the empathetic reading model, in which postcolonial literature offers mainstream Western readers a window into the traumatic lives of others. For example, Libin has argued that *Cockroach* pushes against 'the reading of postcolonial literature as a vehicle for enacting cross-cultural ethics' (71), as the protagonist 'actively demonstrates how soliciting personal narratives of an other is an invasion, an infiltration, an infestation' (86). Genevieve's attempts to gain the protagonist's trust are, in this reading, instructive as an example of the ethical issues involved in the consumption of traumatic narratives as a form of edification. Yet the games the protagonist plays with Genevieve are also similar to his antagonistic relationship to Reza and the professor, in which the protagonist sabotages the possibility of intimacy in order to protect himself against confronting emotion. As the narrative unfolds, and as the reader becomes increasingly able to read between the lines of the protagonist's behaviour, our ethical engagement becomes more complex. We come to understand not only the limitations of the model of empathetic therapy, but the human resistance to confronting difficult emotions, whether traumatic or nostalgic, or both.

It is not only trauma and nostalgia that are manipulated in the novel; the exotic, too, is an underlying theme, with the protagonist reflecting, in a comment which has a meta-dimension addressing the reader, that '[t]he exotic has to be modified here – not too authentic, not too spicy or too smelly, just enough of it to remind others of a fantasy elsewhere' (20). Marchi argues that the protagonist becomes '[l]ike a resourceful and audacious Scheherazade' during therapy sessions 'perform[ing] artful manoeuvres to hold his therapist's curiosity, gain her indulgence, and constantly delay his adverse fate' (53). It is notable however that when the protagonist does explicitly invoke Scheherazade, he does so in a scene where he is inspired and transported into the Arabian Nights fantasy by the Orientalist setting of the restaurant, and, significantly, he imagines himself to be not Scheherazade but rather a rescuer of the women Shahriyar kills, wondering whether he 'could have saved any of those women' by sticking 'a dagger through [Shahriyar's] silky purple robe' (67). Rather than identifying with the storyteller, the protagonist aligns Scheherazade with Shohreh, as a woman to rescue, playing out the damsel-in-distress fantasy through which he can briefly recuperate his self-worth. That he is himself impacted by the fantasy of the exotic which he elsewhere wields as a cynical tool to manipulate others again highlights the complexity of the protagonist's struggle to dissociate himself from notions of heritage and cultural memory through identifying with the survivor figure of the cockroach. In this scene, the protagonist himself proves susceptible to the fantasy, though this moment of escapist daydream is brief.

We see exactly how the cockroach figure allows the protagonist to pull himself away from daydreams in the next sentence, when the heroic figure he imagines himself to be is transfigured back into the insect alter-ego, the Arabian Nights setting turned back into the snowy landscape of Montreal: '[t]he smell of food from the kitchen brought me back to the land of forests and snow. And then all I wished was to crawl under the swinging door and hide under the stove, licking the mildew, the dripping juice from the roast lamb' (67). The association between consuming and forgetting suggested here is one we see repeatedly in the novel, relating to the capacity of the cockroach to hide and to survive. For example, at one point, the narrator speaks of how 'at the first sip of beer, the first fries' he 'forget[s] and forgive[s] humanity for its stupidity' as well as 'forget[ing] about [his] mother, [his] father' (226). Following this remark, the protagonist repeats to himself a consumerist mantra as though he wills himself to believe it: 'I deserve to spend. I deserve every drop of substance, every drip of intoxication. I deserve not only to forgive but also to forget' (228). This reiteration of 'I deserve' speaks to a marketing language where consumerism is a replacement for therapy, an easy substitute for confronting deeper sources of emotional and psychological need and hunger.

At the end of the novel, we return to the fantasy of the heroic figure in an attempted rescue of Shohreh, though as Libin notes, the conclusion is 'deliberately muted, flattened, rendered more banal and commonplace than redemptive or heroic' (88). Whether the ending is to be understood as fantasy or reality, its brevity suggests that soon enough the protagonist will once again push back from genuine emotional engagement to inhabiting his cockroach alter-ego, reminding himself of the inefficacy of being bound to the past. The novel ends on an openness reminiscent of Dominick LaCapra's concept of 'empathic unsettlement', which 'poses a barrier to closure in discourse and places in jeopardy harmonizing or spiritually uplifting accounts of extreme events from which we attempt to derive reassurance or a benefit' (41–2). We are not certain if the rescue the protagonist imagines is successful, or even if it is real. What the ending does leave us with however is the recognition that, for all his insistent performance of anti-nostalgia, the protagonist remains susceptible to the draw of the past: although he seems to aspire to the model of therapeutic forgetting, he lapses repeatedly into fantasies, memories and resentments oriented towards what happened before.

In the novels discussed here, the writers represent characters adapting their lives in the diaspora in relation to present-day political crises in the Arab world that frame their own and others' understandings. *Cockroach* deals with the trauma of the Lebanese civil war, *Out of It* is partially set in and concerned with Palestine, specifically Gaza, during the intifada and its aftermath, while *Road from Damascus* is concerned with both the Gulf War and with the repercussions of recurrent regime brutality in Syria. In each case, the novels explore how political instability continues to impact lives in the diaspora, and how the characters negotiate their attachment to the past and their fear of, or desire for, a future where they have lost their identity to assimilate into the dominant culture. The novels examine how distance from collective national belonging motivates the desire to retain a distinct difference from the dominant culture, casting forms of nostalgic attachment and the ossifications of authenticity against more ambivalent reflections on belonging, as the categories employed to construct belonging are challenged by distance from the homeland. The novels I have examined in this chapter therefore dramatize not only the nostalgic attachment to homeland, but also the attempt to turn away from it, a rejection stemming from a recognition that home is no longer a place of refuge and shelter.

In an article published in April 2013, Hisham Matar writes of a return to his homeland, Libya, thirty-three years after leaving. At the beginning of the article, Matar weighs the arguments of those who try to 'cure [themselves] of [their] country' and those who returned: '[r]eturn and you will face the absence or the defacement of what you treasured [. . .] Leave and your connections to the source will be severed [. . .] What do you do when you cannot leave and cannot return?' ('The Return'). Matar goes on to relate that he had believed that by returning to his birthplace, he would be able to provide a concise answer, pinpoint a place of origin:

> I had pictured myself one day calm and settled in that far-away island, Manhattan, where I was born. I would imagine a new acquaintance asking me that old question 'Where are you from?' and I would casually reply, 'New York.' In these fantasies, I saw myself taking pleasure in the fact that such a statement would be both true and false, like a magic trick. ('The Return')

This 'magic trick' response seeks to circumvent the difficulties of giving an account of oneself, in the situation of being unable to leave and unable to return that sums up the condition of the characters in the novels I have discussed. As the protagonist Yasin reflects in Jamal Mahjoub's *Travelling with Djinns*, 'coming back was not just a matter of physically returning, there were other adjustments to be made, gaps that had to be compensated for. You are no longer one person [. . .] but two – both of them strangers' (204). This in-betweenness is inexorably linked to the instabilities of the homeland, and the implicit obligation to the place of origin. Hout, speaking of the literature of the Lebanese diaspora, suggests that making a life outside the homeland involves 'a complex relationship between self-love and love for a bleeding nation' (*Post-War* 25). It is the conflict between political engagement and personal fulfilment which makes nostalgia a central problem and a recurrent theme explored by the diaspora literature that I have discussed here.

As Maleh notes, 'Anglophone Arab literature is haunted by the same "hybrid", "exilic", and "diasporic" questions that have dogged fellow postcolonialists' (x). My aim in this chapter has been to explore these questions in relation to representations of nostalgia, and to particular political contexts. The novels I have examined explore the transformation of identity in the diaspora in relation to the turmoil of the homeland, and deal with the postcolonial themes of cultural loss and the myth of return. Through representing the divergent choices made by the characters in relation to how to relate to their homelands and their new homes, Yassin-Kassab, Dabbagh and Hage explore different ways of making lives in diaspora liveable. In emphasizing the performative aspects of those choices, the writers undermine the representation of immigrants as, in Ghassan Hage's words, 'passive pained people' (417). In each of the novels, nostalgia proves to be a multifarious and complex emotional recourse and a means through which the protagonists create their lives in diaspora. The writers I have discussed are often keenly aware of the dangers of a romanticized view of the past that produces a solipsistic identity politics. Through depicting characters constructing hybridized identities in diaspora, from incorporating nationalist symbols within a radical aesthetic to subscribing to ideologies from Ba'athism or Islamism, each of these writers negotiate how authenticity is always based on invention and performance. At the same time however, they show nostalgia to be an important way of experiencing and creating a relationship to history, both personal and public, as a coherent narrative, a link to the past that provides stability, particularly in the context of the alienation resulting from displacement and political and cultural crises. Though nostalgia has been regarded with suspicion as a sentimental and reactionary force, nostalgic discourses also respond to the erasures of history, providing continuity and coherence and affective claims of belonging.

CONCLUSION

In an article published in August 2015, Jamal Mahjoub writes about his memories of living in Khartoum during the 1970s, at the time of the Nimeiry regime. Mahjoub describes looking back at the early years of Nimeiry's government as 'a reminder of what might have been', yet immediately questions his impulse to romanticize the past: 'so much of what we wanted to believe turned out to be part of an elaborate fairy tale. Did we hear what we wanted to hear?' ('Rumble on the Nile'). Here, even in expressing nostalgia for what could have been, Mahjoub raises the possibility that the national project was always an illusion, even when it seemed within reach. Self-reflexively questioning why he is drawn back to remember his childhood in Khartoum, Mahjoub writes:

> [i]t's as if the past will not go away. So much has happened in this country's history and yet we can't seem to get over it and move on. It refuses to go away. Instead it keeps coming back, challenging us, asking us to try and understand what it is we haven't yet grasped. ('Rumble on the Nile')

In these remarks, Mahjoub captures the simultaneous and contradictory imperative to move beyond the past and the responsibility to remember. Richard Sennet has suggested that 'regret is a dangerous sentiment. While it produces empathy for the past, and so a certain insight, regret induces resignation about the present and so a certain acceptance of its evils' (259). However, in this case the look back to the past is not one that focuses on resignation about the present but precisely the inability to be resigned to that present. Mahjoub's nostalgic memories frame the analytical dissection of the processes that, in his view, have led to the contemporary political impasse. Nostalgia is leveraged as a strategic way to 'return, in a spirit of revision and reconstruction, to the political conditions of the present' (Bhabha *Location of Culture* 3). The inability to forget, to 'get over it and move on', is shown to stem from the lack of resolution to political crises, and the need to analyse and understand the sources of present conflict. Mahjoub's personalization of a past that returns and asks to be understood, that recurrently challenges us in the present, encapsulates the complex and self-doubting dynamics of nostalgic emotions that permeate Anglophone Arab literature.

The need to overcome nostalgia and aspire to more critical forms is often reiterated within the field of Anglophone Arab literary criticism, yet nostalgia itself often works as a form of critique. This book has sought to pursue several threads of ambivalence in the treatment of nostalgia in Anglophone Arab novels, between acknowledging the irreducible otherness of the past that cannot be recovered and bearing witness to histories that cannot be forgotten. The texts that I have examined push against common assumptions around immigrant fiction, reflecting not only on the negotiation of new modes of belonging but also on the extent to which migrants remain deeply imbricated in the politics and histories of their homelands. The nostalgic narratives in these novels are not always synonymous with a conservative mode that sees the past as a reassuring bulwark against distressing change. Instead, different forms of nostalgia give resonance to the juxtapositions of past and present and provide a lens for the interpretation and questioning of historical narratives. The nostalgia that yearns to return to the past is often inseparable from, and charged by, the awareness of an unhealable rift, the *ghurba* (or estrangement) that makes such a return impossible. It is the ambivalence that this recognition engenders which characterizes the Anglophone Arab novels I have examined, as they explore the yearning for a distant idealized past, for a precolonial authenticity, for the nation as family and for the homeland as refuge. Strategically undercutting these emotionally resonant but one-dimensional narratives, Anglophone Arab novels simultaneously linger on the forms of metaphorical and literal estrangement, the experiences of *ghurba*, that complicate any affiliation to foundational origins.

As discussed in the opening chapter, the notion of a golden age offers both a consoling vision of an idealized distant past and the melancholic awareness of its irrevocable pastness. The overcharged 'chaos of lost empires', as Yasmin Zahran puts it, juxtaposes premodern and pre-Islamic civilizations and the medieval golden age against Arab (post)modernity (49). The golden age thus serves the needs of the present imaginary by bringing a more illustrious past into conversation with the failures and disappointments of the contemporary period. The writers I discussed in the first chapter explore how the melancholic view of a stagnant present emerges from the gap between the golden age and the 'ugliness', in Khemir's words, of contemporary realities ('Mobile Identity' 46). Though Khemir, Zahran and Alameddine are interested in the melancholic nostalgia for a distant, allegedly perfect past, their texts also subvert this romanticization by highlighting the processes of translation, adaptation and retelling, which force a confrontation with the irrevocable disconnection from origins. That is, their texts play out the various gradations on a spectrum between yearning for a distant idealized time and confronting the impossibility of reconnecting with that past. The focus on the traces through which the past surfaces in the present ultimately undermines the notion of restoring the glory of the past, and the emphasis is placed instead on a future-oriented reconstruction of the past for the present. Such a recognition speaks to the extent to which the distant past continues to communicate with the unfolding present. As Stuart Hall puts it:

> [t]he past continues to speak to us. But it no longer addresses us as a simple factual 'past', since our relations to it, like a child's relation to the mother, is always, already, 'after the break.' It is always constructed through memory, fantasy, narrative and myth. (226)

The narrative constructions of the pasts that continue to speak to us are vital to cultural discourse, telling us more about the present than about the past. Demystifying the fantasies and myths that are spun to construct this past requires recognizing (rather than dismissing as sentimental) the complicated nostalgic emotions driving such narratives, including the nostalgia that accompanies the recognition that the idea of a matchless past is in fact a fantasy.

Fantasies of authenticity and tradition are central to the rewriting of the history of colonial occupation. In their novels, Mahjoub, Faqir and Soueif explore the dichotomous understandings of modernity and tradition that continue to drive internal ideological conflicts in the present. On the one hand, the historical focus seeks to heal the dislocation from the precolonial past and bear witness to the traumas of colonialism. On the other, the relevance of this history for the present is captured in an ongoing repetition of the 'war between yesterday and tomorrow' where the ideological investment in tradition becomes a pathway to coherent self-definition (*In The Hour of Signs* 230). As Richard Wolin puts it, 'unless the labour of coming to terms with the past has been undertaken in earnest' there is a compulsion 'to protect the idealized image of national greatness from the traumatic blows it has most recently endured' (86). The idealization of a precolonial past offers a fictional authenticity that heals the fractures of postcolonial, national and diasporic realities. The parallels drawn between colonial and postcolonial regimes suggest an effort on the part of the writers to negotiate contested relationships with the distant homeland and with a painful colonial and postcolonial history. To borrow a phrase from Walter Benjamin, the use of nostalgia in these novels results in the writers 'telescoping the past through the present' ('Berlin Chronicle' 305). That they do so from a geographical and linguistic distance adds to the sense of disconnection from the precolonial past, and from a hopeful time of anti-colonial nationalism that aspired to an independent state.

The nostalgia for the post-independence era is again predominant when it comes to novels that explore the failures of the nationalist postcolonial project. Matar, Aboulela and Jarrar explore the breakdown of the illusionary separation between the public and the private sphere through narratives that subvert the notion of being 'at home', which is commonly taken to impart a sense of stable subjectivity. The myth of the homeland as a home and the nation as a family, and the nostalgia for these concepts, is refracted in exile through the realization that any notion of protective separations between the spheres of public and private life have always been an illusion. This disruption complicates the relationship to nationalist forms of identity, since the romanticized narrative of the 'homeland' falls apart at the level of the most intimate sites of memory, the family and the home. Re-centring the national narrative on the private sphere as it is undermined by the violence of the autocratic state and focusing on the unhomely intrusion of violence results in a questioning of traditional and nostalgic understandings of the nation as secure home.

The disruption of the homeland as refuge precipitates a rethinking of identity-making in diaspora. In the writing of Dabbagh, Mahjoub and Hage, the paradigmatically transnational characters negotiate national subjectivity outside the bounds of autochthonous belonging, and in contexts of political instability that destabilize the myths of nationhood. The superimposition of physical displacement with endemic political violence shapes the narrative of the immigrant capacity for self-creation. The diasporic hope of finding belonging involves a constant negotiation of multiple aspects of identity, including the refusal to forget the conditions which dictate one's leaving and arrival. Nostalgia is a crucial part of immigrant narratives, represented as central to performing identity and to creating 'liveable' lives. The nostalgic strategies of constructing belonging are presented as creative processes rather than solely in terms of the melancholy immigrant narrative of what Ghassan Hage calls 'passive pained people' (417). Having moved from a 'desire for home' to a 'homing desire' in Avtar Brah's terms, nostalgic discourses function as strategies reconfiguring ways to be 'at home' in the diaspora. Nostalgic modes are not always driven by rigid concepts of identity but can also be born of the tenuousness of connection to a sense of home.

The use of nostalgic discourses highlights the rift between the immigrant and the homeland, and the impossibility of return. That is, nostalgia is an integral part of the destabilization of the link between who we are and where we belong territorially, and the need 'to overcome' what Said describes as 'the crippling sorrow of estrangement' (*Reflections* 173). As an aesthetic strategy, the deployment of nostalgic tropes can add complexity to the representation of immigrants and the experiences of diaspora communities. The writers I have discussed explore how nationalist ideologies are transplanted, rejected or reshaped by other modes of orientation and belonging. In doing so, they dramatize the flexibility of nostalgic strategies which make diasporic life liveable. The novels thus both call for a reading that cuts across national boundaries and for an understanding of the located and specific histories migrants carry with them.

This book has made the case that understanding the range of possible nostalgic emotions beyond the binaries of good (complex) and bad (simple) forms of nostalgia challenges some of the assumptions about immigrant writing as a catch-all term. The reconstructions of the past through nostalgic frameworks can offer new ways of thinking diaspora, the variety of nostalgic emotions and associations presenting writers with a spectrum of feelings linked to working through the complex ongoing repercussions of violent histories which continue to drive immigration. I have argued that the common assumption that nostalgia is limited to the romanticizing of the past is confining and leaves unexamined the many creative and performative ways that nostalgia is invoked in literary texts. Moreover, failing to acknowledge the varieties of nostalgic discourses dismisses the urgent political and personal demands to which nostalgia responds, inextricable as it is from the problematics of belonging and citizenship. Nostalgic narratives give us a psychological and intimate point of access to the human experience of migrancy and exile. My argument has been that nostalgia is often a politically motivated act and psychological state. Bringing the politics of nostalgia into sharper focus allows for more nuanced understandings of the impact of the past on the present and future. More generally, I have sought to underline that, as the political and social processes of migration and displacement are increasingly no longer exceptional, there is a need to examine the appeal of nostalgia as an ideological force, and to consider how the dynamics of nostalgia modulate identity narratives in transnational contexts.

The convergence of two seemingly antithetical currents, the rise of memorial consciousness alongside anti-historicist discourses of globalization, prompts further questions regarding what a careful understanding of nostalgia might offer postcolonial and migrant literature more broadly. What critical inferences might result from paying closer attention to nostalgia, rather than arguing for the need to 'get beyond' the nostalgic mode as the stereotypical trope of immigrant narratives? What does the critical re-visioning of nostalgia within memory and trauma studies offer in terms of contemporary discussions about the limitations of postcolonial criticism? How does rethinking nostalgia help to negotiate the areas of crossover between theorizations of identity within postcolonial, transnational and cosmopolitan frames?

Over the past few decades, terms like cosmopolitan, transnational and diaspora have become increasingly ubiquitous and consolidated as areas of study. As Maureen Anne Moynagh has argued, 9/11 'added to the urgency with which many intellectuals are currently promoting cosmopolitanism' as part of a progressive alternative to the discourse of the War on Terror (18). For example, Kwame Anthony Appiah has argued for more focus on 'the idea that we have obligations to others [...] that stretch beyond those to whom we are related by ties of kith and kind or even the more formal ties of a shared citizenship' (xv). The ascendancy of these frameworks raises a number of questions about what we mean by 'postcolonial' today. David Chariandy articulates this concisely when he asks whether the development of 'cosmopolitics' should be considered 'a breakthrough in cultural politics and social justice' or 'the final stage in the ascendancy of migrant, cosmopolitan, and first-world metropolitan biases in representations of the post-colonial experience' ('Postcolonial Diasporas'). Here, we return to a subject of fraught debate since the inception of postcolonial studies, the development of analytical frameworks from the academic centres of the West and their remoteness from the material realities of what was once called the third world. As Neil describes it, the term 'third world', which has now been eclipsed by the term postcolonial (and the term postcolonial perhaps itself eclipsed by other terms) 'conjures up an entire historical conjuncture and accompanying political culture, in which one naturally went on to utter the [...] slogans of "national liberation," etc' (24–5). Implicit and sometimes explicit in the theorization of an ethical cosmopolitics are the negative consequences of clinging to national frameworks, which are perceived to be not only hegemonic, homogenizing and discriminatory but increasingly irrelevant. Yet as Arif Dirlik notes, while '[n]ational liberation movements are now of the past', the issues of identity and history they were addressing remain relevant, albeit in altered form:

> the question of cultural identity is still very much there [...] rephrased now in the language of globalisation that has replaced modernisation as a paradigm of change, but without providing any solutions to either the problems inherited from the past, or the proliferation of cultural conflict under its regime. (Culture, 170)

Making a similar assertion, Said argues for a future-oriented mode of reading difference, noting that we need 'a heightened critical consciousness not only of what difference can do, but of where its politics can lead' (*The Politics of Dispossession* 89–90). Said's argument for an unresolved identity and flawed history as furthering 'narratives of integration not separation' critiques the use of identity to construct and police boundaries (*Culture and Imperialism* xxx). Yet this argument against the emphasis on origins in mythologies of nationalism is in tension with Said's own work in relation to Palestinian national identity and self-determination. The question that emerges from this productive tension is how best to 'reinterpret ideologies of difference' from 'an awareness of the supervening actuality of "mixing" or crossing-over, of stepping beyond boundaries, which are more creative human activities than staying inside rigidly policed borders' (*The Politics of Dispossession* 90). How can such a transnational postcolonialism be constructed in the current climate?

Patrick Williams presents several possible answers for the place of postcolonialism today in the form of rhetorical questions: 'is postcolonialism [. . .] to be construed as propping up identities that are marginalised or demonised in the contemporary world? Is it rather about the historical recovery of lost or damaged identities? Or is it perhaps about the articulation of new possibilities, new modes of identification or belonging?' (48). The implicit suggestion is that postcolonialism should move from past-based modes that offer emotional anchors to new possibilities and modes of identification. A similar drive to overcome the attachment to and the yearning for the past and the homeland characterizes contemporary criticism on Anglophone Arab literature. As discussed in the introduction, Lisa Suhair Majaj for example has written of the 'the problem of nostalgia,' contrasting one mode of 'deploying nostalgia as a way to retrieve ethnic identity' against 'exploring new visions for the future' ('Arab American Literature'). My approach has been to suggest that a more receptive approach to the scope of nostalgia, the spectrum of nostalgic feelings and the psychological needs that they respond to, can provide a useful framework for reading a wide range of texts within the growing body of Anglophone Arab literature, and connecting this literature to the fields of memory, trauma and postcolonial studies.

I have focused on a limited number of novels in this study. However, an investigation of the broader context should include other genres to address more expansively the strategies deployed in fictions of memory by Arab writers writing in English and from the diaspora. In addition to expanding the scope of this study, future work on nostalgia in the Arab diaspora might be extended in terms of the countries represented in the literature. In my examination, I have not discussed in any depth writers who write about or from the Gulf region, due to the particularity of the narratives of alternative modernity and oil politics that structure contemporary novels set in that region. However, the growing popularity of English-language education and popular culture in the Gulf provide the opportunity to examine a different context for Arab writing in English. An example of an Anglophone text that deals with these trends and this region is Sophia al-Maria's memoir *A Girl Who Fell To Earth* (2012), which in part focuses on the dynamics of tradition and modernity in the region. Al-Maria has also examined this tension through her research on what she terms 'Gulf futurism' where urban planning and technology is conjoined to narratives of utopia and prosperity. Though the politics of nostalgia is an integral part of these narratives, the themes and narratives of yearning and memory take different shapes in relation to the construction of a Gulf modernity, and this would make for a rewarding study, particularly in the context of the scale of the museum boom in this region.

This book has sought to connect between Anglophone scholarship and literature and the Arabic literary tradition. I believe that as with Francophone Arab literature, Anglophone Arab literature needs to be read together with Arabic texts, and particularly when it comes to issues of memory and nostalgia, as the need to memorialize, to create alternative archives, in part responds to the sense that 'there is a long-standing crisis in Arab society that awaits a solution [. . .] an underlying assumption that something must be done to break the deadlock in the current situation' (Abu-Rabi' 8). The relationship between identity and language plays a crucial role, but the role of the past in formulating the future is often strikingly similar in English and Arabic texts, especially when contemporary Arabic-language literature already often reflects on themes of exile, diaspora and translation. Let me give as one example the following scene from Elias Khoury's *Gate of the Sun*, where the narrator reflects on his role as a translator and the untranslatability of a certain form of rhetoric:

> I was required to translate whatever I said in Arabic into English and I discovered that I could dispense with half the expressions we use [. . .] I started to avoid the lengthy introductions we usually put in front of whatever we have to say and went straight to the point instead [. . .] How was I to translate the words for suffering, torment, oppression and persecution that the man used one after another? He'd string together adjectives without indicating what he was describing, so I summarised his long Arabic sentences into brief English ones. (266)

This passage, with its focus on translation, and the impossibility of translating the history of a political struggle, is strikingly similar to another scene of translation that occurs in British-Lebanese author Tony Hanania's first novel *Homesick* (1998). Hanania's novel moves between the protagonist's time at boarding school in England and the Lebanese civil war. At one point, the narrator witnesses the following exchange about the challenge of translation in the context of violence:

> A group of foreign reporters [. . .] are asking questions in English about the weight of the SAM's warhead and its range and capabilities [. . .] a Mourabitoun spokesman wanders over with his hands behind his back and grins at the foreign correspondents. All begin asking their questions at the same time. What is the range of the warhead? Where is its projected deployment? Who has supplied it? When they have piped down the spokesman begins a long and convoluted speech in Arabic about the nobility of the revolutionary struggle and the hard road to freedom. None of the correspondents understand a word of this and call

out for a translation. Finally one local journalist steps in. 'The man,' he explains to the foreigners, 'is saying no comment.' (172)

These two passages, the first originally written in Arabic and the second in English, one by a Lebanese writer living in Lebanon, the other by a writer of Lebanese and British parentage living in Britain, reflect the difficulty, if not the impossibility, of cultural and linguistic translation. The two scenes capture the transformation of complex political history into the rhetoric of nationalist struggle, the repression of 'flaws', in Said's terms, that allow for a coherent narrative. As Khoury's narrator puts it, '[h]istory has dozens of versions and for it to ossify into one leads only to death' (297). The process of forming history into ideological narrative is however intrinsic to a worldview bound up in language. The 'no comment' that the local journalist resorts to in Hanania's novel ironically bears witness to this dislocation between contexts. The journalist uses a familiar media phrase in English to sum up the extended rhetorical flourishes in Arabic, capturing the unintelligibility of the 'revolutionary struggle' if considered in another language, from another standpoint. There is a particular narrative around 'the words for suffering, torment, oppression and persecution' that are ideologically deployed within a particular context. In both novels, the narrator brings our attention to the taken-for-granted constructions of belonging, where '[p]eople inherit their countries as they inherit their languages' (*Gate of the Sun* 382). In contexts of physical and linguistic dislocation, outside the comfortable inheritance of identity, nationality, of language, nostalgia as a psychological emotion can underline and respond to the precariousness of these constructs.

The nostalgic tropes I have examined in this book speak to global conditions of displacement and the dilemmas confronting those who must work to produce a sense of being 'at home'. As Boym puts it, today the nostalgic subject is 'a displaced person who mediates between the local and the universal' (15). The detachment from identity, language and territory instigate both persistent yearning and inevitable transformation. In Mahjoub's *Travelling with Djinn*, for example, the protagonist Yasin simultaneously seeks to resist the fixing of identity and to expand assumptions about what home signifies, and it is this attempt to connect his future to his past that is the reason for his travelling across Europe, which he calls 'this trip, this flight, this *hejira* [sic]' (6). The use of the word *hijrah* here is noteworthy. As Richard van Leeuwen notes, the word *hijrah* in Islam is primarily used to refer to the migration of the prophet Muhammad and his followers from Mecca to Medina, but it also provides a framework to speak about 'the exile of those who have been displaced in their homelands, by war, occupation, defeats and traumatic experiences' (29). The positive framework of the *hijrah* complicates the exilic longing for origins that is suffused with sadness. In his review of Soeuif's novel *In the Eye of the Sun*, Edward Said uses the same concept to praise Soueif's ability to 'work out' rather than replicate stereotypical narratives of East and West:

> Soueif does not fall for the East versus West, or Arab versus European, formulas. Instead, she works them out patiently [...] The fine thing, though, is that Soueif

can present such a *hegira* [sic] [...] thereby showing that what has become almost formulaic to the Arab (as well as Western) discourse of the other need not always be the case. In fact, there can be generosity, and vision, and overcoming barriers, and, finally, human existential integrity. (*Reflections* 410)

In this passage, Said points to the potential for postcolonial narratives to explore and enable the reconfiguration of belonging, rather than furthering the attachment to '[i]dentity, always identity, over and above knowing about others' (*Culture* 299). This working out does not however invalidate the fact that Soueif's novel is a profoundly nostalgic text, ending with the protagonist Asya reflecting on the illusive source of her yearning. When Asya asks how she can be 'yearning for Cairo and the feel of the Cairo night and the voice of Ummu Kulthoum [sic] while she is actually here in the middle of it all?' she complicates the double exposure of nostalgia, overlaying the nostalgia for place and nostalgia for the past to encapsulate the confused sense of alienation, the *ghurba*, that inspires Asya's object-less yearning (780). Asya is unable to identify the object of and reason for the nostalgic emotion rising up within her, but the fact that she does feel nostalgic drives her to question what this feeling might mean and why she is experiencing such sentimentality. This invocation and questioning of nostalgia points to the protagonist's conflicted stance on where she should locate herself. In her critical deployment of complex nostalgic themes, Soueif, like the other writers examined in this book, highlights the centrality of literature to the reimagining and reinterpreting of the past and to place. Nostalgic modes narrativize loss, make memories portable and make remembrance and self-creation inextricable. Combined with the experience of exile, nostalgia involves an attempt to recreate the sense of home through language.

In July 2016, speaking at a translation workshop entitled 'The Bearer-Beings: Portable Stories in Dislocated Times', Palestinian Egyptian poet Tamim Barghouti read from his book-length poem written in the wake of the 2003 invasion of Iraq. Barghouti noted that 'the names Baghdad, Kufa, Basra [. . .] to anyone who is literate [. . .] come with images of decorations on mosques and palaces, sounds of poetry, rules of grammar' (Humanitas). Capturing the connotations of Baghdad of the golden age, even for someone who had never visited Iraq, Barghouti comments: 'the idea of these places being obliterated by fire [meant] my formative images being violently changed and altered.' Barghouti then goes on to discuss the feeling of temporariness, the chaos and instability that the invasion engendered, and how this affects the need to remember and record:

the feeling is [. . .] you want to save whatever you can save, to salvage. To take a snapshot of time and space, because everything you see is temporary; the building that now is there will not be there tomorrow. So look at it, keep it in memory, codify it somehow and do that in language, because language is the most portable form [. . .] the most portable camera. (Humanitas)

Barghouti describes here how the precariousness of war engenders a nostalgic need to 'salvage' memories, as though they are physical objects, and to 'codify' time and space in language. The title of the workshop at which Barghouti was speaking is taken from the following lines in Wallace Stevens's 'An Ordinary Evening in New Haven': '[s]o much ourselves, we cannot tell apart/The idea and the bearer-being of the idea' (466). The notion of a 'bearer-being', of a form that contains an idea and allows it to travel, interweaves language, mobility and memory. Invoking this concept, Barghouti likens language to a 'portable camera', a metaphor that hinges on the illusion of a direct contact point with experience, the access to all that is 'temporary' and 'will not be there tomorrow'. As nostalgic modes narrativize loss, they make memories portable and make remembrance and creation inextricable.

Barghouti describes the experience of exile as 'trying to recreate home in language, so you have a country of words', an idea which gives geographical parameters to the pathos of past time (Humanitas). As Darwish puts it in his poem 'We Travel Like Other People':

> We have a country of words. Speak, speak
> So we may know the end of this travel. (31)

The title of this poem normalizes the state of exile as that of travelling 'like other people', highlighting that travel as much as origins are constitutive of identity. Yet there is an irony to this understated assertion, since the travel of exile has no end. The lines above juxtapose the anchoring, political function of a country with the ambiguities of language, and how language might imagine and articulate an 'end' to, or aim of, an endless exile. Even as the end is imagined however, as the repetition of the word 'speak' suggests, the speaker recognizes that this travelling is never-ending. To construct a country of words is to recognize that nostalgia is not only about the past but also about speaking, and creating, the longed-for future.

NOTES

Preface

1. Ahmed Ben Bella, a leader of the war of independence, later became the first president of independent Algeria (1963–5).

Introduction

1. The poem was translated by Mona Anis under the title 'Edward Said: A Contrapuntal Reading'.
2. As Samira Aghacy points out: '[t]he post-1967 era has been punctuated with wars: the 1970 Black September War in Jordan, the 1973 Arab-Israeli war, the Civil War in Lebanon, the 1982 Israeli invasion of Lebanon, the first and second Palestinian intifadas, and the first and second Gulf wars' (15).
3. Yasir Suleiman elaborates on these reflections in his work *Arabic, Self and Identity: A Study in Conflict and Displacement* (2011), in which he argues for the need to investigate 'the link between language and identity as this link is forged under conditions of personal and national trauma' (79).

Chapter 1

1. Samir Kassir argues that 'the ideology of the moment preaches a refusal of the universal. Ideology is [...] a very grand word for the current amalgam of the fossilised remains of Arab nationalism, which [...] have cut themselves off from their original, universalist sources of inspiration, and an "Islamic nationalism" that explicitly sets out to differentiate itself from the universal, if not supplant it' (82). Similarly, Lebanese journalist Hisham Melhem argues that 'both political currents – Arab nationalism and Islamism – are driven by atavistic impulses and a regressive outlook on life that is grounded in a mostly mythologized past'. Discussing the emergence of ISIS, Melhem describes them as a 'gruesome manifestation' of this 'deeper malady' ('The Barbarians Within Our Gates').
2. Some of the main genres of these historical television dramas are named with reference to the historical setting which determines the plot, some of the most popular being the historical drama (*musalsal tārīkhī*) which often focuses on political events and court life in the Islamic golden age, Bedouin dramas (*musalsal badawī*) using a romanticized Bedouin camp as a background to a story of star-crossed lovers, and the 'Damascus environment drama' (*musalsal bi'a shāmiyya*) which have dominated Ramadan TV seasons in the last decade, and which present a picturesque view of everyday life in a traditional Damascus quarter in the late nineteenth or early twentieth century.

3 For example, a writer in *Dabiq*, the online magazine of ISIS, attempted to justify the destruction of artifacts at Nineveh and Mosul's archaeological museum in February 2015 in the following way: 'The kuffār [disbelievers] had unearthed these statues and ruins in recent generations and attempted to portray them as part of a cultural heritage and identity that the Muslims of Iraq should embrace and be proud of' (Dabiq 8, 'Erasing the legacy of a ruined nation', 22–4).

4 Seigneurie notes that '[t]ypically, whereas the ancient poet stands by the ruins of the abandoned campsite and yearns for his lover reft from him by fate, the protagonist in the modern novel stands by war ruins and yearns for a past prior to war' (38).

5 Yasunari Kawabata was a Japanese short story writer and winner of the Nobel Prize for Literature in 1968, who committed suicide in 1972.

6 Hutcheon elaborates: '[i]]rony is not something in an object that you either "get" or fail to "get": irony "happens" for you (or better, you make it "happen") when two meanings, one said and the other said, come together, usually with a certain critical edge. Likewise, nostalgia is not something you perceive in an object; it is what you "feel" when two different temporal moments, past and present, come together for you and often, carry considerable emotional weight' (199).

7 For example, in Palestinian Egyptian poet Tamim Barghouti's poem 'Fī al-Quds' (In Jerusalem), the *aṭlāl* trope of passing by the campsite of the beloved is transposed into the theme of exile in the opening lines: '[b]y the beloved's house we passed but we were turned away/By the enemy's laws and walls' (T. Barghouti, my translation).

8 A very similar chain appears in Robin Yassin-Kassab's *The Road from Damascus* (2008): 'By the Arab nation he didn't refer merely to its latest embodiment, the Muslim Arabs who had ridden out from the Hijaz. He meant all the Semitic peoples in their eternal consecutive march. Sumerians, Akkadians, Assyrians, Canaanites, Phoenicians, Hebrews, Nabateans' (51).

Chapter 2

1 The Mahdist War was initially fought between the Mahdist Sudanese (following a religious leader known as the Mahdi) and the Khedivate of Egypt, with later British participation leading to the joint-rule state of Anglo Egyptian Sudan (1899–1956).

2 The novel refers to Kadaro as part of the *bashi-buzuq*, irregular Ottoman troops.

3 Jacob Norris notes that while 'historians have generally been reluctant to classify Ottoman control over Arab land as colonial', that control fits Jurgen Osterhammel's expansive definition of colonialism as a 'system of domination' predicated upon 'the expansion of society beyond its original habitat' (16). Although the Ottoman period continues to be deemed an occupation of Arab lands in nationalist discourse, Islamist groups in particular have rehabilitated the Ottoman period as part of an expansive and overlapping 'golden age' of Islamic civilization.

4 Waïl Hassan notes that '[i]t was not simply Arab intellectuals' fascination with modern European civilisation but also, and more urgently, its colonial threat that led to the movement known as *Nahḍa* (or "revival") in the mid-nineteenth century' ('Postcolonial Theory' 57).

5 As Nadje al-Ali states, 'the period of direct colonial occupation and rule by imperial powers has passed but we are still left with processes and practises of domination as well as economic exploitation, all signifying present day imperialism' (19). Derek Gregory

uses the term 'colonial present' to refer to places where hegemony and exemplary violence is legitimized through marking 'other people as irredeemably Other' (16).

6. In her review of Taher's novel, Maya Jaggi points out that 'Taher was spurred [on] by the 2003 invasion of Iraq, which he vehemently opposed, to explore earlier occupations, of Egypt by Britain, and of Berber lands by Egyptian Arabs'. Jaggi quotes Taher's explanation of the temple destruction scene: '"I imagined [the police chief] destroyed the temple," says Taher, "because he had taken part in the Orabi [sic] revolution against British occupation." This was a failed nationalist uprising in 1881 that led to the Anglo Egyptian war and colonial rule. For Mahmoud, who shatters the glorious past to open people's eyes to the present, it is a bitter irony that "our ancestors were great men, but their grandchildren are fit only for occupation"' ('Cairo's Greatest Literary Secret').

7. The move from the city to the village is a recurrent theme of anti-colonial nostalgia. As Alaistair Bonnet suggests, '[t]o turn away from the West is also to turn away from an urban, industrial economy' (91).

8. The focus on the material objects and mores of modernity is a recurring theme in Leila Aboulela's *Lyrics Alley*, set in Sudan in the 1950s. Aboulela's text is similar to *Pillars of Salt* in that it reimagines the period of the end of colonialism, and it is similar to Soueif's *The Map of Love* as it focuses on one family saga. Here however, as M. Lynx Qualey discusses in her review of this novel, '[t]he clash, where there is one, is between European and Egyptian-inspired "sophistication" and Sudan's traditional "crudeness"'. Qualey goes on to critique the limitations of this approach: '[t]his narrative might lead us to believe that the future would take us into a struggle between dresses and robes, those who dine with forks and those who eat with their fingers. We would not expect civil wars, sectarian conflict, corruption, repression or a thirst for freedom' (Qualey).

9. Though this is beyond the scope of this study, there are gendered implications to Faqir's use of a metaphor Ann Heilmann and Mark Llewellyn describe as the 'subversive stitch' (91), whereby weaving, whether literal or metaphorical, relates to the need to connect the past in tangible ways. As Heilmann and Llewellyn put it: '[f]or women, historical fiction offers them and their female characters a means of reclamation, a narrative empowerment to write women back into the historical record' (144).

10. Tellingly, the study of history is represented as a luxury in a developing country: '[h]istory was not a priority [. . .] we were a developing country [. . .] we learned about the importance of bridges, railways and dams. The message was clear; we were to become engineers and doctors and help this country onto its feet, to turn it, as the slogan went, into the breadbasket of Africa. What was the point of looking backwards?' (*Travelling* 64).

11. Here, Mahjoub's character echoes a passage from Tayeb Salih's *Mawsim al-hijra ilā al-shamāl* (1966, *Season of Migration to the North*, 1969): '[s]ooner or later they will leave our country, just as many people throughout history left many countries [. . .] and we'll speak their language without either a sense of guilt or a sense of gratitude' (49–50).

Chapter 3

1. Jameson does however discuss aesthetic judgements on the part of first-world readers of this literature: '[t]he third-world novel will not offer the satisfactions

of Proust or Joyce; what is more damaging than that, perhaps, is its tendency to remind us of outmoded stages of our own first-world cultural development and to cause us to conclude that "they are still writing novels like Dreiser or Sherwood Anderson"' (65).

2 These attempts included the short-lived merger between Egypt and Syria known as the United Arab Republic (UAR), formed in 1958, which lasted until Syria seceded in 1961, and the even more short-lived Arab Federation between Jordan and Iraq that lasted for all of six months, between February and July of 1958.

3 Elie Podeh similarly points out that 'the fact that most Arab states are modern creations means that their rulers have continuously engaged in the twin processes of nation building and state formation' (3).

4 Naguib Mahfouz illustrates this logic in his novel *Karnak Café* (1974) when the narrator asks: 'should we not be willing to endure a bit of pain and inconvenience in the process of turning our state [. . .] into a model of a scientific, socialist, and industrial nation?' (17).

5 For example, Lisa Wedeen describes Hafiz al-Assad's role as head of the Syrian 'national family': '[t]he official narrative communicates understandings of obedience and community in terms of a chain of filial piety and paternal authority that culminates, and stops, in Assad. The language of the family suggests that citizens, (both male and female) should behave *as if* they were children and Assad were their father' (65).

6 The claustrophobic bond of mother/child and its relationship to nostalgia for the homeland is also a theme in Yasmin Zahran's *A Beggar at Damascus Gate*, discussed in the first chapter: 'when she spoke of Palestine, she would say "but my mother is buried there." The process has been reversed; the child is carrying the mother, and the mother is equated with Palestine, and this closeness hardly allows for any other' (58–9).

7 A *kunīa* is an honorific title where parents are referred to as the father (*abū*) or mother (*umm*) of either their eldest child, or, more typically, their eldest son.

8 The representation of the failures of nationalist politics through gendered narratives is encapsulated in an exchange at the end of Tony Hanania's first novel *Homesick* (1998), when the protagonist visits Lebanon with his schoolfriend, who has become obsessed by the Palestinian issue. Walking through the refugee camps, they come across an old man who complains about the inhospitality of the country: 'Lubnan, Lubnan, land of milk. Bad mother. Dry like deserts' (227). Since 'Lubnan' and 'laban' (milk) share the same root (l-b-n) the old man sees them as etymologically linked, using the notion of Lebanon as a 'land of milk' to liken the country to a 'bad mother' who is unable to nurture her children.

9 There is enough information that the reader might guess that the country is Iraq, since we are told that Nuri's father was once a diplomatic advisor until the king is killed, and Faisal II was killed in a similar fashion in 1958. These clues and others, such as the mention of Badr Shakir al-Sayyab as Nuri's mother's favourite writer, suggest the unnamed country is Iraq. However, in only hinting at the country, the allegorical aspects of the narrative are foregrounded.

10 Nuri outlines a list of what he believes his father stands for, quoting him on his beliefs: 'I wanted to have believed in and indeed served a constitutional monarchy. I wanted to hate, with the same passion, what he used to call "that infantile impertinence that passes for a revolution," then suddenly to reemerge,

with all my refinement intact, a Marxist, "because each age calls for its own solution"' (90).
11 As Maria Joseph notes, in Matar's first novel, '[t]he line between public and private life breaks down in a regime where politics can enter, even invade, a private household' ('Country of Men').
12 Early on, Nuri associates his mother with the northern 'unpeopled places of Europe' that the family travels to during holidays: 'I have come to think of those places, no matter where they were, as having taken place in a single country – her country – and the silences that marked them her melancholy' (8). Later, Nuri describes his mother's lack of involvement in politics in terms of the delineation of different spaces, her own territory. These geographical markers highlight the masculinist frameworks of the nation, and the exclusion of women as agents, rather than symbols, within those frameworks.
13 There is also a suggestion that his father might be a friend of the family, Taleb, who appears in only one scene to obliquely explain and justify the family secret to a still ignorant Nuri, letting him know that his mother 'never ceased to be tender with Naima, who was innocent, of course. Ultimately, everyone is innocent, including your father' (61).
14 Jaballa Matar was a member of the Libyan delegation to the United Nations and, after Gaddafi's coup, a political dissident living in exile. Abducted in 1990 by the Egyptian secret service, he was handed over to the Libyan government and imprisoned. His fate remains unknown.
15 Nimeiry himself came to power through a military coup in 1969. He was ousted in 1985 in a coup led by his defence minister.
16 Similarly, in Mohja Kahf's *Girl in the Tangerine Scarf*, which again represents the Gulf War as a turning point for the protagonist, Khadra reflects that '[f]rom a distance, all Arab cities looked like home. A place you could have been in when the bomb came down. A brown or olive face that could have been your little sister's, your father's, broken in sorrow' (338–9).
17 In Abouelal's earlier novel, *The Translator* (2007) the Gulf War again features as a catalyst for defining allegiances and claiming identity. According to Sadia Abbas, *The Translator*, first published in 2001, was 'clearly meant to be a response' to the discourse building since the 1990s, from the Rushdie affair to the first Gulf War and ongoing sanctions (Abbas 436).
18 Aboulela is unambiguous about her desire to detach Islam from political frameworks which she sees as limited: '[i]n a secular climate (such as British/European society and I can even include the intellectual and literary Arab circles where religion is almost a taboo subject), faith is seen as either part of tradition/culture or it is seen as political. So therefore, in a secular climate, Muslims need, for practical purposes, to talk in this (postcolonial, adherence to tradition/culture) language. (Incidentally, this is how secular intellectuals in the Muslim world talk about religion – in terms of it being a culture and tradition). But this language to me has been and is very limited and I do not feel that it could show readers the kind of faith I knew and grew up in. I wanted to write about this space [. . .] that is beyond the political because I feel that this space is important, and it is neglected' ('Interview').
19 My translation of '*bilādī wa-in jārat 'alayya 'azīzatun/wa ahlī wa-in ḍannū 'alayya kirāmu*'. The source of this line is debated. It has been ascribed to an alteration of lines by Qatāda Ibn Idrīs from the seventh century.

Chapter 4

1. A very similar nostalgic reimagining occurs in Mahja Kahf's *The Girl in the Tangerine Scarf,* where upon her return to Damascus, the protagonist Khadra reflects on the 'Damascus of possibility' under 'today's misshapen city cringing under the giant-sized glances of its president [. . .] A Damascus that stirred the imagination, beneath the scarred face of the present' (292).
2. For example, in Elias Khoury's novel *Gate of the Sun* (2007, *Bāb al-Shams,* 2000), one of the characters living in a Palestinian refugee camp mocks an academic's obsession with Andalusia: 'God help us, now we're collecting the keys of the Andalusians! He said the descendants of the people of Andalusia who were chased out of their country and who migrated to Meknes still keep the keys to their houses in Andalusia and he's rounding up keys to put on an exhibition and wants to write a book about them [. . .] he says we have to collect the keys of our houses in Jerusalem [. . .] Collect our keys when the doors are already broken!' (118).

WORK CITED

Abbas, Sadia. 'Leila Aboulela, Religion, and the Challenge of the Novel'. *Contemporary Literature* 52.3 (2011): 430–61.
Abdelhady, Dalia. *The Lebanese Diaspora: The Arab Immigrant Experience in Montreal, New York, and Paris*. New York: New York University Press, 2011.
Abdo, Diya M. 'How to Be a Successful Double Agent: (Dis)placement as Strategy in Fadia Faqir's Pillars of Salt'. *Arab Voices in Diaspora: Critical Perspectives*. Ed. Layla Al Maleh. Amsterdam: Rodopi, 2009. 237–71.
Abdul-Jabbar, Wisam Kh. 'The Internalized Vermin of Exile in Montréal: Rawi Hage's Cockroach'. *The Journal of Commonwealth Literature* 52.1 (2017): 168–82.
Abi Samra, Muhammad. *Al-Rajul al- Sābiq*. Beirut: Dār al-Jadīd, 1995.
Aboulela, Leila. *Coloured Lights*. Edinburgh: Polygon, 2001.
Aboulela, Leila. Interview. University of Aberdeen, King's College, 2007. Web. 12 Jan. 2012. web.archive.org/web/20120130120228/http://www.abdn.ac.uk/sll/complit/leila.shtml
Aboulela, Leila. 'Keep the Faith'. *The Guardian*. Guardian News and Media, 5 June 2005. Web. 16 Nov. 2015.
Aboulela, Leila. *Minaret: A Novel*. London: Bloomsbury Publishing, 2015.
Aboulela, Leila. *The Translator*. New York: Grove Atlantic, 2007.
Aboulela, Leila and Mildred Barya. 'A Certain Beauty and a Certain Happiness: An Interview with Leila Aboulela'. *Pambazuka News*, 27 May 2009. Web. 16 Nov. 2015.
Abu-Jaber, Diana. *Arabian Jazz*. New York: Harcourt Brace, 1993.
Abu-Rabi', Ibrahim M. *Contemporary Arab Thought: Studies in Post-1967 Arab Intellectual History*. London: Pluto Press, 2004.
Aciman, André. *Letters of Transit: Reflections on Exile, Identity, Language, and Loss*. New York: New Press, 1999.
Admiraal, Lucia. 'Booze, Tragedy, and Satire: Why *Beer in the Snooker Club* Shares Shelf Space With *1984*'. *Arabic Literature in English*. Wordpress, 5 Mar. 2015. Web. 30 Nov. 2015.
Adnan, Etel. *In the Heart of the Heart of Another Country*. San Francisco: City Lights Books, 2005.
Adunis. [Ali Esber]. *An Introduction to Arab Poetics*, Trans. Catherine Cobham. London: Saqi Books, 2013.
Aghacy, Samira. *Masculine Identity in the Fiction of the Arab East Since 1967*. Syracuse: Syracuse University Press, 2009.
Ahmed, Sara. *The Promise of Happiness*. Durham: Duke University Press, 2010.
Aksikas, Jaafar. *Arab Modernities: Islamism, Nationalism, and Liberalism in the Post-Colonial Arab World*. New York: Peter Lang, 2009.
Al-Ali, Nadje. *Secularism, Gender and the State in the Middle East: The Egyptian Women's Movement*. Cambridge: Cambridge University Press, 2000.
Al-Barghouthi, Hani. 'Arab yaktubūn bī al-inglīzīyya'. *7iber*, 22 July 2016. Web. 5 Aug. 2016.

al Barghouti, Tamim. 'The Bearer-Beings': Portable Stories in Dislocated Times. *Youtube*, uploaded by The Weidenfeld-Hoffmann Trust. 13 Jul 2016. https://www.youtube.com/watch?v=dHiY2XAKEGE

Al-Ghadeer, Moneera. *Desert Voices: Bedouin Women's Poetry in Saudi Arabia*. London: I.B.Tauris, 2009.

Al Jazeera. 'The Arabs: A People's History'. *Al Jazeera English*. Al Jazeera Media Network, n.d. Web. 10 Jan. 2013.

Al-Maria, Sophia. *The Girl Who Fell to Earth: A Memoir*. New York: Harper Perennial, 2012.

Al-Shaykh, Hanan. 'In the Court of the Lions I Sat Down and Wept'. *Gobshite* 2.31 (Winter 2003): 15–19.

Alaidy, Ahmad. *Being Abbas El Abd*. Trans. Humphrey T. Davies. Cairo: AUC Press, 2006.

Alameddine, Rabih. *The Hakawati*. New York: Knopf Doubleday Publishing Group, 2008.

Alameddine, Rabih. *I, The Divine: A Novel in First Chapters*. New York: Norton, 2002.

Alameddine, Rabih. *Koolaids: The Art of War*. New York: Picador USA, 1998.

Alameddine, Rabih. 'Rabih Alameddine: "My Existence Is Uncomfortable for People"'. Interview by John Freeman. *Literary Hub*, 26 Oct. 2016. https://lithub.com/rabih-alameddine-my-existence-is-uncomfortable-for-people

Alameddine, Rabih. 'Talking to Rabih Alameddine'. Interview by Yasmina Hatem. *NOW News*. Mercury Media Inc., 12 May 2013. Web. 15 Aug. 2013.

Alameddine, Rabih. *An Unnecessary Woman*. New York: Grove Atlantic, 2014.

Albakry, Mohammed and Jonathan Siler. 'Into the Arab-American Borderland: Bilingual Creativity in Randa Jarrar's Map of Home'. *Arab Studies Quarterly* 34.2 (2012): 109–21.

Alghaberi, Jameel. 'The Concepts of Home and Statelessness in Palestinian Diaspora Fiction: Reflections in Randa Jarrar's A Map of Home'. *Transnational Literature* 11.1 (2018): 1–13.

Allen, Roger M. A. *The Arabic Novel: An Historical and Critical Introduction*. Syracuse: Syracuse University Press, 1995.

Aly, Ramy M. K. *Becoming Arab in London: Performativity and the Undoing of Identity*. London: Pluto Press, 2015.

Alyan, Talal. 'Nakba: Recollection, Retelling and Existential Vertigo'. *Al Jazeera English*. Al Jazeera Media Network, 16 May 2014. Web. 30 July 2014.

Appiah, Kwame Anthony. *Cosmopolitanism: Ethics in a World of Strangers*. London: Penguin UK, 2015.

Armstrong, Richard H. 'Last Words: Said, Freud, and Traveling Theory'. *Alif: Journal of Comparative Poetics* 25 (2005): 120–48.

Ashcroft, Bill, Gareth Griffiths and Helen Tiffin. *The Empire Writes Back: Theory and Practice in Post-Colonial Literatures*. London: Routledge, 2003.

Ashour, Radwa. 'Eyewitness, Scribe and Storyteller: My Experience as a Novelist'. *The Massachusetts Review* 41.1 (2000): 85–92.

Ashour, Radwa. *Specters*. Trans. Barbara Romaine. Northampton: Interlink Books, 2010.

Ashour, Radwa. *Thulāthiyyat Gharnāṭa*. Cairo: Dār al-Shurūq, 2001.

Assman, Jan. 'Communicative and Cultural Memory'. *Cultural Memory Studies: An International and Interdisciplinary Handbook*. Eds. Astrid Erll and Ansgar Nünning. Berlin: Walter De Gruyter, 2008. 109–18.

Athanasiadis, Iason. 'Book Review: "The Road from Damascus"'. *Washington Times*. The Washington Times, 26 Feb. 2010. Web. 16 May 2014.

Attar, Samar. *Līnā: lawḥat fatāh Dimashqiyyah*. Beirut: Manshūrāt Dār al-Āfāq al-Jadīdah, 1982.

Attar, Samar. *Lina: A Portrait of a Damascene Girl*. Trans. Samar Attar. Colorado Springs: Three Continents Press, 1994.
Ayubi, Nazih N. *Over-Stating the Arab State: Politics and Society in the Middle East*. London: I.B.Tauris, 1995.
Bahrani, Zainab. *The Graven Image: Representation in Babylonia and Assyria*. Philadelphia: University of Pennsylvania Press, 2011.
Ban, Kah Choon. 'Nostalgia and the Scene of the Other'. *Perceiving Other Worlds*. Eds. Edwin Thumboo and Thiru Kandiah. Singapore: Marshall Cavendish Academic, 2005. 1–12.
Barakat, Halim. *Al-Ightirāb fī al-thaqāfah al-'Arabiyyah, matāhāt al-insān bayna al-ḥulm wa-al-wāqi'*. Beirut: Markaz Dirāsāt al-Waḥdah al-'Arabīyah, 2006.
Barakat, Halim. *The Crane*. Cairo: AUC Press, 2008.
Barakat, Halim. *Ghurbat al-kātib al-'Arabī*. Beirut: Dār al-Sāqī, 2011.
Barghouthi, Mourid. *I Saw Ramallah*. New York: Anchor Books, 2003.
Barghouthi, Tamim. 'Fī al-Quds'. *Adab*, n.d. Web. 12 Aug. 2015. http://www.adab.com/modules.php?name=Sh3er&doWhat=shqas&qid=76853
Baudrillard, Jean. *The Gulf War Did Not Take Place*. Bloomington: Indiana University Press, 1995.
Bayeh, Jumana. *The Literature of the Lebanese Diaspora: Representations of Place and Transnational Identity*. London: I.B.Tauris, 2014.
Benjamin, Walter. *A Berlin Chronicle: In One Way Street*. London: Verso, 1979.
Benjamin, Walter. *Illuminations*. Trans. Harry Zorn. New York: Schocken Books, 1968.
Berger, Mark T. *After the Third World?* London: Routledge, 2013.
Berlant, Lauren. 'Austerity, Precarity, Awkwardness'. *Supervalent Thought*. Web. 20 Feb. 2019. https://supervalentthought.files.wordpress.com/2011/12/berlant-aaa2011final.pdf
Berrada, Mohamed. *The Game of Forgetting: A Novel*. London: Quartet Books, 1997.
Bevan, David. *Literature and Exile*. Amsterdam: Rodopi, 1990.
Bhabha, Homi. *The Location of Culture*. London: Routledge, 2012.
Bhabha, Homi. 'The World and the Home'. *Social Text* 31/32 (1992): 141–53.
Bilal, Parker. [Jamal Mahjoub]. *The Golden Scales*. London: A&C Black, 2012.
Bonnett, Alastair. *Left in the Past: Radicalism and the Politics of Nostalgia*. New York: Continuum, 2010.
Boullata, Issa J., Kamal Abdel-Malek and Wael B. Hallaq. *Tradition, Modernity, and Postmodernity in Arabic Literature: Essays in Honor of Professor Issa J. Boullata*. Leiden: BRILL, 2000.
Boym, Svetlana. *The Future of Nostalgia*. New York: Basic Books, 2008.
Bradbury, Jill. 'Narrative Possibilities of the Past for the Future: Nostalgia and Hope'. *Peace and Conflict: Journal of Peace Psychology* 18.3 (2012): 341–6.
Brah, Avtar. *Cartographies of Diaspora: Contesting Identities*. London: Routledge, 1996.
Bright, Gillian. 'On Being the "Same Type": Albert Camus and the Paradox of Immigrant Shame in Rawi Hage's *Cockroach*'. *The Cambridge Journal of Postcolonial Literary Inquiry* 5.1 (2018): 69–89.
Brooks, Lily. 'Lifting the Veil: Interview with Ahdaf Soueif'. *The Guardian*. Guardian News and Media, 2 Aug. 1999. Web. 13 May 2012.
Bujupaj, Ismet. 'Parents and Daughters in Two Novels by Arab American Authors: Khalas, Let Her Go'. *Anafora* 3.2 (2016): 185–210.
Butler, Judith. *Giving an Account of Oneself*. New York: Fordham University Press, 2005.
Butler, Judith. *Precarious Life: The Powers of Mourning and Violence*. London: Verso, 2006.

Camillia Fawzi El-Solh. 'Arab Communities in Britain: Cleavages and Commonalities'. *Islam and Christian-Muslim Relations* 3 (1992): 236–58.
Casini, Lorenzo. *Beyond Occidentalism: Europe and the Self in Present-Day Arabic Narrative Discourse'*. Florence: European University Institute, 2008. Web. 3 Mar. 2013.
Certeau, de Michel. *The Writing of History*. Trans. Tom Conley. New York: Columbia University Press, 1988 [1975].
Chakrabarty, Dipesh. *Provincialising Europe: Postcolonial Thought and Historical Difference*. Princeton: Princeton University Press, 2009.
Chambers, Iain. *Migrancy, Culture, Identity*. London: Routledge, 2008.
Chariandy, David. 'Postcolonial Diasporas'. *Postcolonial Text* 2.1 (2006): n. pag. Web. 15 Nov. 2015.
Chatterjee, Partha. *The Nation and Its Fragments: Colonial and Postcolonial Histories*. Princeton: Princeton University Press, 1993.
Chatterjee, Partha. *Our Modernity*. Rotterdam: SEPHIS, 1997.
Clark, Peter. 'Marginal Literatures of the Middle East'. *Literature and Nation in the Middle East*. Ed. Yasin Suleiman. Edinburgh: Edinburgh University Press, 2006. 179–89.
Cooke, Miriam. 'Mothers, Rebels and Textual Exchanges: Women Writing in French and Arabic'. *Postcolonial Subjects: Francophone Women Writers*. Eds. Mary Jean Matthews Green et al. Minneapolis: University of Minnesota Press, 1996. 140–56.
Craps, Stef. *Postcolonial Witnessing: Trauma Out of Bounds*. New York: Palgrave Macmillan, 2013.
Craps, Stef and Gert Buelens. 'Introduction: Postcolonial Trauma Novels'. *Studies in the Novel* 40.1/2 (2008): 1–12.
Creet, Julia. *Memory and Migration: Multidisciplinary Approaches to Memory Studies*. Toronto: University of Toronto Press, 2011.
Crossen, Cynthia. 'A New "Arabian Nights"'. *Wall Street Journal*, 27 Apr. 2008. *The Wall Street Journal*. https://www.wsj.com/articles/SB120916642423246209
Dabbagh, Selma. 'Focusing on Dispersal'. *Wasafiri* 33.1 (2018): 40–1.
Dabbagh, Selma. 'New Texts Out Now: Selma Dabbagh, *Out of It: A Novel*'. *Jadaliyya*. The Arab Studies Institute, 17 July 2013. Web. 16 Nov. 2015.
Dabbagh, Selma. *Out of It*. London: A&C Black, 2011.
Dabiq. 'Erasing the Legacy of a Ruined Nation'. *Dabiq Magazine*. Issue 8. Jumada al-Akhira 1436. April 2015. Web. 11 May 2015. http://www.blazingcatfur.ca/wp-content/uploads/2015/03/Dabiq_8.compressed.pdf
Dabydeen, David. 'In the Country of Men by Hisham Matar'. *The Independent*, 13 July 2006. Web. 17 Nov. 2018. https://www.independent.co.uk/arts-entertainment/books/reviews/in-the-country-of-men-by-hisham-matar-6095437.html
Dahab, Elizabeth. *Voices of Exile in Contemporary Canadian Francophone Literature*. Lanham: Lexington, 2009.
Daif, Rashid. *Dear Mr Kawabata*. Trans. Paul Starkey. London: Quartet Books, 1999.
Darraj, Muaddi Susan. 'Writing Relocation: Arab Anglophone Literature of the Last Decade'. *Iowa Journal of Cultural Studies* 2.1 (2002): 123–30.
Darwish, Mahmud. 'Edward Said: A Contrapuntal Reading: Translated by Mona Anis'. *Cultural Critique* 67.1 (2007): 175–82.
Darwish, Mahmud. 'We Travel Like Other People'. *Victims of a Map: A Bilingual Anthology of Arabic Poetry*. Ed. and trans. Abdullah al-Udhari. London: al-Saqi Books, 1984. 30–1.
Davis, Emily. 'Romance as Political Aesthetic in Ahdaf Soueif's *The Map of Love*'. *Genders OnLine Journal* 45 (2007): n. pag. Web. 2 Aug. 2013.
Davis, Fred. *Yearning for Yesterday: A Sociology of Nostalgia*. New York: Free Press, 1979.

Dawisha, Adeed. *Arab Nationalism in the Twentieth Century: From Triumph to Despair*. Princeton: Princeton University Press, 2009.
Decter, Jonathan P. *Iberian Jewish Literature: Between Al-Andalus and Christian Europe*. Bloomington: Indiana University Press, 2007.
Deleuze, Gilles and Félix Guattari. *Kafka: Toward a Minor Literature*. Minneapolis: University of Minnesota Press, 1986.
Derrida, Jacques. *Archive Fever: A Freudian Impression*. Chicago: University of Chicago Press, 1998.
Derrida, Jacques. *Of Hospitality: Anne Duformantelle Invites Jacques Derrida to Respond*. Trans. Rachel Bowlby. Stanford: Stanford University Press, 2000.
Dirlik, Arif. 'Culture Against History? The Politics of East Asian Identity'. *Development and Society* 28.2 (December 1999): 167–90.
Dirlik, Arif. 'Modernity as History: Post-Revolutionary China, Globalization and the Question of Modernity'. *Social History* 27.1 (2002): 16–39.
Downey, Anthony. *Dissonant Archives: Contemporary Visual Culture and Competing Narratives in the Middle East*. London: I.B.Tauris, 2015.
Dunphy, Graeme. 'Migrant, Emigrant, Immigrant. Recent Developments in Turkish-Dutch Literature'. *Neophilologus* 85.1 (2001): 1–23.
Durrant, Sam. *Postcolonial Narrative and the Work of Mourning: J.M. Coetzee, Wilson Harris, and Toni Morrison*. New York: SUNY Press, 2012.
Eco, Umberto. 'Stefano Rosso. A Correspondence with Umberto Eco Genoa–Bologna–Binghamton–Bloomington August–September, 1982, March–April, 1983'. Trans. Carolyn Springer. *Boundary 2* 12.1 (1983): 1–13.
El-Ariss, Tarek. 'Hacking the Modern: Arabic Writing in the Virtual Age'. *Comparative Literature Studies* 47.4 (2010): 533–48.
El-Enany, Rasheed. *Arab Representations of the Occident: East-West Encounters in Arabic Fiction*. London: Routledge, 2006.
El Shakry, Omnia. *The Great Social Laboratory: Subjects of Knowledge in Colonial and Postcolonial Egypt*. Stanford: Stanford University Press, 2007.
Eng, David L. and David Kazanjian. *Loss: The Politics of Mourning*. Berkeley: University of California Press, 2003.
Erll, Astrid. *Memory in Culture*. Basingstoke: Palgrave Macmillan, 2011.
Erll, Astrid and Ansgar Nünning. *A Companion to Cultural Memory Studies: An International and Interdisciplinary Handbook*. Berlin: Walter De Gruyter, 2010.
Fadda-Conrey, Carol. *Contemporary Arab-American Literature: Transnational Reconfigurations of Citizenship and Belonging*. New York: NYU Press, 2014.
Fanon, Frantz. *The Wretched of the Earth*. Trans. Constance Farrington. New York: Grove, 1968.
Faqir, Fadia. 'Interview with Fadia Faqir, 23 March 2010'. Interview by Rachel Bower. *Journal of Postcolonial Writing* 48.1 (2012): 3–12.
Faqir, Fadia. *Pillars of Salt: A Novel*. New York: Interlink Books, 1997.
Faqir, Fadia. 'Stories from the House of Songs'. *In the House of Silence: Autobiographical Essays by Arab Women Writers*. Eds. Fadia Faqir and Shirley Eber. Reading: Garnet, 1998.
Fayad, Mona. 'Reinscribing Identity: Nation and Community in Arab Women's Writing'. *College Literature* 22.1 (1995): 147–60.
Freud, Sigmund. 'The "Uncanny"'. *The Standard Edition of the Complete Psychological Works of Sigmund Freud. Volume XVII (1917-1919): An Infantile Neurosis and Other Works*. Trans. James Strachey et al. London: Hogarth Press (1955): 217–56.

Gallien, Claire. 'Minding (About) the Gazan Border in Contemporary Palestinian Literature'. *Commonwealth: Essays and Studies* 39.1 (Autumn 2016): 57–68.

Gana, Nouri. 'Introduction'. *The Edinburgh Companion to the Arab Novel in English: The Politics of Anglo Arab and Arab American Literature and Culture*. Eds. Nouri Gana, Waïl S. Hassan and Mara Naaman. Edinburgh: Edinburgh University Press, 2013.

Gana, Nouri. *Signifying Loss: Toward a Poetics of Narrative Mourning*. Lewisburg: Bucknell University Press, 2011.

Gardner, Katy. 'Mullahs, Migrants, Miracles: Travel and Transformation in Sylhet'. *Contributions to Indian Sociology* 27.2 (1993): 213–35.

Gelder, van, G. J. H. 'Satire, Medieval'. *Encyclopedia of Arabic Literature*. Eds. Julie Scott Meisami and Paul Starkey. London: Routledge, 1998.

Gendy, Nancy El. 'Trickster Humour in Randa Jarrar's *A Map of Home*: Negotiating Arab American Muslim Female Sexuality'. *Women: A Cultural Review* 27.1 (2016): 1–19. https://doi.org/10.1080/09574042.2015.1122484

Genetsch, Martin. *The Texture of Identity: The Fiction of MG Vassanji, Neil Bissoondath and Rohinton Mistry*. Toronto: TSAR, 2007.

George, Rosemary Marangoly. *The Politics of Home: Postcolonial Relocations and Twentieth-Century Fiction*. Berkley: University of California Press, 1999.

Ghali, Waguih. *Beer in the Snooker Club*. 1964. New York: Vintage International, 2014.

Ghattas, Kim. *Black Wave: Saudi Arabia, Iran and the Rivalry That Unravelled the Middle East*. London: Wildfire Books, 2020.

Ghazoul, Ferial. 'Comparative Literature in the Arab World'. *Comparative Critical Studies* 3.1–2 (2006): 121–2.

Gibbons, Luke, Peadar Kirby and Michael Cronin. *Reinventing Ireland: Culture, Society, and the Global Economy*. London: Pluto Press, 2002.

Gikandi, Simon. 'African Literature and Modernity'. *Texts, Tasks, and Theories: Versions and Subversions in African Literatures*. Eds. Tobias Robert Klein and Viola Pruschenk. Amsterdam: Rodopi, 2008. 3–19.

Gikandi, Simon. *Maps of Englishness: Writing Identity in the Culture of Colonialism*. New York: Columbia University Press, 1996.

Gilroy, Paul. *The Black Atlantic: Modernity and Double Consciousness*. London: Verso, 1993.

Gilsenan, Michael. *Recognising Islam: An Anthropologist's Introduction*. London: Routledge, 2013.

Gopinath, Gayatri. *Impossible Desires: Queer Diasporas and South Asian Public Cultures*. Durham: Duke University Press, 2005.

Gopnik, Adam. 'Does It Help to Know History?' *The New Yorker*. Condé Nast Digital, 28 Aug. 2014. Web. 14 Nov. 2014.

Grainge, Paul. 'Nostalgia and Style in Retro America: Moods, Modes, and Media Recycling'. *The Journal of American and Comparative Cultures* 23.1 (2000): 27–34.

Grainge, Paul. 'TIME's Past in the Present: Nostalgia and the Black and White Image'. *Journal of American Studies* 33.3 (1999): 383–92.

Green, Andre. *Key Ideas for a Contemporary Psychoanalysis: Misrecognition and Recognition of the Unconscious*. London: Routledge, 2012.

Gregory, Derek. *The Colonial Present: Afghanistan. Palestine. Iraq*. Oxford: Wiley-Blackwell, 2004.

Gurr, Andrew. *Writers in Exile: The Identity of Home in Modern Literature*. Brighton: Harvester Press, 1981.

Gurría-Quintana, Ángel. 'Anatomy of a Disappearance'. *Financial Times*. Financial Times, 21 Feb. 2011. Web. 31 July 2014.

Habibi, Emile. *The Secret Life of Saeed, the Ill-Fated Pessoptimist: A Palestinian Who Became a Citizen of Israel*. Trans. Salma Khadra Jayyusi and Trevor Le Gassick. New York: Readers International, 1989.

Haddad, Lutfi. *Anthūlūjiyā al-adab al-'Arabī al-mahjarī al-muʿāṣir*. Beirut: Dār Ṣādir, 2004–2006.

Hage, Ghassan. 'Migration, Food, Memory and Home-Building'. *Memory, Histories, Theories, Debates*. Eds. Suzannah Radstone and Bill Schwarz. New York: Fordham University Press, 2010. 419–27.

Hage, Rawi. *Cockroach*. Toronto: House of Anansi Press, 2008.

Hage, Rawi. 'From the Ground Up'. *The National*. https://www.thenational.ae/arts-culture/books/from-the-ground-up-1.562054. Accessed 29 Mar. 2019.

Hall, Stuart. 'Cultural Identity and Diaspora'. *Identity: Community, Culture, Difference*. Ed. Jonathan Rutherford. London: Lawrence & Wishart, 1990. 222–37.

Halliday, Fred. *Britain's First Muslims: Portrait of an Arab Community*. London: I.B.Tauris, 2010.

Hanafi, Hasan. *Al-Turāth wa-al-tajdīd: mawqifunā min al-turāth al-qadīm*. Cairo: Maktabat al-Anglū-al-Miṣriiyya, 1980.

Hanania, Tony. *Unreal City*. London: Bloomsbury, 1999.

Harlow, Barbara. 'From Flying Carpets to No-Fly Zones: Libya's Elusive Revolution(s), According to Ruth First, Hisham Matar, and the International Criminal Court'. *Journal of Arabic Literature* 43.2–3 (2012): 431–57.

Hassan, Robert. *The Chronoscopic Society: Globalization, Time, and Knowledge in the Network Economy*. New York: Peter Lang, 2003.

Hassan, Waïl S. *Immigrant Narratives: Orientalism and Cultural Translation in Arab American and Arab British Literature*. New York: Oxford University Press, 2011.

Hassan, Waïl S. 'Postcolonial Theory and Modern Arabic Literature: Horizons of Application'. *Journal of Arabic Literature* 33.1 (2002): 45–64.

Heilmann, Ann and Mark Llewellyn. 'Hystorical Fictions: Women (re)Writing and (re)Reading History'. *Women: A Cultural Review* 15.2 (2004): 137–249.

Himmich, Bensalem. *The Theocrat*. Trans. Roger Allen. Cairo; New York: American University in Cairo Press, 2005.

Hirsch, Marianne. *Family Frames: Photography, Narrative, and Postmemory*. Cambridge, MA: Harvard University Press, 1997.

Hirsch, Marianne. *The Generation of Postmemory: Writing and Visual Culture After the Holocaust*. New York: Columbia University Press, 2012.

Hirsch, Marianne and Leo Spitzer. 'The Witness and the Archive'. *Memory: History, Theories, Debates*. Eds. S. Radstone and B. Schwarz. New York: Fordham UP, 2010. 390–405.

Hirst, David. 'Gaddafi Cruelly Resists, but this Arab Democratic Revolution is Far from Over'. *Sydney Morning Herald*. Fairfax Media, 20 Feb. 2011. Web. 15 Nov. 2012.

Hout, Syrine. 'Cultural Hybridity, Trauma, and Memory in Diasporic Anglophone Lebanese Fiction'. *Journal of Postcolonial Writing* 47.3 (2011): 330–42.

Hout, Syrine. 'Memory, Home, and Exile in Contemporary Anglophone Lebanese Fiction'. *Critique: Studies in Contemporary Fiction* 46.3 (2005): 219–33.

Hout, Syrine. *Post-War Anglophone Lebanese Fiction: Home Matters in the Diaspora*. Edinburgh: Edinburgh University Press, 2012.

Huggan, Graham. *The Oxford Handbook of Postcolonial Studies*. Oxford: Oxford University Press, 2013.
Hutcheon, Linda. 'Irony, Nostalgia, and the Postmodern'. *Methods for the Study of Literature as Cultural Memory*. Eds. Raymond Vervliet and Annemarie Estor. Atlanta: Rodopi, 2000. 189–207.
Hutchings, Kimberly. *Time and World Politics: Thinking the Present*. Manchester: Manchester University Press, 2013.
Huttunen, Laura. '"Home" and Ethnicity in the Context of War: Hesitant Diasporas of Bosnian Refugees'. *European Journal of Cultural Studies* 8.2 (2005): 177–95.
Huyssen, Andreas. 'Nostalgia for Ruins'. *Grey Room* 23 (Spring 2006): 6–21.
Huyssen, Andreas. *Twilight Memories: Marking Time in a Culture of Amnesia*. New York: Routledge, 2012.
Jabra, Ibrahim Jabra. *Hunters in a Narrow Street*. 1960. Boulder: Lynne Rienner, 1990.
Jabra, Ibrahim Jabra. *In Search of Walid Masoud: A Novel*. Trans. Roger Allen and Adnan Haydar. Syracuse: Syracuse University Press, 2000.
Jabra, Ibrahim Jabra. *The Ship*. Colorado Springs: Three Continents Press, 1985.
Jackson, Tina. 'Robin Yassin-Kassab Goes beyond the Veil'. *Metro*, 5 June 2008. http://metro.co.uk/2008/06/05/robin-yassin-kassab-goes-beyond-the-veil-172360/
Jaggi, Maya. 'Beyond Belief'. *The Guardian*. Guardian News and Media, 14 June 2008. Web. 16 Nov. 2015.
Jaggi, Maya. 'Cairo's Greatest Literary Secret'. *The Guardian*. Guardian News and Media, 11 Apr. 2008 Web. 13 Nov. 2015.
Jaggi, Maya. 'Djinn Genie'. *The Guardian*. Guardian News and Media, 20 Sept. 2003. Web. 16 Nov. 2015.
Jameson, Frederick. 'Postmodernism and Consumer Society'. *The Anti-Aesthetic: Essays On Postmodern Culture*. Ed. Hal Foster. Seattle: Bay Press, 1983. 111–25.
Jameson, Frederick. 'Third-World Literature in the Era of Multinational Capitalism'. *Social Text* 15 (Autumn 1986): 65–88.
Jarrar, Randa. 'Beirut39: Nomadic Words: An Interview with Randa Jarrar'. *Beirut39*, 11 Apr. 2010. http://beirut39.blogspot.com/2010/04/nomadic-words-interview-with-randa.html
Jarrar, Randa. *A Map of Home*. New York: Other Press, LLC, 2008.
Jones, Jane Anderson. 'The Blue Manuscript by Sabiha Khemir'. *Belletrista* 7 (2010): n. pag. Web. 13 Aug. 2015.
Joseph, Maria. 'In the Country of Men'. *The Sydney Morning Herald*. Fairfax Media, 22 Feb. 2013. Web. 15 Nov. 2015.
Joseph, Suad and Afsana Najmabadi, eds. *Encyclopedia of Women and Islamic Cultures: Family, Law and Politics*. Leiden: BRILL, 2003.
Jouiti, Abdelkrim. 'Medina Nuhhas'. *Al-Mutawasidiat* 11 (1999/2000): 98–101.
Kahf, Mohja. *The Girl in the Tangerine Scarf: A Novel*. New York: Carroll and Graf, 2006.
Kaldas, Pauline and Khaled Mattawa. *Dinarzad's Children: An Anthology of Contemporary Arab American Fiction*. Fayetteville: University of Arkansas Press, 2009.
Karim, Karim Haiderali. *The Media of Diaspora*. New York: Routledge, 2003.
Kassab, Elizabeth Suzanne. *Contemporary Arab Thought: Cultural Critique in Comparative Perspective*. New York: Columbia University Press, 2010.
Kassir, Samir. *Being Arab*. 2006. Trans. Will Hobson. London: Verso, 2013.
Khatibi, Abdelkébir. *Tattooed Memory*. Trans. Peter Thompson. Paris: L'Harmattan, 2016.
Khemir, Sabiha. *The Blue Manuscript*. London: Verso, 2008.

Khemir, Sabiha. 'Cairo, the Triumphant'. Institute of International Visual Arts. Iniva, n.d. Web. 13 Nov. 2015.

Khemir, Sabiha. 'Mobile Identity and the Focal Distance of Memory'. *Displacement & Difference: Contemporary Arab Visual Culture in the Diaspora*. Ed. Fran Lloyd. London: Saffron Books, 2001.

Khemir, Sabiha. *Waiting in the Future for the Past to Come*. London: Quartet Books, 1993.

Khoury, Elias. *Gate of the Sun*. Hanover: Steerforth Press, 2012.

Khoury, Elias. *Kingdom of Strangers*. Fayetteville: University of Arkansas Press, 1996.

Kilito, Abdelfattah. *Thou Shalt Not Speak My Language*. Trans. Waïl S. Hassan. Syracuse: Syracuse University Press, 2008.

Kilpatrick, Hilary. 'Arab Fiction in English: A Case of Dual Nationality'. *New Comparison* 13 (1992): 46–55.

Kilpatrick, Hilary. 'Literary Creativity and the Cultural Heritage: The Aṭlal in Modern Arabic Fiction'. *Tradition, Modernity and Postmodernity in Arabic Literature*. Eds. Kamal Abdel-Malek and Wael B. Hallaq. Leiden: BRILL, 2000. 28–45.

King, Diane. 'Lineal Masculinity: Gendered Memory within Patriliny'. *American Ethnologist* 37.2 (2010): 323–36.

Kohl, Philip L., Mara Kozelsky and Nachman Ben-Yehuda. *Selective Remembrances: Archaeology in the Construction, Commemoration, and Consecration of National Pasts*. Chicago: University of Chicago Press, 2008.

Kumaraswamy, P. R. 'Who Am I? The Identity Crisis in the Middle East'. *Middle East Review of International Affairs* 10.1 (March 2006): 63–73.

LaCapra, Dominick. *Writing History, Writing Trauma*. Baltimore: JHU Press, 2014.

Lalami, Laila. *Hope and Other Dangerous Pursuits*. Chapel Hill: Algonquin Books, 2005.

Lalami, Laila. Interview by Andrew Lawless. *Three Monkeys Online Magazine*, 1 Sept. 2008. Web. 30 July 2015.

Lalami, Laila. 'So to Speak'. *World Literature Today* 83.5 (2009): 18–20.

Laroui, Abdallah. *The Crisis of the Arab Intellectual: Traditionalism or Historicism?* Berkley: University of California Press, 1977.

Larsen Neil. 'Imperialism, Colonialism, Postcolonialism'. *A Companion to Postcolonial Studies*. Eds. Henry Schwarz and Sangeeta Ray. Oxford: Blackwell Publishers, 2008.

Libin, Mark. 'Marking Territory: Rawi Hage's Novels and the Challenge to Postcolonial Ethics'. *English Studies in Canada* 39.4 (2013): 71–90.

Ludescher, Tanyss. 'From Nostalgia to Critique: An Overview of Arab American Literature'. *MELUS* 31.4 (2006): 93–114.

Mahfouz, Naguib. *Children of the Alley*. 1981. Trans. Peter Theroux. New York: Doubleday, 1996.

Mahfouz, Naguib. *Karnak Cafe*. Trans. Roger Allen. New York: Anchor, 2011.

Mahjoub, Jamal. '"The Accidental Arab": Alexander Siddig Interviewed by Jamal Mahjoub'. *Bidoun Projects*, n.p., n.d. Web. 15 Nov. 2015. http://www.bidoun.org/magazine/18-i nterviews/the-accidental-arab-alexander-siddig-interviewed-by-jamal-mahjoub/

Mahjoub, Jamal. *The Golden Scales*. London: New York: Bloomsbury, 2014.

Mahjoub, Jamal. *In the Hour of Signs*. Oxford: Heinemann International, 1996.

Mahjoub, Jamal. 'Jamal Mahjoub: Novelist, Nomad and Not Martin Amis'. *Al Jazeera America*. Al Jazeera Media Network, 23 May 2014. Web. 10 Nov. 2015.

Mahjoub, Jamal. *Navigation of a Rainmaker*. Oxford: Heinemann International, 1989.

Mahjoub, Jamal. 'Rumble on the Nile'. *Nederlands Letterenfonds*. Dutch Foundation for Literature. 10 Aug 2015. Web. 15 Nov. 2015.

Mahjoub, Jamal. *Travelling with Djinns*. London: Chatto & Windus, 2003.

Mahjoub, Jamal. 'Which Africa Are We Talking About?' Interview by Stacy Hardy. *The Chronic*. Chimurenga. 19 Mar. 2015. Web. 10 May 2016.
Mahjoub, Jamal. *Wings of Dust*. Oxford: Heinemann Educational, 1994.
Mahjoub, Jamal. 'The Writer and Globalism'. IFLA Satellite Meeting. Århus. 26 Aug. 1997. Speech. Monikultuurinen kirjasto (Multicultural Library). Web. 12 May 2015. http://www.lasipalatsi.fi/~karilam/mcl/uusi/articles/mahjoub.htm
Majaj, Lisa Suhair. 'Arab American Literature: Origins and Developments'. *American Studies Journal* 52 (2008): n.pag. Web. 20 Aug. 2014.
Majaj, Lisa Suhair. 'The Hyphenated Author: Emerging Genre of "Arab-American Literature" Poses Questions of Definition, Ethnicity and Art'. *Al Jadid* 26 (1999): n.pag. Web. 12 Mar. 2015.
Majaj, Lisa Suhair. 'New Directions: Arab-American Writing at Century's End'. *Post Gibran: Anthology of New Arab American Writing*. Eds. Munir Akash and Khaled Mattawa. Syracuse: Syracuse University Press, 1999. 66–77.
Majid, Anouar. *Si Yussef*. Northampton: Interlink Books, 1992.
Maloul, Linda F. 'The Construction of Palestinian Muslim Masculinities in Two Novels by Laila Halaby and Randa Jarrar'. *NORMA* 14.3 (2019): 183–98.
Makdisi, Saree. '"Postcolonial" Literature in a Neocolonial World: Modern Arabic Culture and the End of Modernity'. *Boundary 2* 22.1 (1995): 85–115.
Malak, Amin. *Muslim Narratives and the Discourse of English*. Albany: SUNY Press, 2004.
Maleh, Layla, ed. *Arab Voices in Diaspora: Critical Perspectives on Anglophone Arab Literature*. Amsterdam: Rodopi, 2009.
Marchi, Lisa. 'From the Dark Territories of Pain and Exclusion to Bright Futures? Rawi Hage's *Cockroach*'. *Canadian Literature* 223 (2014): 50–7.
Matar, Hisham. *Anatomy of a Disappearance*. London: Penguin, 2011.
Matar, Hisham. *In the Country of Men*. London: Penguin UK, 2007.
Matar, Hisham. 'An Interview with Hisham Matar'. Interview by Nouri Gana. *Words Without Borders*, August 2007. Web. 15 July 2013.
Matar, Hisham. 'Libya's Reluctant Spokesman'. Interview by Hari Kunzru. *Guernica*. Guernica, A Magazine of Art and Politics, 15 Oct. 2011. Web. 15 Nov. 2015.
Matar, Hisham. 'The Return'. *The New Yorker*. Condé Nast Digital, 8 Apr. 2013. Web. 16 Nov. 2015.
Matar, Hisham. *The Return: Fathers, Sons, and the Land in Between*. New York: Random House Publishing Group, 2016.
Matar, Hisham. 'The Weight of Inconclusive Grief'. *Times*. Times Newspapers Limited, 11 Oct. 2006. Web. 15 Apr. 2012.
Mbembé, Achille. *On the Postcolony*. Berkeley: University of California Press, 2001.
McClintock, Anne. *Imperial Leather: Race, Gender, and Sexuality in the Colonial Contest*. New York: Routledge, 2013.
McClintock, Anne, Aamir Mufti and Ella Shohat. *Dangerous Liaisons: Gender, Nation, and Postcolonial Perspectives*. Minneapolis: University of Minnesota Press, 1997.
Melhem, Hisham. 'The Barbarians Within Our Gates'. *Politico Magazine*. Politico LLC, 18 Sept. 2014. Web. 16 Nov. 2015.
'Memory of The Arab Arab-American Literature: Origins and Developments'. *American Studies Journal* 52 (2008): n.pag. Web. 31 June 2014.
'Memory of The Arab World'. Bibliotheca Alexandrina, n.d. Web. 12 Oct. 2013. http://www.bibalex.org/en/Project/Details?DocumentID=244&Keywords=
Menocal, Maria Rosa. 'The Finest Flowering: Poetry, History, and Medieval Spain in the Twenty-First Century'. *A Sea of Languages: Rethinking the Arabic Role in Medieval*

Literary History. Eds. Suzanne Conklin Akbari and Karla Mallette. Toronto: University of Toronto Press, 2013. 242–53.

Micklethwait, Christopher. 'Zenga Zenga and Bunga Bunga: The Novels of Hisham Matar and a Critique of Gadhafi's Libya'. *The Edinburgh Companion to the Arab Novel in English: The Politics of Anglo Arab and Arab American Literature and Culture*. Eds. Nouri Gana, Waïl S. Hassan and Mara Naaman. Edinburgh: Edinburgh University Press, 2013. 171–97.

Mishra, Pankaj. 'The West Will Not Prevent a Palestinian State's Eventual Birth'. *The Guardian*. Guardian News and Media, 14 Sept. 2011. Web. 16 Nov. 2012.

Mitchell, W. J. T. *What do Pictures Want? The Lives and Loves of Images*. Chicago: University of Chicago Press, 2005.

Mohsen, Caroline A. 'Narrating Identity & Conflict: History, Geography, and the Nation in Jamal Mahjoub's Portrayal of Modern-Day Sudan'. *World Literature Today* 74.3 (2000): 541–54.

Moore, Lindsey. 'A Conversation with Selma Dabbagh'. *Journal of Postcolonial Writing* 51.3 (2015): 324–39. doi:10.1080/17449855.2014.954755

Moore, Lindsey. '"You Arrive at a Truth, Not the Truth": An Interview with Fadia Faqir'. *Postcolonial Text* 6.2 (2011): 1–13.

Mounir, Walid. 'The Journey of Exile in Modern Arabic Poetry: Isolated Place and Memory'. *Alif: Journal of Comparative Poetics* 26 (2006): 193–211.

Moynagh, Maureen Anne. *Political Tourism and Its Texts*. Toronto: University of Toronto Press, 2008.

Naaman, Mara. 'Invisible Ethnic: Mona Simpson and the Space of the Ethnic Literature Market'. *The Edinburgh Companion to the Arab Novel in English: The Politics of Anglo Arab and Arab American Literature and Culture*. Ed. Nouri Gana. Edinburgh: Edinburgh University Press, 2013. 363–85.

Nagel, Caroline and Lynn Staeheli. 'British Arab Perspectives on Religion, Politics and "the Public"'. *Muslims in Britain: Race, Place and Identities*. Eds. Peter Hopkins and Richard Gale. Edinburgh: Edinburgh University Press, 2009. 95–112.

Naqvi, Fatima. *The Literary and Cultural Rhetoric of Victimhood: Western Europe, 1970–2005*. 2007 edition. New York: Palgrave Macmillan, 2007.

Nash, Geoffrey. *The Anglophone Arab Encounter: Fiction and Autobiography by Arab Writers in English*. New York: Peter Lang, 2007.

Nash, Geoffrey. *The Arab Writer in English: Arab Themes in a Metropolitan Language, 1908–1958*. Portland: Sussex Academic Press, 1998.

Nash, Geoffrey. *Writing Muslim Identity*. London: Continuum. 2012.

Neumann, Birgit. 'The Literary Representation of Memory'. *A Companion to Cultural Memory Studies: An International and Interdisciplinary Handbook*. Eds. Astrid Erll and Ansgar Nünning. Berlin: De Gruyter, 2010. 333–43.

Newmark, Kevin. 'Traumatic Poetry: Charles Baudelaire and The Shock Of Laughter'. *Trauma: Explorations in Memory*. Ed. Cathy Caruth. Baltimore: Johns Hopkins UP, 1995. 236–55.

Nikro, Saadi Norman. 'The Arab Australian Novel: Situating Diasporic and Multicultural Literature'. *The Edinburgh Companion to the Arab Novel in English: The Politics of Anglo Arab and Arab American Literature and Culture*. Eds. Nouri Gana, Waïl S. Hassan and Mara Naaman. Edinburgh: Edinburgh University Press, 2013. 298–321.

Nikro, Saadi Norman. 'Situating Postcolonial Trauma Studies'. *Postcolonial Text* 9.2 (2014): 1–21.

Norris, Jacob. *Land of Progress: Palestine in the Age of Colonial Development, 1905–1948*. Oxford: Oxford University Press, 2013.

Nyman, Jopi. 'Europe and Its Others: The Novels of Jamal Mahjoub'. *The Edinburgh Companion to the Arab Novel in English*. Eds. Nouri Gana, Waïl S. Hassan and Mara Naaman. Albany: State University of New York Press. 2013. 217–46.

Nyman, Jopi. *Home, Identity, and Mobility in Contemporary Diasporic Fiction*. Amsterdam: Rodopi, 2009.

Olivier, Laurent. *The Dark Abyss of Time: Archaeology and Memory*. Lanham: AltaMira Press, 2011.

O'Riley, Michael F. *Postcolonial Haunting and Victimisation: Assia Djebar's New Novels*. New York: Peter Lang, 2007.

Ouyang, Wen-chin. 'Intertextuality Gone Awry? The Mysterious (Dis)appearance of Tradition in the Arabic Novel'. *Intertextuality in Modern Arabic Literature Since 1967*. Eds. Luc Deheuvels, Barbara Michalak-Pikulska and Paul Starkey. Durham: Durham University Press, 2006. 45–64.

Ouyang, Wen-chin. *Poetics of Love in the Arabic Novel: Nation-State, Modernity and Tradition*. Edinburgh: Edinburgh University Press, 2012.

Ouyang, Wen-chin. *Politics of Nostalgia in the Arabic Novel: Nation-State, Modernity and Tradition*. Edinburgh: Edinburgh University Press, 2013.

Papastergiadis, Nikos. *The Turbulence of Migration: Globalisation, Deterritorialisation and Hybridity*. Hoboken: Wiley, 2013.

Phillips, Mike. 'Faith Healing'. *The Guardian*. Guardian News and Media, 11 June 2005. Web. 15 Nov. 2015.

Podeh, Elie. *The Politics of National Celebrations in the Arab Middle East*. New York: Cambridge University Press, 2011.

Puri, Jyoti. *Encountering Nationalism*. New York: Wiley, 2008.

Qualey, M. Lynx. 'Lyrics Alley by Leila Aboulela'. *The Guardian*. Guardian News and Media, 9 Apr. 2011. Web. 15 Nov. 2015.

Qutait, Tasnim. '"Like His Father Before Him": Patrilineality and Nationalism in the work of Hisham Matar, Jamal Mahjoub and Robin Yassin-Kassab'. *Postcolonial Interventions: An Interdisciplinary Journal of Postcolonial Studies* 2.2 (2017): 130–60.

Qutait, Tasnim. 'Qabbani versus Qur'an: Arabism and the Umma in Robin Yassin-Kassab's *The Road from Damascus*'. *Open Cultural Studies* 2.1 (2018): 73–83.

Ra'ad, Walid. 'The Atlas Group Archive'. *Atlas Group*, n.p, n.d. Web. 10 Jan. 2012. http://www.theatlasgroup.org

Rabinow, Paul. *French Modern: Norms and Forms of the Social Environment*. Chicago: University of Chicago Press, 1995.

Radstone, Susannah and Bill Schwarz. *Memory: Histories, Theories, Debates*. New York: Fordham University Press, 2010.

Ricoeur, Paul. *Memory, History, Forgetting*. Chicago: University of Chicago Press, 2009.

Rooke, Tetz. *In My Childhood: A Study of Arabic Autobiography*. Stockholm: Almqvist and Wiksell International, 1997.

Rosenfeld, Gavriel D. 'A Looming Crash or a Soft Landing? Forecasting the Future of the Memory "Industry"'. *Journal of Modern History* 81.1 (2009): 122–58.

Rothberg, Michael. 'Remembering Back: Cultural Memory, Colonial Legacies, and Postcolonial Studies'. *The Oxford Handbook of Postcolonial Studies*. Ed. Graham Huggan. Oxford: Oxford University Press, 2013. 359–79.

Rushdie, Salman. *Imaginary Homelands: Essays and Criticism 1981–1991*. London: Vintage Books, 2012.

Sadiki, Larbi. *The Search for Arab Democracy: Discourses and Counter-Discourses*. London: C. Hurst & Co. Publishers, 2004.

Said, Edward W. 'Andalusia's Journey'. *Travel + Leisure*. Time Inc. Affluent Media Group, Dec. 2002. Web. 12 Nov. 2015.
Said, Edward W. *Culture And Imperialism*. New York: Vintage Books, 2014.
Said, Edward W. *Freud and the Non-European*. New York: Verso, 2003.
Said, Edward W. *Humanism and Democratic Criticism*. New York: Columbia University Press, 2004.
Said, Edward W. 'Invention, Memory, and Place'. *Critical Inquiry* 26.2 (2000): 175–92.
Said, Edward W. 'Living in Arabic'. *Al-Ahram Weekly*. Al-Ahram Publishing House, 12–18 Feb. 2004. Web. 6 Jan. 2013.
Said, Edward W. *Out of Place: A Memoir*. New York: Vintage Books, 1999.
Said, Edward W. *The Politics of Dispossession: The Struggle for Palestinian Self-Determination, 1969–1994*. New York: Vintage Books, 1995.
Said, Edward W. *Reflections on Exile and Other Essays*. Cambridge, MA: Harvard University Press, 2000.
Said, Edward W. 'Travelling Theory'. *The World, the Text, and the Critic*. Cambridge, MA: Harvard University Press, 1982. 226–47.
Salaita, Steven. *Modern Arab American Fiction: A Reader's Guide*. Syracuse: Syracuse University Press, 2011.
Salameh, Franck. *Language, Memory, and Identity in the Middle East: The Case for Lebanon*. Washington, DC: Lexington Books, 2010.
Salhi, Zahia Smail and Ian Richard Netton. *The Arab Diaspora: Voices of an Anguished Scream*. London: Routledge, 2006.
Salih, Tayeb. *Season of Migration to the North*. 1969. Trans. Denys Johnson-Davies. Oxford: Heinemann, 1991.
Schlack, Julie Wittes. 'Storytellers Share the Power of Words'. *The Boston Globe*. http://archive.boston.com/ae/books/articles/2008/06/14/storytellers_share_the_power_of_words/. Accessed 28 Mar. 2019.
Sedikides, Constantine and Tim Wildschut. 'Nostalgia: A Bittersweet Emotion that Confers Psychological Health Benefits'. *The Wiley Handbook of Positive Clinical Psychology: An Integrative Approach to Studying and Improving Well-Being*. Ed. Alan Wood and Judith Johnson. Hoboken: John Wiley & Sons Incorporated. 2016. 125–36.
Seigneurie, Ken. *Standing by the Ruins: Elegiac Humanism in Wartime and Postwar Lebanon*. New York: Fordham University Press, 2011.
Selim, Samah. 'Jabra: In Search of Walid Masoud'. *Journal of Palestine Studies* 31.2 (2001/2): n.pag. Web. 15 Nov. 2015.
Sellman, Johanna Barbro. *The Biopolitics of Belonging: Europe in Post-Cold War Arabic Literature of Migration*. Aug. 2013. *repositories.lib.utexas.edu*. https://repositories.lib.utexas.edu/handle/2152/21155
Sennett, Richard. *The Fall of Public Man*. Cambridge: Cambridge University Press, 1977.
Shabout, Nada. 'What Role can the Archive Play in Developing and Sustaining a Critical and Culturally Located Art History?' *Ibraaz*. Ibraaz, 6 Nov. 2013. Web. 24 July 2015.
Shakir, Evelyn. 'Coming of Age: Arab American Literature'. *Ethnic Forum* 13.2/14.1 (1993–4): 63–88.
Shalakany, Amr. 'Sanhuri and the Historical Origins of Comparative Law in the Arab World'. *Rethinking the Masters of Comparative Law*. Ed. Annalise Riles. Oxford: Hart Publishing, 2001. 152–88.
Sharabi, Hisham. *Neopatriarchy: A Theory of Distorted Change in Arab Society*. Oxford: Oxford University Press, 1992.

Skinner, David. 'The New Here, A Visit with Sabiha Khemir'. *Humanities* 30.1 (Jan/Feb. 2009): n.pag. Web. 13 Apr. 2016.
Smith, Anthony D. *National Identity*. Reno: University of Nevada Press, 1991.
Sontag, Susan. *Regarding the Pain of Others*. New York: Picador, 2013.
Soueif, Ahdaf. 'Ahdaf Soueif on Colonialism in Egypt'. Radio Interview by Steve Paulson. *To the Best of Our Knowledge*. Public Radio International, 4 Nov. 2001. Web. 14 Nov. 2015.
Soueif, Ahdaf. *Aisha*. London: Bloomsbury, 1995.
Soueif, Ahdaf. 'A Correspondence with Ahdaf Soueif'. *Wasafiri* 24.3 (2009): 56–61.
Soueif, Ahdaf. *In the Eye of the Sun*. London: Bloomsbury, 2012.
Soueif, Ahdaf. *Mezzaterra: Fragments from the Common Ground*. London: Bloomsbury, 2012.
Soueif, Ahdaf. *The Map of Love: A Novel*. New York: Anchor Books, 2000.
Soueif, Ahdaf. *My City, Our Revolution*. London: Bloomsbury, 2014.
Srinivas, Siri. 'Rabih Alameddine: Right Now in the West, Arabs Are the Other'. *The Guardian*. Guardian News and Media, 09 Jan. 2015. Web. 12 July 2016.
Stein, Mark. *Black British Literature: Novels of Transformation*. Columbus: Ohio State University Press, 2004.
Stetkevych, Jaroslav. *Zephyrs of Najd*. Chicago: University of Chicago Press, 1993.
Stevens, Wallace. *The Collected Poems of Wallace Stevens*. New York: Alfred A. Knopf, 2011.
Stewart, Kathleen. 'Nostalgia – A Polemic'. *Cultural Anthropology* 3.3 (1988): 227–41.
Strehle, Susan. *Transnational Women's Fiction: Unsettling Home and Homeland*. New York: Palgrave Macmillan, 2008.
Su, John J. *Ethics and Nostalgia in the Contemporary Novel*. Cambridge: Cambridge University Press, 2005.
Suleiman, Yasir. *Arabic, Self and Identity: A Study in Conflict and Displacement*. Oxford: Oxford University Press, 2011.
Suleiman, Yasir and Ibrahim Muhawi. *Literature and Nation in the Middle East*. Edinburgh: Edinburgh University Press, 2006.
Szeman, Imre. 'Who's Afraid of National Allegory? Jameson, Literary Criticism, Globalisation'. *The South Atlantic Quarterly* 100.3 (2001): 803–27.
Tabar, Paul. *Lebanese Diaspora: History, Racism and Belonging*. Beirut: Lebanese American University, 2005.
Taha, Mahmoud Mohamed. *The Second Message of Islam*. Syracuse: Syracuse University Press, 1987.
Taher, Bahaa. *Sunset Oasis*. London: Hodder and Stoughton, 2009.
Tannock, Stuart. 'Nostalgia Critique'. *Cultural Studies* 9/3 (1995): 453–64.
Tarabichi, Georges. *Al-Muthaqqafūn al-'Arab wa-al-turāth*. London: Riad El-Rayyes, 1991.
Taras, Ray. 'Manichean Taxis and Murderous Readers: A Conversation with Rawi Hage'. *World Literature Today* 87.4 (2013): 12–17.
Tazini, al-Tayyib. *Min al-turāth ilā al-thawrah: ḥawla naẓariyya muqtaraḥa fī qaḍīyat al-turāth al-'Arabī*. Beirut: Dār Ibn Khaldūn, 1978.
Tölölyan, Khachig. "'From Exilic Nationalism to Diasporic Transnationalism." The Call of the Homeland'. *Diaspora Nationalisms, Past and Present*. Eds. Allon Gal et al. Leiden: Brill, 2010. 27–45.
Tousignant, Isa. 'Good Times for Montreal Writers'. *Hour Community*. Urbacom, 9 Nov. 2006. Web. 12 Nov. 2015.

Van Leeuwen, Richard. 'The Narrative of the Ship'. *Intertextuality in Modern Arabic Literature Since 1967*. Eds. Luc Deheuvels, Barbara Michalak-Pikulska and Paul Starkey. Durham: Durham University Press, 2006. 13–33.
Vertovec, Steven and Robin Cohen. *Migration, Diasporas, and Transnationalism*. Cheltenham: Edward Elgar, 1999.
Virilio, Paul and Sylvère Lotringer. *Pure War*. New York: Semiotext(e), 1997.
Walder, Dennis. *Postcolonial Nostalgias: Writing, Representation and Memory*. New York: Routledge, 2010.
Wang, Qin. 'Fredric Jameson's "Third-World Literature" and "National Allegory": A Defense'. *Frontiers of Literary Studies in China* 7.4 (2013): 654–71.
Wedeen, Lisa. *Ambiguities of Domination: Politics, Rhetoric, and Symbols in Contemporary Syria*. Chicago: University of Chicago Press, 1999.
Werbner, Richard P. *Memory and the Postcolony: African Anthropology and the Critique of Power*. London: Zed Books, 1998.
Werman, David S. 'Normal and Pathological Nostalgia'. *Journal of the American Psychoanalytic Association* 25.2 (1977): 387–98.
Wildschut, Tim, et al. 'Nostalgia: Content, Triggers, Functions'. *Journal of Personality and Social Psychology* 91.5 (Nov. 2006): 975–93.
Williams, Patrick. 'Postcolonialism and Orientalism'. *Postcolonialism and Islam: Theory, Literature, Culture, Society and Film*. Eds. Geoffrey Nash, Kathleen Kerr-Koch and Sarah Hackett. London: Routledge, 2013. 48–63.
Wolin, Richard. *Labyrinths: Explorations in the Critical History of Ideas*. Amherst: University of Massachusetts Press, 1995.
Worth, Robert. 'Anatomy of a Disappearance'. *New York Times*. The New York Times, 11 Sept. 2011. Web. 15 Nov. 2015.
Yassin-Kassab, Robin. Foreword. *In Praise of Hatred*. By Khaled Khalifa. London: Transworld Publishers, 2012. ix–xiv.
Yassin-Kassab, Robin. 'Out of It, by Selma Dabbagh'. *The Guardian*. Guardian News and Media, 6 Jan. 2012. Web. 16 Nov. 2015.
Yassin-Kassab, Robin. *The Road from Damascus*. London: Penguin UK, 2008.
Youssef, Saadi. *Nostalgia, My Enemy: Poems*. Minneapolis: Graywolf Press, 2012.
Zahran, Yasmin. *A Beggar at Damascus Gate*. Sausalito: Post Apollo Press, 1995.
Zaydan, Yusuf. *Azazeel*. Trans. Jonathan Wright. London: Atlantic Books, 2012.
Ziadah-Seely, Ghada. 'An Archaeology of Palestine: Mourning a Dream'. *Selective Remembrances: Archaeology in the Construction, Commemoration, and Consecration of National Pasts*. Eds. Philip Kohl, Mara Kozelsky and Nachman Ben-Yehuda. Chicago: University of Chicago Press, 2007. 326–45.
Žižek, Slavoj. *Living in the End Times*. London: Verso, 2011.

INDEX

Abi Samra, Muhammad 95
Aboulela, Leila, *Minaret* 22, 30, 105–14
   Lyrics Alley 165 n.8
   "The Museum" 113
   The Translator 105, 112, 167 n.17
Abu Jaber, Diana 19
Abu-Rabi', Ibrahim 65, 159
Aghacy, Samira 163 n.2
Ahmed, Sara 9
Alaidy, Ahmed 66
Al-Ali, Nadje 164 n.5
Alameddine, Rabih 23, 28, 30
   Hakawati 44–52
   I, The Divine 50
   Koolaids 50
   An Unnecessary Woman 46
Al-Barghouthi, Hani 27
Al-Daif, Rashid 39
Algeria 6–7, 67, 74, 146, 163 n.1
Al-Ghadeer, Moneera 14, 38
Allen, Roger 38, 95
Al-Shaykh, Hanan 2, 34
Alyan, Talal 130
Aly, Ramy 2, 93
Admiraal, Lucia 66
Adnan, Etel 49, 130
Adunis 35
Aksikas, Jaafar 63, 72
Andalusia 33–4, 36, 37, 43–4, 60, 65, 168 n.2
Anderson, Benedict 88
Arab nationalism 3, 5, 24, 58, 86, 92–6, 128, 163 n.1
Armstrong, Richard 10
Ashour, Radwa 36–7, 138
Assman, Jan 35
Attar, Samar 95
Ayubi, Nazih 93

Bahrani, Zainab 65
Barakat, Halim 26, 126–7, 135

Barghouti, Mourid 67, 72
Barghouti, Tamim 161–2, 164 n.7
Bayeh, Joumana 20
Benjamin, Walter 23, 75, 155
Berrada, Mohammed 94

Dabbagh, Selma 3, 31, 124, 137–43, 151
D'Alessandro, Sabina 70
Darraj, Susan 21
Davis, Emily 76
Davis, Fred 12
Dawisha, Adeed 92
Decter, Jonathan P. 25
Deleuze, Gilles 91
Derrida, Jacques 17, 57, 127
Downey, Anthony 16
Durrant, Sam 79

Egypt 5, 6, 25, 35, 36, 49, 50, 52, 56, 63, 65–76, 79, 84, 86, 87, 100, 102, 108, 114, 115, 118, 120, 137, 160, 164 n.1, 165 n.6, 166 n.2, 167 n.14
El-Ariss, Tarek 66
El-Enany, Rashid 63, 67, 95
El Solh, Camillia 111
Erll, Astrid 6, 13

Fadda-Conrey, Carol 20
Fanon, Frantz 62, 65, 75, 83, 86–7
Faqir, Fadia 22
   Pillars of Salt 30, 61, 68, 76–81, 87, 111, 155, 165 n.8
   "Stories from the House of Songs" 77, 80, 81
   "You Arrive At A Truth" 19, 77
Fayad, Mona 94, 99, 135
Freud, Sigmund 9–10, 60, 103

Gana, Nouri 14, 18, 19, 97
Ghali, Waguih 18, 66

Ghazoul, Ferial   88
Ghurba   25–6, 31, 33, 46, 127, 145, 154, 161
Gikandi, Simon   75
Gilroy, Paul   65
Grainge, Paul   6, 12
Granara, William   33
Gulf war   19, 22, 37, 87, 110–11, 115, 118, 125, 150, 163 n.2, 167 n.16, n.17

Habibi, Emile   23
Hage, Ghassan   9, 151, 156
Hage, Rawi   3, 28
   Cockroach   31, 124, 143–51
Halbwachs, Maurice   7, 12
Hanania, Tony   47, 159–60, 166 n.8
ḥanīn   1, 5, 11, 15, 47
Hassan, Waïl   14, 18, 21, 29, 45, 79, 111–12, 113, 164 n.4
Himmich, Bensalem   36
Hirsch, Marianne   6, 68, 82
Holmberg, Bo   15
Hout, Syrine   20, 44, 50, 90, 127, 144, 151
Hutcheon, Linda   6, 11, 41, 44, 53, 59, 164 n.6
Huyssen, Andreas   6, 58

Iraq   7, 13, 17, 22, 25, 41, 42, 51, 74, 87, 93, 95, 111, 131, 132, 133, 138, 161, 164 n.3, 165 n.6, 166 n.2

Jabra, Ibrahim Jabra   18
   Hunters in a Narrow Street   23, 40–1
   The Search for Walid Masoud   93–4
   The Ship   16
Jameson, Frederic   6, 91, 165 n.1
Jarrar, Randa   3, 24, 30, 90, 114–20
Jordan   19, 25, 76–80, 87, 163, 166 n.2
Jouaiti, Abdelkarim   34, 39

Kahf, Mohja   89, 167 n.16, 168 n.1
Kassab, Elizabeth   63
Kassir, Samir   2, 5, 34, 130, 163 n.1
Khatibi, Abdelkebir   37
Khemir, Sabiha
   The Blue Manuscript   30, 35, 52–7
   "From Cordoba to Samarkand"   55
   "Mobile Identity and the Focal Distance of Memory"   33, 52, 154

Waiting in the Future for the Past to Come   52
Khoury, Elias   24, 96, 159, 160, 168 n.2
Kilito, Abdelfettah   54
Kilpatrick, Hilary   2, 38

Lalami, Laila   27, 28, 43
Laroui, Abdallah   64
Lebanese civil war   46, 47, 150, 159
Lebanon   74, 138, 160, 163 n.2, 166 n.8
Libya   6–7, 26, 74, 96, 97, 101, 105, 150, 167 n.14
Ludescher, Tanyss   7–8

McClintock, Anne   92
Mahfouz, Naguib   37, 166 n.4
Mahjoub, Jamal   3
   "Accidental Arab"   27
   Golden Scales   86
   In the Hour of Signs   30, 61, 68, 81–8
   Navigation of a Rainmaker   82
   "Novelist, Nomad"   26
   "Rumble on the Nile"   114, 153
   Travelling with Djinns   31, 88, 123, 151
   "Which Africa"   28
   Wings of Dust   82–3, 86
   "The Writer and Globalism"   29
Majaj, Lisa Suheir   4, 19–20, 158
Majid, Anouar   126
Makdisi, Saree   3, 43, 53
Maleh, Layla   18, 19, 20, 27, 151
Matar, Hisham   3, 90, 120
   Anatomy of a Disappearance   19, 103–5
   In the Country of Men   30, 97–103
   "Inconclusive Grief"   105
   "An Interview"   26, 28
   "Reluctant Spokesman"   26, 96, 103
   "The Return"   105, 150
Mbembé, Achille   70
Melhem, Hisham   163 n.1
Menocal, María Rosa   43
Micklethwait, Christopher   97
Mohsen, Caroline   82, 83
Moore, Lindsey   7, 19, 138, 139, 143
Mounir, Walid   16

Index

Naqvi, Fatima 7
Nash, Geoffrey 18, 20, 21, 69, 84
Neumann, Bridget 5, 8, 143
Nikro, Saadi 14, 19, 20
Nyman, Jopi 87

Olivier, Laurent 55
O'Riley, Michael 85, 87
Ouyang, Wen-chin 7, 37, 38

Palestine 37, 57, 58, 59, 68, 115, 116, 129, 133, 140–3, 150, 166 n.6
Pieprzak, Katarzyna 39

Qabbani, Nizar 129, 134

Rooke, Tetz 98
Rose, Jacqueline 10
Rothberg, Michael 12
Rushdie, Salman 28, 45, 78, 120, 125, 128, 167 n.17

Said, Edward 1, 3, 8, 9, 10, 13–18, 25, 29, 30, 34, 36, 37, 39, 43, 60, 65, 82
Salaita, Steven 20
Seigneurie, Ken 39, 40, 164 n.4
Shabout, Nada 17
Shalakany, Amr 64–5, 84
Sharabi, Hisham 92–3
Soueif, Ahdaf
   Cairo, My City, Our Revolution 114
   "On Colonialism" 67–8
   "A Correspondence" 27
   In the Eye of the Sun 3, 5, 17, 160–1

   The Map of Love 30, 42, 61, 69–76, 165 n.8
   Mezzaterra 21, 22, 66
Spivak, Gayatri 62
Standing by the ruins 16, 38, 39, 40, 42, 46, 56, 58, 60
Sudan 27, 29, 61, 74, 81–84, 87, 94, 105, 107, 108, 109, 111–114, 123, 164 n.1, 165 n.8
Suleiman, Yasir 25
Syria 7, 35, 38, 42, 44, 89, 95, 126, 128, 129, 131, 132, 137, 150, 166 n.2

Tabar, Paul 111
Taher, Baha 63, 65, 165 n.6
Tarabichi, Georges 63
Tunisia 33, 52

Umm Kulthum 5, 48, 50, 51, 161

Walder, Dennis 123
War on Terror 87, 157
Werbner, Richard 13, 95

Yassin-Kassab, Robin 3
   Foreword to *In Praise of Hatred* 137
   The Road from Damascus 5, 24, 41, 42, 124, 128–37, 151, 164 n.8
Youssef, Saadi 36, 95, 129

Zahran, Yasmina 30, 35, 57–60
Zeidan, Youssef 36
Ziadeh-Seely, Ghada 57
Žižek, Slavoj 68, 88

www.ingramcontent.com/pod-product-compliance
Lightning Source LLC
Chambersburg PA
CBHW070639300426
44111CB00013B/2179